CISTERC
NUMBER ON

John Moschos

THE SPIRITUAL MEADOW
(Pratum Spirituale)

Library of Congress Cataloguing-in-Publication Data:
Moschus, John, *ca.* 550-619.

[Pratum spirituale. English]

The spiritual meadow = Pratum spirituale / by John Moschos (also known as John Eviratus) : introduction, translation, and notes by John Wortley.

p. cm.

Includes bibliographical references.

ISBN 0-87907-439-6 (alk. paper). — ISBN 0-87907-539-2 (pbk.: alk. paper).

1. Monastic and religious life—History—Early church, *ca.* 30-600—Anecdotes. 2. Orthodox Eastern Church—Anecdotes. 3. Spiritual life—Orthodox (Orthodox Eastern Church) authors. I. Wortley, John. II. Title.

BX385.A1M6716 1992
271'.009'021--dc20 92-31885
CIP

CISTERCIAN STUDIES SERIES:
NUMBER ONE HUNDRED THIRTY-NINE

THE SPIRITUAL MEADOW
(Pratum Spirituale)

by

John Moschos

(also known as John Eviratus)

Introduction, Translation and Notes by

John Wortley

Cistercian Publications
Kalamazoo, Michigan

A translation of *Pratum spirituale* by John Moschos (Moschus), from the Greek text of J.-P. Migne, *Patrologia Graeca* 87: 2851-3116, compared with the Latin text in Migne, *Patrologia Latina* 74:119-240, with supplementary texts from Elpidio Mioni, 'Il Pratum Spirituale di Giocanni Mosco: gli episodi inediti del Cod. Mariano greco II.21', *Orientalia Christiana Periodica* (1951), and from Theodor Nissen, 'Unbekannte Erzählungen aus dem Pratum Spirituale', *Byzantinische Zeitschrift* 38 (1938).

The work of Cistercian Publications is made possible in part
by support from Western Michigan University to
The Institute of Cistercian Studies

Cistercian Publications
Editorial Offices
Institute of Cistercian Studies
Western Michigan University
Kalamazoo, Michigan 49008

Distribution:
Saint Joseph's Abbey
Spencer, Massachusetts 01562

Printed in the United States of America

For W.S.M.

TABLE OF CONTENTS

CORRIGENDA

Page	*line*
xv	B-5: *Οοκουμένη* ▸*Οἰκουμένη*
xvi	n 1: PL 74:119-**121**
32	l.9: **Athanasios**
34	B-9: **Thessalonican**
69	l. 10: What
71	B-2: and ▸ an
95	l. 6: is ▸ it
99	Raïthou [no note]
156	l. 9: God **of** the Christians
162	l. 6: too ▸ to
170	l. 7: delete <
176	B-13: may ▸ many
179	B-11: gave ▸ give
189	B-11: the brother had **not** stowed
202	B-2: guiless ▸ guileless
243	c. 41, l.3: delete (
250	c. 127, l. 2: lieutenant **or** adjutant
251	c. 147, l. 3: Constantinople l. 4: of Chalcedon

TRANSLATOR'S NOTE

It would be misleading to suggest that the present work is any other than a temporary measure. It has no pretensions to do anything else but supply the English reader with a general idea of what is contained in that delightful collection of tales dating from about the year 600 AD generally known as *Pratum spirituale,* 'The Spiritual Meadow'. No matter how good the translator may be, no translation can be better than the text from which it is made; and there simply is no adequate edition of the Greek text yet in existence. One is in preparation to be sure, and in due course it will appear. But to trace, collect, evaluate, collate and edit the many manuscripts of a work of this complexity and magnitude is a major undertaking requiring many years of thankless toil. All credit is due to those who undertake such projects but, alas, whilst they create their meticulous editions which the translators impatiently await, the texts in question remain inaccessible to the many who can no longer read the ancient languages. This is particularly regrettable in the case of John Moschos' incomparable collection of sayings and stories; for even the French translation of Rouët de Journel (Paris, 1946) has been so long out of print that it is almost unobtainable. (There is, however, an excellent Italian translation by Riccardo Maisano, *Giovanni Mosco, Il Prato,* Naples, 1982.) Yet good translations of other great collections of early monastic lore are readily available (see the bibliography for details:) *The History of the Monks in Egypt* written before 400 AD; Palladios' *Lausiac History* written towards 419; both collections of *apophthegmata,* the *Systematikon,* alias 'Pelagius and John', (early sixth century perhaps, not yet in English but available in French) and the *Alpha-*

betikon (mid-sixth century) can all be easily obtained. In fact, of the seven known major collections (of tales and *apophthegmata) of the* fathers) only three remain unavailable in modern translation: the sixth-century *Tales of Daniel of Scêtê,* the late-seventh century *Tales* attributed to Anastasios the Sinaïte, and John Moschos' *Spiritual Meadow.*

As many readers are aware since the publication of Derwas Chitty's excellent book, *The Desert a City: an introduction to the study of Egyptian and Palestinian Monasticism in the Christian Empire* (Oxford, 1966), the work attributed to John Moschos is the sixth of the seven Greek *Paterika;* but it is also, in a number of ways, the most remarkable of them. It is thus not only lamentable that so many generations of students and readers have been denied direct access to its contents; it is also a serious deprivation for those who seek to gain a balanced picture of the entire tradition of eremitic monachism down to and beyond the Moslem cataclysm. This is why the present translation, imperfect and unsatisfactory though it must be, has been made and published. It would appear to be better to 'see through a glass darkly' than not at all. For no matter how grimy the glass, there is no doubt that the contents of the *Pratum* are of great value from many points of view, not least to those who would gain a glimpse of life as it was being lived just before the Christian empire sustained the blow which might well have been the *coup de grâce* of any less well-founded state.

Yet the question of what exactly its contents are is a daunting one. Even the number of sections is unsure; the published edition includes only two hundred and nineteen, But Photios *(Bibliotheca,* cod.198) described a volume which is obviously Mochos' *Pratum,* containing three hundred and four stories. The reader will in fact find two hundred and thirty-one stories in the present volume, for we have included tales which two modern scholars, Theodor Nissen and Elpidio Mioni, have edited and which they believe—rightly or wrongly—to belong to this collection.

Equally complex, however, is the question of what the text should actually *say.* It is an inescapable fact of life that manuscripts vary; the editor's task is to compare all the extant manuscripts and to determine as nearly as possible what the original text said. As indicated above, this task (though under way) has not yet been accomplished for the *Pratum.* Although there are known to be very many manuscripts of all or parts of the collection in existence, the translator had only the published texts to guide him, and these are a trumpet which gives forth an uncertain sound.

The *Pratum* was first published in Italian translation at Venice in 1475; a Greek text of the work was not published until 1624—by Fronto Ducaeus at Paris *(Bibliotheca Veterum Patrum* t.2:1057-1159)—which is said to be very unsatisfactory. It was superseded half a century later by an improved edition which made use of some Paris manuscripts, the work of Jean Baptiste Cotelier *(Ecclesiae Graecae monumenta* t.2:341-456, Paris, 1681)—and that is almost as far as the matter has gone. Cotelier's edition was reprinted and somewhat augmented by Jacques Paul Migne in volume 87:2851-3116 of his celebrated *Patrologia Graeca* and it is on the basis of Migne's text that the present translation has been made. It is not by any stretch of the imagination a satisfactory edition but, for the time being, it is almost all there is to work from.

Fortunately, however, accompanying Migne's edition is a Latin translation which first appeared in Venice, in 1558. It is reprinted in *Patrologia Latina* 74:119-240 from Heribert Rosweyde, *Vitae Patrum* t.10, Antwerp 1615, the *pierre fondamontale* of the *Acta Sanctorum.* This Latin version (from which the above-mentioned Italian translation was made) is a source of considerable help to the translator, for two reasons. First, it is the work of a careful and intelligent scholar, Ambrose Traversari ('Fra Ambrogio', 1346-1439) the Florentine humanist. Secondly, he used a Greek text (or texts) which was/were independent of the ones the Paris scholars were to know. Thus (for instance) it is his, and not the published Greek text, which supplies the section headings. These have been retained here even though the Greek originals (if such there are) have not yet been published. There are also significant passages which are found only in the Latin text (indicated by square brackets in the translation), and there are many other passages where the Greek would make little or no sense without the Latin to shed some light on what was misunderstood, omitted or distorted by the Greek scribe(s).

Yet even with Fra Ambrogio's Latin text to hand, there are places where the meaning is less than clear; where a *lacuna* is suspected, or where the text is manifestly in disarray. In these circumstances, common sense sometimes indicates what in all probability needs to be supplied; at other times, one's knowledge of the general literature of this genre suggests the most likely reading, given the context and the situation. Yet the reader must be cautioned: there are still a few places in this translation which are little better than guesswork; intelligent guesswork one hopes, but no more than that. The translator's *prostheses* are indicated thus: <...>. The reader will easily perceive whether it is a simple case of replacing an ambiguous (English) pronoun with something more precise, or a more radical piece of reconstruction.

It might not be unhelpful to add a word here about why the Greek text is in such disarray, because this will also indicate why the editor's task is such a difficult one, a task likely to take far more time than the editing of texts in general. Anybody who has anything whatsoever to do with the Greek texts of what may be generally labelled *paterika,* fathers' tales, is both impressed and frustrated by the degree of variation encountered. Even a copyist who is well known to be capable of giving a fairly faithful reproduction of the exemplar before him, will, when it comes to tales, grant himself complete licence to change whatever he likes into almost anything he chooses.

This licence operates at two levels. So far as collections of tales are concerned, he will omit or include at will: hence the variation in the number of items in manuscripts containing collections bearing the same name. But the texts themselves will often be handled with the same nonchalance: abbreviations, expansions, stylistic retouchings are common. Names of places and persons are often changed indiscriminately; stories may be conflated or divided, circumstances transformed and so forth. Such and many other similar variants are commonplace in collections of tales. A good example is the later part of Cod. Paris. Graec. 1596. This eleventh-century codex contains (amongst other things) an apparently arbitrary selection of tales from *Pratum Spirituale,* more or less in the order of the present translation, but often so changed that they are difficult to recognise. For instance: c. 60 is merely summarised; in c. 130 Athanasios has become Thalassios, and so forth.

The explanation of this degree of variation may be a simple one: it may be that, in the case of this monastic folk-lore, we are dealing with something which not only started out as, but also *remained,* an oral tradition for many years after the first written texts were made. Hence, a copyist might well have *both* a written form of a tale before him *and* an oral version registered in his head, of which the second would obviously be the more familiar. Small wonder then if he preferred 'his' version in what he wrote. But it does mean that the quest for a stable text is a very difficult, if not an impossible, one. It may be that there was not one *Meadow,* but as many *Meadows* as there were 'copies', which in truth are *versions* in many cases, rather than copies. The quest for an *Urtext* will, nevertheless, continue; but until it is successful, we have no choice but to make do with temporary measures—such as Migne's text and the present translation.

There are those who will cry that the translation is inaccurate, and they will be right. But in this it does no more than reflect the inaccuracy and variability of the tales-tradition itself. For, in the final analysis, those who passed these tales down to succeeding generations did so, not to transmit an accurate text, but to convey a message; a message which is contained in the dimensions of the story itself, rather than in the precision of its wording. Therefore, its undeniable (and undenied) imperfections apart, this translation is offered in the hope that it will, nevertheless, be of some use to a generation of readers who would otherwise remain largely unfamiliar with this fascinating chapter in the history of eremitic monachism and of western civilisation.

The author wishes to express his sincere appreciation of the work of Ms. Helga Dyck of the Institute for the Humanities at the University of Manitoba, who prepared the camera-ready copy of this book and improved it considerably in the process.

GLOSSARY OF THE TRANSLATION

The word *gerôn* is translated *elder* as usual; it should however be noted that it does not necessarily mean one who is old in years, but one who has seniority of some kind or other (usually spiritual here).

The Aramaic word *abba,* sometimes *appa* (father, hence *abbot),* has been retained in its original form, as it was in the Greek text *(cf* Mark 14:36; Romans 8:15; Gal. 4:6). *Abba* usually means a monk, but it is sometimes used (in the form *abbas)* to mean the chief monk (c. 54, c. 80), in which case it *could* be translated to *abbot. Abba* can even designate a bishop, presumably a monk-bishop (c. 79), but there is some indication that towards the end of the seventh century it was beginning to be used generally of clerics, much like the French *abbé.*

The word *hêgoumen* is represented by the usual English form of the word (higoumen), meaning the monk in charge of a community. This is because none of the English expressions *(e.g.* 'father superior', 'prior') exactly responds to the eastern office. The text will sometimes refer to 'him who ruled the community' *(koinobiarchês)* rather than use the word *higoumen* and on rare occasions, this person is referred to as *the* abba.

Many of the sections are titled '*vita/bios* of Abba NN' and this we have not hesitated to translate literally, 'life'. But it must be understood that this does not mean *biography* or anything like it. It means rather 'the way of life', how he lived *(politeia)*.

Koinobion we have rendered *community; monê* and *monastêrion* (which are used interchangeably in the text) are both represented by *monastery; laura* is represented by *lavra.* Strictly speaking a lavra is a base for anchorites whereas a *koinobion* is (as suggested above) an integrated community, but in fact John sometimes uses the terms interchangeably.

Demons and devils have been differentiated as in the text, but in fact the terms are used interchangeably (see c. 63).

The following equivalents have been consistently used even though, especially in the case of the monastic virtues, they are scarcely adequate (see the notes):

ἀκτημοσύνη	aktêmosunê	poverty
ἀναχωρητής	anachorêtês	anchorite
ἄσκησις	askêsis	asceticism
διάκρισις	diakrisis	discernment
ἔγκλειστος	egkleistos	recluse
ἔρημος	erêmos	wilderness*
ἡσυχαστής	hêsuchastês	solitary
θεῖος	theios	godly
ὁ ἐν ἁγίοις	ho en hagiois	saintly
οἰκονομία	oikonomia	providence
οἰκουμένη	oikoumenê	urban/village society
προσκυν-έω	proskunô	venerate

*—the more usual translation 'desert' has been avoided on account of its connotations of sand-dunes and cacti. Parts of the monastic wilderness were undoubtedly like that, but not by any means all. What they all had in

common was their wildness; the fact that man had not yet set his taming, civilising stamp on them, which creates οἰκουμένη, *oikoumenê*.

JOHN MOSCHOS

John Moschos, surnamed Eucrates, is obviously more than a name, although the task of discovering what lies behind the name is not an easy one. There are two documents which supply the main outlines of John's life, including a few valuable details: a brief anonymous biography[1] and the description of *Pratum Spirituale* in Photios' *Bibliotheca* (Cod.199) composed in the second half of the ninth century. But by far the greater part of our knowledge of John is to be gleaned from his own work, of which the *Pratum* is almost the only surviving example. The watchful reader will detect many autobiographical details in the tales he set down. But as John was not in the least concerned to write about himself, these may easily escape notice, or be given less than their full importance. To Siméon Vailhé goes the credit of having first drawn attention to these details. Combining them with the documentation mentioned above, he was able to construct a comprehensive *curriculum vitae* of John Moschos, 'ce juif-errant monastique' as he called him ['this wandering Jew-of-a-monk].[2] Subsequent writers have further elucidated Vailhé's pioneering effort; English readers will discover for themselves that the articles of Norman H. Baynes and Henry Chadwick

[1] See *Bibliotheca veterum patrum* (Paris, 1624) t.2:1054-1055; Latin translation of Fra Ambrogio in *PL* 74:119-112.

[2] S. Vailé. 'Jean Mosch', *Echos d'Orient* #5 (1901) 107-116.

are particularly informative[3]. What follows here is little more than a summary of Vailhé's *curriculum.*

It appears that both John and his disciple Sophronios, the future Patriarch of Jerusalem, hailed from Damascus. Sophronios was almost certainly born there[4], and at one point (c. 171) John speaks of their affection for a certain Zoïlos: 'because we shared the same homeland and upbringing' <διὰ τὸ κοινῆν ἔχειν πατρίδα καὶ τῆν ἀναστροφήν.> Unfortunately, if this indicates where John was born, it gives no indication of when. It can be assumed that he was somewhat older than Sophronios since they seem to have stood in the relationship of spiritual father and son. One does not have to be an exact contemporary to share another's homeland and upbringing; witness the affinity one feels for somebody who 'went to the same school', or came from the same town—albeit a generation later or earlier than oneself. Since Sophronios is known to have lived on beyond 634 (to 638?) and John to have died (at the earliest) in 619, it would not be unreasonable to suppose that they were born, the one a little before, the other somewhat after, the middle of the sixth century; at all events, both in the reign of Justinian I (527-565).

At some point, John must have left his family (of whom he says nothing) and embraced the religious life, or 'renounced the world' as he and most Greek writers express it. He was tonsured at the Monastery of Saint Theodosios (Deir Dosi) five miles west of Bethlehem on the road to the Great Lavra of Saint Saba (Mar Saba). Saint Theodosios' was founded after 478 on a conspicuous

[3] Norman H. Baynes, 'The Pratum Spirituale', *Orientalia Christiana Periodica* 13 (1947) 404-414, reprinted in *Byzantine Studies* (1955) pp. 261-270; H. Chadwick, 'John Moschos and his friend Sophronios the Sophist', *Journal of Theological Studies,* New Series 25 (1974) 41-74.

[4] See G. Bardy, 'Sophrone de Jérusalem', *DThC* 14/2 (1941) 2379-2383.

hill-top containing a cave in which the Magi were believed to have rested on the return journey from Bethlehem. It became the largest and best-organised of the Judaean communities and, with over four hundred brethren, it was also famed for its hospitality and its care for those in need. Both the anonymous *Life* and Photios affirm that this was John's home-monastery and this is born out by the inference of his own words: he refers to the superior of that monastery (Abba George) as *our* father (cc. 92, 93, 94;) he had Sophronios professed there[5] and in no part of the world is he more familiar with so many monks as in the vicinity of Saint Theodosios'. In short, this would appear to have been his spiritual home.

After undergoing basic training there, in accordance with the then prevalent custom, he withdrew to a remoter station: Paran (Pharôn) in the Judaean desert, the first monastic foundation of Saint Charitôn, with a history going back to the time of Constantine the Great (d.337). Here he stayed for ten years (c. 40), possibly 568/9–578/9. It is not improbable that here he was joined by Sophronios the Sophist, his inseparable friend and disciple for the rest of his life (John calls him ὁ ἑταῖρος μοῦ, 'my companion', in c. 92). Then, at the beginning of the reign of Tiberius, he (and Sophronios?) undertook a journey to Egypt for the purpose of collecting the lore of the great elders, whom he believed to be the guardians of a monastic tradition which was fast being eroded away by the slackness of the new generation of monks and ascetics. He made the rounds of the communities of the Thebaïd and even visited the Desert of the Oasis. From there he went to the Lavra of the Æliotes on Mount Sinaï, and there he stayed for ten more years (c. 67). This was at the time when another John was Patriarch of Jerusalem, 575-593.

[5] Sophronios attests to this himself: see *PG* 87:3380, 3421, 3664.

John then left Sinaï and he was present when Amos was installed as Patriarch of Jerusalem in 594. He seems then to have spent some time travelling around and staying at various Palestinian communities, in search of examples of great holiness such as the fathers describe. But in 602 two things happened which led him to leave the Holy Land for good—although Sophronios would return. The first was the murder of the God-fearing Emperor Maurice (602) by the bloodthirsty tyrant, Phocas: an event which promised (and brought) evil days to the whole empire. The second was the renewed antagonism of the Persians whom Maurice had successfully held in check. John was not being unduly pessimistic; in fact, scarcely a decade later, they occupied the Holy City. As early as 603-604 Persian raids were sufficiently alarming for John (and Sophronios) to leave. They travelled north up the coast, through Phoenicia, Syria Maritima and so came to Antioch. From there they visited Cilicia whence they sailed to Alexandria. They arrived there before 607 as Eulogios was still pope (as they called the patriarch of that city). John and Sophronios seem to have been taken into the patriarchal service and to have served not only Eulogios but also his two successors, John the Almsgiver and Theodore Scribo. It was particularly under the second of these popes that they carried on the struggle against Severus Akephalos, whose heresy and co-religionists are mentioned in several tales.

The fall of Jerusalem to the Persians in 614 interrupted whatever had been the normal course of life for the two in Egypt. There were refugees to be cared for by the thousand, and all too soon the Persians were at the threshold of Egypt. In 615 John and Sophronios fled, possibly with the pope, to Rome. It was here that John put the finishing touches to the *Pratum* and it was here that he died (in 619). The faithful Sophronios fulfilled his wishes and brought back his remains to be buried at Saint Theodosios, in September of 619.

It should however be noted that this date is by no means certain. We have a firm statement that Sophronios came to Jerusalem with the remains of his friend 'at the beginning of the eighth indiction'. That could mean either September 619 or September 634. For the most part, learned opinion has tended to accept the earlier date, but a recent study of the matter has shown that it is still not possible to state with certainty which is the correct one[6].

A NOTE ON THE SIGNS USED IN THIS TEXT

[...] indicates text which is found in the Latin text but not in the Greek, but please note that since all the titles of the chapters fall into this category, these have not been placed in square brackets.

<...> indicate words added by the translator which are either necessary to make the meaning clear or desirable to fill a real or suspected lacuna in the text.

An asterisk (*) indicates that there is a brief note on the word or passage by which an asterisk stands. Please see pages 231-256 for the endnotes.

There is a general note on money and currency beginning on page 231.

[6] Enrica Follieri, 'Dove e quando morì Giovanni Mosco?' *Rivista di Studi Bizantini e Neoellenici NS* 25 (1988) 3-39, seeks to demonstrate that John Moschos died at Rome after 11 November 620 but before spring-summer 634.

JOHN MOSCHOS EUCRATES

THE SPIRITUAL MEADOW

(Pratum spirituale)

JOHN EVIRATUS
TO HIS BELOVED IN CHRIST,
SOPHRONIOS THE SOPHIST

In my opinion, the meadows in spring present a particularly delightful prospect. They display to the beholder a rich diversity of flowers which arrests him with its charm, for it brings delight to his eyes and perfume to his nostrils. One part of this meadow blushes with roses; in another place lilies predominate, drawing one's attention to themselves and away from the roses. In another part the colour of violets blazes out, resembling the imperial purple. In short, the diversity and variety of innumerable flowers affords delights both to nostril and to eye on every side.

Think of this present work in the same way Sophronios, my sacred and faithful child. For in it, you will discover the virtues of holy men who have distinguished themselves in our own times; men, as the Psalmist says, *planted by the waterside* <Ps 1:3>. They were all equally beloved of God (by the grace of Christ),—yet there was a diversity in the virtues from which the beauty and the charm of each derived. From among these I have plucked the finest flowers of the unmown meadow and worked them into a crown which I now offer to you, most faithful child; and through you, to the world at large.

I have called this work *meadow* on account of the delight, the fragrance and the benefit which it will afford those who come across it. For the virtuous life and habitual piety do not merely consist of studying divinity; not only of thinking on an elevated plain about things as they are here and now. It must also include the description in writing of the way of life of others. So I have striven to complete this composition to inform your love, oh child; and as I have put together a copious and accurate collection, so I have emulated the most wise bee, gathering up the spiritually beneficial deeds of the fathers. Now I will begin to tell <you> those things.

1. The life of John the elder and the cave of Sapsas

There was an elder living in the monastery of Abba Eustorgios* whom our saintly Archbishop of Jerusalem wanted to appoint higoumen of the monastery. <The candidate> however would not agree and said: 'I prefer prayer on Mount Sinaï'. The archbishop* urged him first to become <higoumen> and then to depart <for the mountain> but the elder would not be persuaded. So <the archbishop> gave him leave of absence, charging him to accept the office of higoumen on his return. <The elder> bid the archbishop farewell and set out on the journey to Mount Sinaï, taking his own disciple* with him. They crossed the river Jordan* but before they reached even the first mile-post the elder began to shiver with fever. As he was unable to walk, they found a small cave and went into it so that the elder could rest. He stayed in the cave for three days, scarcely able to move and burning with fever. Then, whilst he was sleeping, he saw a figure who said to him: 'Tell me, elder, where do you want to go'? He replied: 'To Mount Sinaï'. The vision then said to him: 'Please, I beg of you, do not go there', but as he could not prevail upon the elder, he withdrew from him. Now the elder's fever attacked him more violently. Again the following night the same figure with the same appearance came to him and said: 'Why do you insist on suffering like this, good elder? Listen to me and do not go there.' The elder asked him: 'Who then are you'? The vision replied: 'I am John the Baptist and that is why I say to you: do not go there. For this little cave is greater than Mount Sinaï. Many times did our Lord Jesus Christ come in here to visit me. Give me your word that you will stay here and I will give you back your health'. The elder accepted this with joy and gave his solemn word that he would remain in the cave. He was instantly restored to health and stayed there for the rest of his life. He made the cave into a church and gathered a brotherhood together there; the place is called Sapsas.* Close by it and to the left is the Wadi Chorath* to which Elijah the Tishbite was sent during a drought; it faces the Jordan.

2. The Elder Who Fed Lions in His Own Cave

There was another elder at that place called Sapsas whose virtue was so great that he would welcome the lions which came into his cave and feed them at his lap, so full of divine grace was this man.

3. The Life of Conon, Priest of the Community of Penthoucla

At the monastery of our holy father Sabas* we met Athanasios. The elder told us this tale:

When I was in the Community of Penthoucla,* there was a priest there who baptised. He was a Cilician and his name was Conon. He had been appointed to administer baptisms because he was a great elder. He would anoint and baptise those who came there; but it was an occasion of acute embarrassment to him whenever he had to anoint a woman. For this reason, he wanted to withdraw from the community. But whenever he thought of withdrawing, Saint John would stand by him, saying: 'Persevere and I will make the struggle easier for you'. One day a Persian damsel came to be baptised and she was so very beautiful that the priest could not bring himself to anoint her with the holy oil. After she had waited two days, Archbishop Peter* heard of it and was very angry with the elder. He wanted to appoint a woman deacon for the task but he did not do so since this would have been contrary to custom.* Conon the priest took up his sheepskin* cloak and went his way saying: 'I will not stay in this place any longer.' However, when he got into the hills, Saint John the Baptist met him and said to him in a gentle voice: 'Go back to your monastery and I will make the struggle easier for you'. Abba Conon replied in anger: 'Believe me, I will *not* return. You have often made that promise to me and you have done nothing about it'. Saint John then made him sit down on one of the hills, stripped him of his clothes and three times made the sign of the cross beneath his navel. 'Believe me, Conon the priest', he said, 'I wanted you to carry away some reward from the struggle. But since you did not wish it to be so, I have caused the struggle to cease. But you shall have no reward for this'. Conon the priest returned to the task of baptising at the community and next day he baptised and anointed the Persian without even being aware that she was of the female sex. For twelve years he anointed and baptised without suffering any physical disturbance and with no awareness of women's femininity; so he drew his life to a close.

4. The vision of Abba Leontios

Abba Leontios of the community of our holy father Theodosios* told us: After the new lavriotes were driven out of the New Lavra* I went and took up residence in the same lavra. One Sunday I went to the church to make my communion and when I went in, I saw an angel standing at the right side of the altar. When I had received <communion> I went back to my cell and a voice came to me saying: 'From the moment that altar was consecrated I was commanded to remain here'.*

5. Abba Polychronios' story of the three monks

Abba Polychronios told us: I saw one of the brothers at the Lavra of the Towers of Jordan* who was not keeping himself up to the mark;* for he never fulfilled his Sunday duties.* Then, some time later, I saw this man who had formerly been so lax devoting himself <to his duties> with all diligence and great zeal. So I said to him: 'Now you are doing well, brother, and looking after your own soul'. He said to me: 'Abba, I am about to die sir',—and three days later he was dead.

This same Polychronios, priest of the New Lavra, also told me this: Once whilst I was staying at the Lavra of the Towers one of the brothers died. The steward said to me: 'Of your charity, brother, come so we can carry that brother's effects into the storeroom'. As we began to move his things I saw the steward weeping. I said to him: 'Come now, abba, why are you weeping in this way, sir'? He replied: 'Because today I am carrying out that brother's effects and two days from now others shall bear away mine'. And so it was; two days later the steward himself died, just as he said.

6. Another story of Abba Polychronios

Abba Polychronios the priest told us that he had heard from Abba Constantine, who was higoumen of the New Lavra of Holy Mary the Mother of God,* that one of the brethren died in the hospital at Jericho.* They brought him back to The Towers to bury him there and from the moment they left the hospital until they arrived at The Towers, a star travelled with them and never ceased shining over the dead brother until they laid him in the earth.

7. The life and death of an elder who would not be higoumen of the Lavra of the Towers

There was an elder dwelling at the Lavra of the Towers and when the higoumen died, the priests and other brethren at the lavra wanted to make him higoumen because of his great virtue. The elder begged them <not to,> saying: 'Let me rather go and weep for my sins, fathers, for I am no fit man to undertake the care of souls. This is a task for great fathers <such as> those who were with Abba Anthony* and the others'. The brethren, however, would not permit this. Each day they came begging him <to accept,> but he would not. When he saw that they were determined to make him change his mind, he said to them all: 'Give me three days for prayer and I shall do whatever God requires of me'. This was on a Friday: He died on the Sunday morning.

8. The life of Abba Myrogenes who had dropsy

At the Lavra of the Towers there was an elder named Myrogenes who had been so harsh in his treatment of himself that he developed dropsy. He would often say to the elders who came by to take care of him: 'Pray for me, fathers, so that I do not develop dropsy in my inner man. I pray to God that I may endure this sickness for a long time'. When Eutychios, the Archbishop of Jerusalem,* heard about this, he wanted to send Abba Myrogenes all that he needed; but he never got anything back in reply to his offer other than: 'Pray for me father, that I might be delivered from eternal torment'.

9. The wondrous charity of an holy elder

At the same Lavra of the Towers there was an elder who practised poverty to an exceptional degree* and yet his particular spiritual gift was that of almsgiving. One day a beggar came to his little tower asking for alms. The elder had nothing but a single loaf of bread which he brought out and gave to the beggar. 'It is not bread I want' said the beggar; 'I need clothing'. Wishing to minister to the man's needs, the elder took him by the hand and led him into his tower. When the beggar found that there was nothing there at all other than what the elder stood up in, he was so impressed by his virtue that he opened his bag and emptied out all its contents in the middle of the cell. 'Take this, good elder', he said; 'I will satisfy my needs elsewhere'.

10. The life of Barnabas the Anchorite

There was an anchorite at The Caves of the holy Jordan called Barnabas. One day he went down to drink at the Jordan and he got something sharp deeply embedded in his foot. But he left it there, and would not let a doctor examine it. His foot turned septic and compelled him to seek assistance at one of the towers of The Towers. His foot became more and more infected and he used to say to everybody who called on him that the more the outer man suffered, the more the inner man flourished.

After Abba Barnabas the anchorite had left the cave, come to The Towers and been there for some time, another anchorite went out to his cave. When he went in there he saw an angel of God standing at the altar which the elder Barnabas had set up and consecrated in the cave. The anchorite said to the angel: 'What are you doing there?' The angel replied: 'I am the angel of the Lord; and from the moment that <this altar> was consecrated, it was entrusted to me by God'.

11. The life of Abba Hagiodoulos

Abba Peter, priest of the Lavra of our holy father Saint Sabas, told us that when Hagiodoulos was higoumen of the Lavra of the blessed Gerasimos,* one of the brethren there died without the elder knowing of it. When the precentor struck the wood <-en signal>* for all the brethren to mourn together and send the dead man on his way, the elder came and saw the body of the brother lying in the church. He grieved at not having been able to take leave of him before he died. Going up to the bier, he said to the dead man: 'Rise up and greet me, brother', and the dead man rose up and greeted him. Then the elder said to him: 'Take your rest* now until the Son of God shall come and raise you up again'. When this same Hagiodoulos had come down to the banks of the holy Jordan he pondered in his mind as to what had become of the stones* which Joshua <the son> of Nun collected and set up before his chosen leaders. As he was pondering these things, the waters suddenly parted to either side and he saw the twelve stones. He humbly prostrated himself before God and went his way.

12. A Saying of Abba Olympios

A brother asked Abba Olympios, the priest of the Lavra of Abba Gerasimos, to say something to him;* this is what he said: 'Do not consort with heretics; keep a watch over the tongue and the belly and wherever you stay, keep on saying <to yourself> "I am a stranger."'*

13. The life of Abba Mark the Anchorite

They said that Abba Mark the anchorite who lived near the Penthoucla monastery practised the austerity of fasting all week long for sixty-nine years, with the result that some people thought he was incorporeal. He also laboured night and day in accordance with Christ's commandments. <What he gained> he gave to the poor and he never accepted anything from anybody. There were some people, friends of Christ, who heard of him and came, intending to give him some charitable donation. But he said to them: 'I do not accept <alms.> The labour of my hands is sufficient both for me and for those who come to me by <the grace of> God'.*

14. A BROTHER ASSAILED BY A LASCIVIOUS SPIRIT WHO WAS STRICKEN WITH LEPROSY

On another occasion Abba Polychronios told us the following tale: In the Community of Penthoucla there was a brother who was extremely ascetic and attentive <to his soul's health>. He had, however, to strive against sexual temptation. As he was not winning the battle, he left the monastery and went off to Jericho to satisfy his desires. Just as he was entering the den of fornication, he was suddenly afflicted with leprosy all over. When he saw himself in such a condition, he immediately returned to the monastery, giving thanks to God and saying: 'God has stricken me with this terrible disease in order that my soul should be saved', and he glorified God exceedingly.

15. THE WONDROUS DEED OF ABBA CONON

They said that Abba Conon, higoumen of the Penthoucla <monastery>, met some Hebrews one day when he was on his way to the holy place of the Bites.* They wanted to kill him; they drew their swords and ran towards the elder. But when they reached him and lifted up their hands to strike at him, their hands remained immobile in the air. The elder made a prayer on their behalf and they went their way, praising and glorifying God.

16. Abba Nicolas' story about himself and his friends

There was an elder living at the Lavra of Abba Peter* near the holy Jordan whose name was Nicolas. He told us that when he was staying at Raïthou,* three of the brethren, <of whom he was one> were sent to perform a service* at the Thebaïd. 'But when we were going through the desert', he said, 'we lost our way and wandered far and wide. Our water was all used up and we went for days without finding any. We began to faint from thirst and heat. When we could not take one more step, we found some tamarisk trees there in the desert and flung ourselves down wherever any shade could be found, fully expecting to die of thirst. As I lay there I fell into an ecstasy and I saw a pool of water full to overflowing. Two people were standing at the edge of the pool, drawing water with a wooden vessel. I began to make a request of one of them in these words: 'Of your charity, sir, give me a little water, for I am faint', but he was unwilling to grant my request. The other one said to him: 'Give him a little', but he replied: 'No, let us not give him any, for he is too easy-going,* and does not take care <of his soul'.> The other said: 'Yes, yes; it is true that he is easy-going but he is hospitable* to strangers',—and so he gave some to me and also to my companions. We drank and went on our way, travelling three more days without drinking until we reached civilisation.*

17. The life of a great elder

The same elder also told us about a certain great elder of the same lavra who spent fifty years in his cave. He never drank wine and the only bread he ate was made from bran. He received <communion> three times a week.

18. The life of another elder at the monastery of the Lavra who slept with lions

Abba Polychronius the priest also told us about another elder living in the same Lavra of Abba Peter who would often go off and stay on the banks of the holy Jordan. There he found a lion's den in which he installed himself. One day he found two lion-cubs in the cave. Wrapping them up in his cloak,* he took them to church. 'If we kept the commandments of our Lord Jesus Christ', he said, 'these animals would fear us. But because of our sins we have become slaves and it is rather we who fear them'. Greatly edified, the brethren returned to their caves.

19. Abba Elijah's story about himself

Abba Elijah the grazer* told us that he was once living in a cave in the area around Jordan because he was not in communion with Abba Macarios, the Bishop of Jerusalem:*

One day, about the sixth hour, when the heat was at its most intense, somebody came knocking at the cave. I went out and saw a woman there. 'What are you doing here?' I asked her, and she answered in these words: 'Abba, I too follow this way of life, sir. I have a little cave in which I live about a stone's throw from your cell'. She pointed out to me where it was located, away to the south. Then she said to me: 'I have travelled across this wilderness and am very thirsty on account of the raging heat. Of your charity, give me a little water'. I took out my water-bottle and gave it to her. She took it and drank, then I sent her on her way. When she had departed, the devil began working against me on her account, putting lewd thoughts* into my mind. The devil gained possession of me and I could not bear the flame of lust. So I took my staff and set out from the cave in the heat of the day, across the burning stones. It was my intention to search for her and to satisfy my desire. When I had gone about a furlong, my passion reached fever-pitch and I went into a trance. I saw the earth open up and I fell down into it. There I saw rotting corpses, badly decayed and burst open, filling the place with an unspeakably foul stench. I then saw a person of venerable appearance who pointed to the corpses and said to me: 'See, this is a woman's <body> and that is a man's; go and enjoy yourself and do whatever your passion dictates. But in return for that pleasure, take note how much labour you intend to destroy. Just look at the sort of sin for which you are prepared to deprive yourself of the kingdom of heaven. Oh, wretched humanity! Would you lose the fruit of all that toil for one hour's <pleasure>?' But I was overcome by the appalling stench and fell to the ground. The holy apparition came and set me on my feet. He caused the warfare to cease and I returned to my cell giving thanks to God.

20. The conversion of a soldier (whose life is briefly described) when God worked a miracle for him

One of the fathers told me that a military standard-bearer* had told him this:

We were in a battle with the Mauritanians in the African provinces; the barbarians defeated us and put us to flight. They pursued us and many of us were slain. One of the barbarians caught up with me and raised his spear to strike at me. When I saw this, I began calling on God. 'Lord God', I said; 'You who appeared to your servant Thecla* and delivered her from impious hands: deliver me from this calamity and save me from this bitter death. Then I will go and lead a life of solitude* in the desert'. When I turned round, there was not a barbarian in sight. I came straight away to this Lavra of Kopratha* and, by the grace of God, I have lived thirty years in this cave.

21. THE DEATH OF AN ANCHORITE AND OF HIS SLAYER

Abba Gerontios, higoumen of the monastery of our holy father Euthymios,* told me this:

There were three of us who were grazers living beyond the Red Sea, over towards Besimon. Once when we were walking around on the mountain-side another grazer was walking along the shore of the sea, down below us. It happened that he met with some Saracens passing through the area. As they passed by him, one of the Saracens turned back and struck off the head of the anchorite. We saw all this from a distance as we were on the mountain. While we were grieving for the anchorite, suddenly a bird came over the Saracen, seized him and carried him up into the air. It then let him drop to the ground, where he was turned into carrion.

22. THE LIFE OF ANOTHER ELDER NAMED CONON

In the community of our holy father Theodosios the Archimandrite* there was an elder named Conon, a native of Cilicia. This is the rule of life which he maintained for thirty-five years: he partook of bread and water once a week, he worked unceasingly and he never went out of the church.

23. THE LIFE OF THEODOULOS THE MONK

We saw another elder in that same monastery, a former soldier* named Theodoulos who fasted every day, never wore shoes and never slept lying down.*

24. An elder who lived at the Cells of Choziba

There was an elder living at the Cells of Choziba* and the elders there told us that when he was in his <home> village, this is what he used to do. If ever he saw somebody in his village so poor that he could not sow his own field, then, unknown to the man who worked that land, he would come by night with his own oxen and seed—and sow his neighbour's field. When he went into the wilderness and settled at the Cells of Choziba this elder was equally considerate <of his neighbours>. He would travel the road from the holy Jordan to the Holy City <Jerusalem> carrying bread and water. And if he saw a person overcome by fatigue, he would shoulder that person's pack and carry it all the way to the holy Mount of Olives. He would do the same on the return journey if he found others, carrying their packs as far as Jericho. You would see this elder, sometimes sweating under a great load, sometimes carrying a youngster on his shoulders. There was even an occasion when he carried two of them at the same time. Sometimes he would sit down and repair the footwear of men and women if this was needed, for he carried with him what was needed for that task. To some he gave a drink of the water he carried with him and to others he offered bread. If he found anyone naked, he gave him the very garment that he wore. You saw him working all day long. If ever he found a corpse on the road, he said the appointed prayers over it and gave it burial.

25. A brother at the Monastery of Choziba, the words of <the prayer of> the holy offering and Abba John

Abba Gregory, a former member of the Imperial Guard, told us of a brother at the Community of Choziba who had learned by heart the words used at the offering of the holy gifts.* One day he was sent to fetch the <eucharistic> oblations and, as he returned to the monastery, he said the offering prayer—as though he were reciting verses. The deacons placed the same oblations on the paten in the holy sanctuary.* The priest at that time was Abba John the Chozibite who later became Bishop of Caesarea in Palestine. When he offered the gifts, he did not perceive the coming of the Holy Spirit* in the accustomed manner. He was distressed, thinking that it might be on account of some sin on his part that the Holy Spirit was absent. He withdrew into the sacristy in tears and flung himself face-down. An angel of the Lord appeared to him and said: 'Because the brother who was bringing the oblations here recited the holy prayer of offering on the way, they are already consecrated and made perfect'. The elder laid down a rule* that from henceforth nobody was to learn the holy prayer of offering unless he had been ordained; nor was it ever to be recited at any time other than in a consecrated place.

26. The life of Theophanes, his wondrous vision and concerning intercourse with heretics

There was an elder residing at the Lavra of Calamôn on the holy Jordan whose name was Cyriacos. He was a great elder in the sight of God. A brother came to him, a stranger from the land of Dara,* named Theophanes, to ask the elder about lewd thoughts.* The elder began to encourage him by talking about self-control and purity. Having benefitted greatly, the brother said to the elder: 'Abba, in my country I am in communion with the Nestorians,* sir; which means I cannot stay with you, even though I would like to'. When the elder heard the name of Nestorios he became very concerned about the destruction of the brother. He urged and besought him to separate himself from that noxious heresy and to go to the catholic, apostolic church. He said to him: 'There is no other way of salvation than rightly to discern and believe that the holy Virgin Mary is in truth the Mother of God'. The brother said to the elder: 'But truly, abba, all the sects speak like that sir: that if you are not in communion with us, you are not being saved. I am a simple person and really do not know what to do. Pray to the Lord that by a deed he will show me which is the true faith'. The elder was delighted to grant the brother this request. He said to him: 'Stay in my cell and put your trust in God that his goodness will reveal the truth to you'. He left the brother in the cave and went out to the Dead Sea, praying for him. About the ninth hour of the second day, the brother saw a person of awesome appearance standing before him and saying to him: 'Come and see the truth'. He took the brother and brought him to a dark and disagreeable place where there was fire—and showed him Nestorios, Theodore, Eutyches, Apollinarios, Evagrios and Didymus, Dioscoros and Severus, Arius and Origen* and some others, there in that fire. The apparition said to the brother: 'This place is prepared for heretics and for those who blaspheme against the holy Mother of God and for those who follow their teachings. If you find this place to your liking, then stay with the doctrine you now hold. If you have no wish to experience the pains of this chastisement, proceed to the holy catholic church in which the elder teaches. For I tell you that if a man practise every virtue and yet not glorify <God> correctly, to this place he will come.' At that saying the brother returned to his senses. When the elder came back, he told him everything that had happened, exactly as he saw it. Then he went and entered into communion with the holy catholic and apostolic church. He stayed with the elder at Calamôn and, having passed several years in his company, he fell asleep in peace.

27. The Life of the Priest of the Mardardos Estate

Ten miles from the city of Ægaion in Cilicia there is an estate called Mardardos and on it there is an oratory of Saint John the Baptist. There resided an elder who was a priest, an elder of great prestige and virtue. One day those who lived on that estate went to complain about him to the Bishop of Ægaion. 'Take this elder away from us', they said, 'for he is objectionable to us. When Sunday comes around, he holds the service at the ninth hour and even then he does not follow the appointed order of service'. The bishop took the elder aside privately and said to him: 'Good elder, why do you behave like this? Do you not know the procedure of holy church?' The elder said to him: 'Truth to tell, great sir, it is just as you say and you have spoken well. But I do not know what to do. After the vigil-service of the holy Lord's Day I remain close by the holy altar; and until I see the Holy Spirit over-shadowing the holy sanctuary, I do not begin the <eucharistic> service. When I see the coming [ἐπιφοίτησις] of the Holy Spirit, then I celebrate the liturgy'. The bishop was amazed at the virtue of the elder. He informed the inhabitants of the estate and dismissed them in peace; they went their way glorifying God.

Abba Julian the stylite sent greetings to this elder, sending him a folded cloth with three coals of fire within. The elder received the greeting and the three coals still not dead. He sent them back to Abba Julian in the same cloth having poured water into it and tied it up. They were about twenty miles distant from each other.

28. A WONDROUS DEED OF ABBA JULIAN THE STYLITE

Abba Cyril, the disciple of the aforementioned Abba Julian the Stylite, told this story:

I and my father and brother, hearing what was said about Abba Julian, came to him from our own country. I had an incurable disease which no doctor was able to heal. The elder healed me with prayer as soon as I arrived. So the three of us stayed with him and renounced <the world>. The elder appointed my father to be in charge of the grain. One day my father came to Abba Julian and said: 'We have no grain'. The elder replied: 'Go, gather together whatever you can find and grind it up. God will take care of tomorrow for us'. My father was troubled by this command for he knew there was nothing left in the granary; he withdrew to his cell. When need became very pressing, the elder indicated that he was to come to him and as soon as he entered, he said to him: 'Brother Conon, go and prepare whatever you find for the brethren'. Almost in anger he took the keys of the granary and went off, intending to bring back some earth. Having released the lock he wanted to open the doors, but he could not do so because the granary was completely filled with grain. When he saw this he humbly prostrated himself before the elder, glorifying God.

29. A MIRACLE OF THE MOST HOLY EUCHARIST

About twenty miles from the city of Ægaion in Cilicia there were two stylites located about six miles from each other. One of them was in communion with the holy catholic and apostolic church. The other, who had been the longer time on his column (which was near an estate called Cassiodora) adhered to the Severan sect.* The heretical stylite disputed with the orthodox one in various ways, contriving and desiring to win him over to his own sect. And having disseminated many words, he seemed to have got the better of him. The orthodox stylite, as though by divine inspiration, intimated that he would like the heretic to send him a portion of his eucharist. The heretic was delighted, thinking that he had led the other astray and he sent the required portion immediately without the slightest delay. The orthodox took the portion which was sent to him by the heretic (the sacrament of the Severan sect, that is) and cast it into a pot which he had brought to the boil before him—and it was dissolved by the boiling of the pot. Then he took the holy eucharist of the orthodox church and cast it into the pot. Immediately the pot was cooled. The holy communion remained safe and undampened. He still keeps it, for he showed it to us when we visited him.

30. The life of Isidore the Monk of Melitene and another miracle of the most holy sacrament

There is a market-town in Cyprus called Tadai which contains a monastery located near a place called Philoxenos. When we arrived there, we found in the monastery a monk called Isidore, a native of Melitene. We noticed that he was always in tears and groaning. Everybody tried to persuade him to desist a little from his lamentation, but he would not be comforted. He told them all: 'I am as great a sinner as there has been from Adam to this day'. We said to him: 'But abba, in truth, sir, nobody is really sinless except one: God himself'. He said: 'Believe me, brethren, I have found no sin amongst men which I have not committed, whether I have learnt it from writing or by hearsay. If you think that I am accusing myself unjustly, hear of my sin so that you can pray for me. In the world', he said, 'I had a wife and both she and I were of the Severan persuasion. One day when I came home I could not find my wife, but I heard that she had gone to a neighbour's to take communion. Now he was a communicant of the holy catholic church, so I ran immediately to stop my wife. As I entered the neighbour's house, I found my wife exactly at the point of receiving the holy portion and making her communion. I grabbed her by the throat and forced her to emit the holy portion. I seized it and threw it up and down and it fell in the mud. All at once I saw a flash of lightening take up the holy communion from the spot where it lay. And two days later I saw a black-faced one wearing rags who said to me: "You and I are alike condemned to the same damnation", and I said: "Who are you"? The black-faced one who had appeared to me replied: "I am he who struck the cheek of the Creator of all things, our Lord Jesus Christ, at the time of his passion". It is on this account' said the monk 'that I cannot desist from weeping'.

31. THE CONVERSION AND LIFE OF MARY THE HARLOT

Two elders set off from Ægaion to Tarsos in Cilicia. By the providence of God, they came to an inn where they could rest, for the heat was intense. There they found three younger men who had a harlot with them going to Ægaion. The three elders sat discreetly apart; one of them took the holy gospel out of his travelling-bag and began to read <aloud>. When the harlot who was with the youths saw the elder begin to read, she came and sat down near him, forsaking the youths. The elder drove her off, saying to her: 'Wretched woman, you seem very indecent. Are you not ashamed to come and sit near us?' In reply she answered: 'Oh father, please do not treat me with loathing. Even if I am filled with every kind of sin, the master of all, our Lord and God, did not send away the harlot who came to him.' The elder answered her: 'But that harlot remained a harlot no longer'. She said to him: 'My hope is in the Son of the living God that from this day forward neither will I continue in this sin'. Forsaking the youths and everything she had, she followed the elders. They placed her in a <women's> monastery called Nakkiba, near Ægaion. I saw her as an old woman of great experience. It was from her that I heard all this and her name was Mary.

32. The conversion and life of Babylas the actor and of Cometa and Nicosa his concubines

There was an actor at Tarsos in Cilicia whose name was Babylas and he had two female companions: one named Cometa, the other Nicosa. He led a disorderly life, performing deeds which were truly worthy of the demons who urged him on. One day he went into church and by the providence of God, the gospel was being read in which there is the verse which says: 'Repent ye, for the kingdom of heaven is at hand'. This struck him forcibly; he began to reproach himself with tears for the evil of his ways. As soon as he came out of church, he called his two companions and said to them: 'You know how I have lived in disorderliness with you and never preferred one of you over the other. Now you are to have everything I possess for your own. Take all that I have and share it; for this very day I am going to renounce <the world> and become a monk'. The women replied as though with one voice and in tears: 'We have shared with you in the experience of sin and in the destruction of our own souls; now that you have decided on this course of action which is pleasing to God, will you keep us out of it and do it alone? Indeed you shall not! Let us also be partakers with you of the good'. The actor immediately shut himself up in one of the towers of the walls of the city. The women sold their property and gave the proceeds to the poor, then they too received the monastic habit. After that they made a cell for themselves near the tower and shut themselves up in it. I happened upon it myself and profited <from the experience>. The man is very compassionate, very forgiving and humble-minded. I wrote this for the benefit of those who chance to come upon it.

33. The Life of the Holy Bishop Theodotos

One of the fathers told us that there was formerly an archbishop of Theoupolis* <=Antioch> whose goodness was such that once when there was a feast-day he invited several of the clergy who had celebrated the feast with him to dinner. There was one of them who refused the invitation. The patriarch made no comment but on another occasion he went personally to find the cleric and invited him to share his table. They also told this story about the same Archbishop Theodotos: such were his humility and lowliness that once he was travelling with one of his clergy, the bishop <reclining> in a litter whilst the cleric rode a horse. The patriarch said to him: 'Let us defray the tedium of the journey by exchanging our modes of travel'. 'It would disgrace the patriarch' said the cleric, 'if I were to get into the litter and he to mount the horse'. The godly Theodotos would have nothing of that. He persuaded his attendant cleric that it would be no disgrace and so prevailed upon him to make the exchange.

34. The Life of the Godly Alexander, Patriarch of Antioch

Theoupolis had another patriarch who was compassionate and merciful; his name was Alexander. One of his secretaries once stole some gold from him, fled in fear and came to the Thebaïd in Egypt. He was found wandering around by the bloodthirsty barbarians of Egypt and of the Thebaïd; they took him to the remotest corner of their land. When the godly Alexander heard about this, he ransomed him from captivity at a cost of eighty-five pieces of gold.* When the captive returned, the bishop was so loving and gentle with him that one of the inhabitants of the city once said: 'There is nothing more profitable or advantageous for me than to sin against Alexander'. On another occasion one of the deacons slandered the godly Alexander before all the clergy. But the godly Alexander prostrated himself before the man saying: 'Brother, forgive me, sir'.

35. The life of Elias, Archbishop of Jerusalem and concerning Flavian, Patriarch of Antioch

Abba Polychronios said of Abba Elias, Archbishop of Jerusalem, that when he was a monk he never drank wine and after he became patriarch he continued to observe the same rule. They said of Archbishop <Elias> of Jerusalem and of Flavian the Archbishop of Antioch that the Emperor Anastasios exiled them both on account of the holy synod of the fathers at Chalcedon: Eilias to Eilat, Flavian to Petra. One day the two patriarchs revealed to each other that Anastasios had died that very day. 'Let us go, too, to be judged with him', they said, and two days later they went to the Lord.

36. The life of Ephraim, Patriarch of Antioch and how he converted a stylite monk from the impiety of the Severan heresy

One of the fathers told us that the blessed Ephraim, Patriarch of Antioch,* had a great deal of zeal and fervour for the orthodox faith. One day he learned that a stylite in one of the regions around Hierapolis was one of Severus' excommunicate Acephalites.* He went to this stylite with the intention of talking him round. When he got there the godly Ephraim began to urge and entreat the stylite to take refuge in the apostolic throne* and to enter into communion with the catholic and apostolic church. In answer the stylite said to him: 'It will never be the case that I will communicate with the <orthodox> Synod'. The godly Ephraim rejoined: 'Well then, what have I got to do to convince you that, by the grace of Christ Jesus our Lord, the holy Church has been set free of every trace of heretical teaching'? The stylite said: 'Let us light a fire, my lord

Patriarch, and let you and me go into it. If one of us comes out unharmed, he is the orthodox and he is the one we ought to follow'. He said this to terrify the patriarch; but the godly Ephraim said to the stylite: 'You ought to have obeyed me as a father, my child, and to have asked nothing of us. Since you have asked something which is beyond my meagre ability, I have put my trust in the mercies of the Son of God that, for the sake of your soul's salvation, I will do what you suggest'. Then the godly Ephraim said to those who stood by: 'Blessed be the Lord! Bring some wood here'. When the wood arrived, the patriarch lit it before the column and he said to the stylite: 'Come down and we will both walk into the fire to carry out your test'. The stylite was amazed at the patriarch's trust in God and he did not want to come down. The patriarch said to him: 'Was it not you who suggested we do this? How is it you no longer want to go through with it'? Then the patriarch took off the *omophorion** he was wearing and, coming close to the fire, prayed in these words: 'Lord Jesus Christ our God, who for our sakes condescended truly to be made flesh of our Lady the holy Mother of God and ever-virgin Mary, show us the truth'. When the prayer was finished, he threw his *omopohorion* into the fire. The fire burned for three hours. Then, when the wood was all burnt up, he retrieved the *omophorion* from the fire—still in one piece. It was undamaged and unmarked and there was no sign to be found on it of having been in the fire. When he saw what had happened, the stylite received instruction, rejected Severus and his heresy with an oath, and entered the holy church. He received communion at the hands of the blessed Ephraim, glorifying God.

37. THE LIFE OF A BISHOP WHO LEFT HIS THRONE AND CAME TO THE HOLY CITY* WHERE HE CHANGED HIS CLOTHES AND BECAME A BUILDER'S LABOURER

One of the fathers told of a bishop who left his own diocese and came into Theoupolis, where he worked as labourer. At that time the Count of the East was Ephraim, a merciful and compassionate man; so much so that he was rebuilding the public edifices (the city having been dilapidated by an earthquake). In his sleep one night Ephraim saw the bishop lying down and a column of fire standing over him which reached up into heaven. As he had this vision not once, but several times, Ephraim was greatly amazed, for it was an awesome and truly astounding apparition. He asked himself what it might be, for he had no idea the workman was a bishop. How could he have known the labourer was a bishop, in view of his uncombed hair and shabby clothing? This was a poverty-stricken man, broken down by much endurance, much asceticism and labour, plus the continuous burden of much toil. One day Ephraim sent for the labourer who was once a bishop, to learn from him who he was. He took him aside and began asking him where he was from and what his name was. The sometime bishop said: 'I am one of the poor men of this city. For lack of any support I work as a labourer and God sustains me by my toil.' God prompted Ephraim to answer him: 'Believe me, I shall not let you go until you tell me the whole truth about yourself'. Since he could conceal himself no longer, the bishop said to him: 'Give me your word that you will never tell anybody what you are about to hear from me as long as I am still alive, and I will tell you about myself. But I will not tell you my name or the name of my city'. The godly Ephraim swore to him: 'I will not tell anybody what you are about to tell me for as long as it pleases God to keep you in this life'. The other said to him: 'I am a bishop. At the behest of God, I left my diocese and came to this place—because it was totally unknown to me. Here I have suffered affliction and laboured at menial tasks. By my toil I earn a little bread, but do you add what you can by way of almsgiving.* For in these days, God is going to raise you up to the throne of Theoupolis to be the shepherd of his people which Christ our true God purchased by his own blood. As I said to you, you are to strive for almsgiving and orthodoxy. By such sacrifices you will be well-pleasing to God'. Within a few days it came about as he had predicted. When the blessed Ephraim had heard the bishop out, he glorified God saying: 'Oh, how many hidden servants God has and they are known only to him alone'!

38. The death of the impious Emperor Anastasios

One of those who loved Christ told us about the Emperor Anastasios who dismissed Euphemios and Macedonios, Patriarchs of Constantinople, and exiled them to Euchaïta in Pontus on account of the holy synod of the fathers at Chalcedon. In his sleep, the Emperor Anastasios saw a man of striking appearance, dressed in white and standing before him, carrying a written book from which he was reading. He turned over five pages of the book, read out the emperor's name and said to him: 'See, because of your faithlessness I am expunging fourteen <years(?)>', and they say he erased them with his own finger. Two days later there was a severe outburst of thunder and lightening. In deep terror <the emperor> surrendered his spirit, greatly distressed. This was his reward for having despised the most holy Church of Christ our God and having exiled her shepherds.

39. The life of a monk of the Monastery of Abba Severian and how he was prudently restrained by a country-girl from sinning with her*

When I was in Antioch the Great I heard one of the priests of the church saying the Patriarch Anastasios had told something of this sort:

A monk of the monastery of Abba Severian was sent to serve in the district of Eleutheroupolis. He put up at the home of a Christ-loving farmer, the father of a daughter (his only child) whose mother was dead. When the monk had been some days in the farmer's house, the devil (he who is always contending with humanity) thrust unclean thoughts upon the brother. He became disturbed concerning the maiden and sought an opportunity to have his way with her. And the devil who was responsible for this disturbance himself took care to provide the desired opportunity. The maiden's father took himself off to Ascalon to deal with some pressing business. Knowing that there was nobody in the house but the maiden and himself, the brother approached her with the intention of forcing his attentions upon her. When she realised how disturbed he was and how he burned with desire for her, the maiden said to him: 'Do not be so excited and do not act ignobly toward me; my father will not return either today or tomorrow. But first listen to what I have to say to you and then, the Lord knows, I will do anything you wish'. And she began to reason with him saying: 'You, brother, how long have you been in your monastery, sir?' He said: 'Seventeen years'. She replied: 'Have you had any experience with a woman?' and he said he had not. The maiden answered the brother: 'And you wish to destroy all your labour for the sake of an hour's pleasure? How many times have you poured out tears that you might present your flesh spotless and without stain to Christ? And now you are willing to dissipate all that labour for the sake of a short-lived pleasure?

And if I do as you wish and you fall <into sin> with me, have you the wherewithal to assume responsibility for me and to support me?' The brother confessed he had not, whereupon the maiden replied and said to him: 'In truth, this is no lie: if you disgrace me, you will be the cause of many evils'. The monk said to her: 'How so?' The maiden replied: 'You will destroy your soul and, in the second place, you will have to answer for my soul. To make you aware of this, I will convince you with an oath. If you disgrace me, <I swear> by Him who said *Thou shalt bear no false witness* that I will hang myself. Thus you will be found guilty of murder too, and in the judgement you will be judged as a murderer. Rather than become the cause of so much evil, go back to your monastery. You will have <plenty> to do in praying for me.' The brother became himself again and recovered his normal state of mind. He left the farm and went away to his monastery where he fell prostrate before the higoumen with the prayer that he might never again for the rest of his life go out of the monastery. He lived for three months and then passed over to the Lord.

40. The life of Abba Cosmas the Eunuch

This story was told to us by Abba Basil, priest of the monastery of the Byzantines:*
When I was with Abba Gregory the Patriarch at Theoupolis,* Abba Cosmas the Eunuch of the Lavra of Pharôn came from Jerusalem. This man was most truly a monk, orthodox and of great zeal, with no small knowledge of the holy Scriptures. After being there a few days, the elder died. Wishing to honour his remains, the patriarch ordered that he should be buried at a spot in the cemetery where a bishop lay. Two days later I came to kiss the elder's grave. A poor man stricken with paralysis was lying on top of the tomb, begging alms of those who came into the church. When this poor man saw me making three prostrations and offering the priestly prayer, he

said to me: 'Oh abba, this was indeed a great elder, sir, whom you buried here three days ago'. I answered him saying: 'How do you know that'? He told me: 'I was paralysed for twelve years and, through this elder, the Lord cured me. When I am distressed, he comes and comforts me, granting me relief. And now you are about to hear yet another strange thing about this elder. Ever since you buried him, I hear him at night calling and saying to the bishop: "Touch me not; stay away! Come not near, thou heretic and enemy of the truth and of the holy catholic Church of God"'. Having heard this from the man cured of his paralysis, I went and repeated it to the patriarch. I besought that most holy man to let us take the body of the elder and lay it in another tomb. Then the patriarch said to me: 'Believe me, my child, Abba Cosmas will suffer no hurt from the heretic. This has all come about that the virtue and zeal of the elder might become known to us after his departure from this world; also that the doctrine of the bishop should be revealed to us, so that we not hold him to have been one of the orthodox'.

The same Abba Basil also told us this concerning this elder, Abba Cosmas:

I visited him when he was staying at the Lavra of Pharôn and he said to me: A doubt once perplexed me concerning the saying of the Lord to his disciples: 'He who has a garment, let him sell it and buy a sword', and they said to him: 'Here are two swords'.* After agonizing unsuccessfully over the meaning of this passage, I went from my cell, out into the heat of the midday sun, driven by a compulsion to go to the Lavra of Pyrgia <=The Towers or Turrets> where Abba Theophilos was, to ask him about the matter. When I came into the desert, near to Calamôn, I saw an exceedingly large dragon coming down from the mountain towards Calamôn. It was so large that it made a great vault of itself as it moved. I suddenly realised that I was passing through its vault unharmed. I knew (he said) that the devil was trying to frustrate my purpose but that the prayer of the elder had prevailed. I went my way (he said) and recited the passage of scripture to Abba Theophilos. He told me the explanation of the two swords* is this: the active and the contemplative [τὸ πρακτικὸν καὶ τὸ θεωρητικόν]. If a person has these two virtues, he is approaching perfection. I visited this Abba Cosmas at the Lavra of Pharôn and stayed there for ten years. Whilst he was speaking to me about the salvation of the soul, we came across an opinion of Saint Athanasios, Archbishop of Alexandria. The elder said to me: 'When you come across a saying of Athansios the Great, if you have no paper, write it on your clothing'—so great was the appetite of this elder for our holy fathers and teachers. They also said this about him: that on the eve of the holy Lord's Day, he would stand from vespers to dawn singing and reading, in his cell or in church, never sitting down at all. Once the sun had risen and the appointed service had been sung, he would sit reading the holy Gospel until it was time for the eucharist.

41. The life of Abba Paul of Anazarbos*

At the same Lavra of Pharôn, we saw Abba Paul too, a holy man of great humility and self-abegnation, wholly devoted to God; a man who wept many tears each day. I don't know whether I ever met his like in all my life. For almost fifty years this elder had led the solitary life* sustained by nothing more than the charitable dole of the church, for he would accept nothing in addition to the rations he received. He came from Anazarbos.

42. The life of Abba Auxanôn

At the same place we saw Abba Auxanôn in his cell, a man of compassion, continence and solitude who treated himself so harshly that over a period of four days he would only eat a twenty-*lepta** loaf of bread, such as we offer at the eucharist. Sometimes this was sufficient for him during a whole week. Towards the end of his life, this ever-memorable father fell ill with a stomach complaint. They carried him to the patriarchal infirmary at the Holy City. One day when we were visiting him, Abba Conon, higoumen of the Lavra of our saintly father Sabas, sent him a small basket containing the church dole and six pieces of gold, with a message: 'Forgive me, but my sickness prevents me from coming to greet you'. The elder accepted the dole but sent the gold back to him with this message: 'If it be the will of God that I be in this life, father, I have ten pieces of gold. If I have need of these others I will let you know, and do you send them to me. But you should know, father, that two days from now I will go forth out of this world'—which indeed he did. We bore him to the Lavra of Pharôn and buried him there. This blessed one had been the fellow-monk of those saintly men Eustochios and Gregory but, leaving them both, he completed his formation in the wilderness.* He was a native of Ancyra in Galatia.

43. The horrible death of Thalilaios, the impious archbishop of Thessalonica

In Thessalonica there was an archbishop named Thalilaios who feared neither God nor the reward which was in store for him. The wretch trampled christian teaching under foot and impiously treated the priestly dignity as nothing worth. He turned out to be a ravening wolf rather than a shepherd. He declined to worship the holy and consubstantial Trinity, turning instead (Oh Lord, forgive me!) to the worship of idols. So those who presided over the holy churches at that time expelled him by a canonical vote. A little while later however this man, so full of iniquity, wished to resume his priesthood. Since (as the most wise Solomon says) *all things are obedient to gold,* he was recalled and ordered to return to his own diocese (for it was at Constantinople that the rulers lived, those of whom Isaiah spoke: *Which justify the wicked for reward and take away the righteousness of the righteous man from him.* <Is 5:23>)

But God did not disregard his church. He reversed the judgement which had been pronounced in the bishop's favour in contravention of the Apostolic canons. On a certain day when he was all dressed up splendidly and ready to go before the rulers in order to regain his priestly dignity by their decision, just as he was about to leave his house, his belly intimated that he was in need of the privy. When he had been two hours in there without coming out, some of those who stood by went in,—for they had to ask him whether he was coming out. They found him with his head down in the drain of the privy and his feet up in the air. He had gained for himself an equally well-matched eternal death as that which bore off Arius, the sacrilegious enemy of God. For Arius too, when his hopes ran high of being arbitrarily restored to the church by the cooperation if those in authority, the wondrous angel of the holy church of God and of the great council, scattered his bowels (bitterly afflicted with the labour-pains of blasphemy) in a privy. When <Thalilaios> hoped to continue the evil he had previously committed by the unjust intervention of those in authority, the angel who governed the Thesslonican church set out together with the great martyr Demetrios. And in the very place where he used to associate with the impure demon which provoked him and to contrive his onslaughts against the holy church of God; there, in that place, he nailed the unhallowed <body> of him, the unprofitable servant, and lifted up into the air those feet which would not walk in the way of righteousness, bearing the marks which indicated the judgement which awaited him; and that *It is a terrible thing to fall into the hands of the living God* <Heb 10:31>.

44. The life of an elder, a monk living near the city of Antinoë* and concerning his prayer for a dead brother

When we came to the Thebaïd one of the elders told us that there was an elder of great repute living outside the city of Antinoë, one who had kept his cell for about seventy years. He had ten disciples but one of them was very careless so far as his own soul was concerned. The elder often besought and entreated him, saying: 'Brother, pay attention to your own soul, for death awaits you and the road to punishment'. The brother always disregarded the elder, refusing to accept what was said by him. Well, after a time, death carried the brother off and the elder was deeply troubled on his account, knowing that he had left this world sadly lacking in faith and devotion. The elder fell to his prayers and said: 'Lord Jesus Christ, our true God, reveal to me the state of the brother's soul'. He went into a trance and saw a river of fire with a multitude <of people> in the fire itself. Right in the middle was the brother, submerged up to his neck. The elder said to him: 'Was it not because of this retribution that I called on you to look after your own soul my child"? The brother answered and said to the elder: 'I thank God, father, that there is relief for my head. Thanks to your prayers I am standing on the head of a bishop'.

45. The life of a Monk, a recluse on the Mount of Olives and concerning the veneration of an icon of the most holy Mother of God

One of the elders told us that Abba Theodore the Aeliote said that there was a certain recluse on the Mount of Olives, a great warrior against whom the demon of sexual desire waged battle. One day when <the demon> attacked with vehemence, the elder began to give up in despair and to say to the demon: 'How much longer are you not going to let me go? Desist from growing old together with me'! The demon appeared to him in visible form, saying: 'Swear to me that you will never reveal to anybody what I am about to tell you and I will no longer wage war against you'. The elder swore: 'By Him who dwelleth in the heavens I will not tell anybody what you say'. The demon said to him: 'Desist from venerating this icon here and I will call off my war against you'. The icon in question bore the likeness of our Lady Mary, the holy Mother of God, carrying our Lord Jesus Christ. The recluse said to the demon: 'Let me go and think about it'. The next day he sent for Abba Theodore the Aeliote (the one who told us this story) for at that time he was residing at the Lavra of Pharôn. When Abba Theodore came, the recluse told him all there was to tell and received this reply: 'In fact you were ensnared when you swore, abba. But you are quite right to speak out. It were better for you to leave no brothel in the town unentered than to diminish reverence from our Lord Jesus Christ and from his Mother'. Abba Theodore strengthened and comforted the recluse with many words and then returned to his own place. The demon re-appeared to the recluse and said to him: 'What is this then, you wicked old man?* Did you not swear to me that you would not tell anybody? Why then have you revealed everything to the man who came to see you? I tell you, you wicked old man, you will be tried as an oath-breaker at the day of judgement'. The recluse answered: 'I know that I gave my oath and broke it, but it was with my Lord and Creator that I broke faith; you I will not obey. As the initiator of evil counsel and of the oath-breaking, you are the one who will have to face the inescapable consequences of the misdeeds you brought about'.

46. The wondrous vision of Abba Cyriacos of the Lavra of Calamôn and concerning two books of the impious Nestorios

We once paid a visit to Abba Cyriacos the priest at the Lavra of Calamôn on the Holy Jordan and he told us this story:
One day, in my sleep, I saw a woman of stately appearance clad in purple and after her <I saw> two reverend and honourable men standing outside my cell. It seemed to me that the woman was our Lady the Mother of God and that the men with her were Saint John the Divine and Saint John the Baptist. I went out of my cell and invited them to come in and offer a prayer in my cell, but she would not agree <to my request.> I persisted at some length, entreating her and saying: *Oh let the simple not go away ashamed* <Ps 73:21> and much else. When she realised that I was importunate with my invitation, she answered me coldly, saying: 'How can you ask me to enter your cell when you have my enemy in there?' With these words she went away. When I awoke, I began to worry and to wonder if I might have offended her in my thoughts, for there was nobody in the cell but me. I examined myself at some length and could find no fault which I might have committed against her. As it seemed that I was about to be overcome with remorse, I rose up and took up a scroll, intending to read it, thinking that perhaps reading would alleviate my distress. It was a book I had borrowed from Hesychios, priest of Jerusalem. I unwound it and found two writings of the irreligious Nestorios written at the end of it—and immediately I knew that he was the enemy of our Lady, the holy Mother of God. So I rose up and went off and gave the book back to him who had given it to me. I said to him: 'Take your book back, brother, for I have not derived as much benefit from it as it has brought adversity upon me'. When he asked me how it had caused me adversity, I told him what had happened. When he had

heard about it all, he immediately cut the writings of Nestorios off from the scroll and threw the piece into the fire, saying: 'The enemy of our Lady, the holy Mother of God, shall not remain in my cell either'.

47. A Miracle of the holy Mother of God against Gaïanas the actor who was blaspheming her in the theatre

[Heliopolis] is a city of Lebanese Phoenicia. There was an actor there named Gaïanas who used to perform at the theatre an act in which he blasphemed against the holy Mother of God. The Mother of God appeared to him saying: 'What evil have I done to you that you should revile me before so many people and blaspheme against me?' He rose up and, far from mending his ways, proceeded to blaspheme against her even more than before. Three times she appeared to him with the same reproach and admonition. As he did not mend his ways in the slightest degree, but rather blasphemed the more, she appeared to him once when he was sleeping at mid-day and said nothing at all. All she did was to sever his two hands and feet with her finger. When he woke up he found that his hands and feet were so afflicted that he just lay there like a tree-trunk. In these circumstances the wretched man confessed to everybody (making himself a public example) that he had received the reward for his blasphemy. And this he did for love of his fellow men.

48. Another miracle of the holy Mother of God by which Cosmiana, wife of Germanos, was compelled to return to the true faith from the Severan heresy

Anastasios, priest and treasurer at the holy <Church of the> Resurrection of Christ our God told us that Cosmiana, the wife of Germanos the Patrician, came one night, wishing to worship alone at the holy and life-giving sepulchre of our Lord Jesus Christ, the true God. When she approached the sanctuary, our Lady the holy Mother of God, together with other women, met her in visible form, and said to her: 'As you are not one of us, you are not to come in here, for you are none of ours'. The woman was in fact a member of the sect of Severus Acephalos.* She begged hard for permission to enter but the holy Mother of God replied: 'Believe me, woman, you shall not come in here until you are in communion with us'. The woman realised that it was because she was a heretic that she was being refused entry; and that nor would she be allowed in until she join the holy catholic and apostolic Church of Christ our God. She sent for the deacon and when the holy chalice arrived, she partook of the holy body and blood of our great God and Saviour Jesus Christ; and thus she was found worthy to worship unimpeded at the holy and life-giving sepulchre of our Lord Jesus Christ.

49. The Wondrous vision of the Duke of Palestine by which he was compelled to renounce the aforementioned heresy and to enter into communion with the Church of Christ

Anastasios the Priest also told us that when Gêbêmer became the military governor of Palestine, his first act was to come and worship at the holy <Church of the> Resurrection of Christ who is God. As he was about to approach, he saw a ram charging at him intent on impaling him on its horns. So great was his fear that he stepped backwards towards the guardian of <the Chapel of> the Cross who was present, and also the lictors who stood by. They said to him: ‘What is the matter, your highness? Why do you not enter”? He said: ‘Why did you bring in that ram”? They were taken aback by this, but they peered into the holy sepulchre and saw nothing. So they spoke to him, urging him to enter and telling him that there was no such thing <as a ram> in there. A second time he made as though to enter and again he saw the ram charging at him and preventing him from entering. This happened several times, at least in *his* eyes. Those who were with him saw nothing and the guardian of <the Chapel of> the Cross said to him: ‘Believe me, your highness, there is something in your soul and it is because of this that you are prevented from worshipping at the holy and life-giving sepulchre of our Saviour. You would do well to confess before God, for he is kindly disposed towards humanity and it was to show mercy on you that he made you see this vision’. Bursting into tears, the governor said: ‘I am responsible for many great sins against the Lord’. He cast himself face down on the ground and remained weeping in that position for a long time, confessing to God. Then he got up and made as though to enter the sepulchre, but he could not <enter>. The apparition of the ram prevented him no less than before. Then the guardian of <the Chapel of> the Cross said to him: ‘There is still some other impediment’. The governor replied: ‘Could it be that I am forbidden to enter because I am in communion with Severus, and not with the holy catholic and apostolic Church”? And he besought the guardian of <the Chapel of the> Cross that he might partake of the holy and life-giving mysteries of Christ our God. When the holy chalice arrived, he made his communion, and thus he entered and worshipped, no longer seeing anything <which deterred him>.

50. The Vision and a Saying of Abba George the recluse

Scythopolis was the second city of Palestine. There I met Abba Anastasios who told us about Abba George the recluse:
One night I got up to beat the wood <-en signal> (for I was the precentor) and I heard an elder weeping. I went and entreated him saying: 'Abba, what is the matter, sir, that you weep so"? He answered me not a word. So I asked him again: 'Tell me the cause <of your grief>.' Sighing from the depths of his heart, he said to me: 'How should I not weep, seeing that our Lord is not willing to be placated on our account? I thought I stood before one who sat on a high throne, my child.' Around him were several tens of thousands who besought and entreated him concerning a certain matter, but he would not be persuaded. Then a woman clothed in purple raiment came and fell down before him saying: 'Please, for my sake, grant this request', but he remained equally unmoved. 'That is why I weep and groan, for I am afraid of what is going to happen to me'. He said this to me at first light on the Thursday. The next day, Friday, about the ninth hour, there was a severe earthquake which overthrew the cities of the Phoenician coast.

This Abba Anastasios spoke to us again and told us this about the same elder:
Some time later, as he stood at the window <of his cell>, he began to weep and to say to me: 'Woe are we, brother, for we have no compunction, but live heedlessly. I fear we are at the gates <of perdition> and that the wrath of God has overtaken us'. The next day, fire appeared in the sky.

51. THE LIFE OF ABBA JULIAN, THE ELDER OF THE EGYPTIANS' MONASTERY

Anazarbos is the metropolis of Cilicia Secunda. About twelve miles away is the so-called 'Lavra of the Egyptians'. The fathers of that place told us that, five years earlier, an elder named Julian had died there. They testified that he spent about seventy years in one little cave and that he possessed nothing of this world's goods other than a hair shirt, a cloak, a book of the gospels, and a wooden bowl. They also said this of him: that all his life long he never lit a lamp to give light, for at night-time a light shone upon him from heaven sufficient for him to discern the sequence of the letters when he was reading.

52. A SAYING OF ABBA ELIAS THE SOLITARY

A brother visited Abba Elias the solitary at the community of the cave of Abba Sabas and said to him: 'Abba, give me a saying!' The elder said to the brother: 'In the days of our fathers, three virtues were cherished: poverty, humility and continence.* Now monks are dominated by avarice, gluttony and audacity. Hold on to which <of these> you will'.

53. THE LIFE OF CYRIACOS THE ELDER FROM THE MONASTERY OF SAINT SABAS*

Abba Stephan Trichinas told us about an elder named Cyriacos living at the Lavra of our saintly father Sabas, who once went down to Coutila. He stayed for a little while <there> beside the Dead Sea; then he started back to his cell. The heat was so intense that the elder was about to faint. So he stretched out his hands to heaven and prayed to God saying: 'Lord, you know that I can hardly walk for thirst'. Immediately there came a cloud about him and it was not taken away from him until he was back at his cell once more. It was a distance of twelve miles. The same Stephan told us this about the same elder: One day some of his relatives came wanting to see him. When they came into the Lavra, they enquired where his cell was. Some people showed them where it was located, so they went and knocked at the door. Realising who they were, the elder prayed God not to let him be seen by them. He opened the door and went out of his cell, but he was not seen by them. He went out into the wilderness and did not return to his cell until they had gone away.

54. The life of the Monks of Scêtê and concerning an elder <named> Ammonios

At Terenuthis we met Abba Theodore of Alexandria. This elder said to us: 'My child, it was by <their> nature that the monks lost Scêtê, just as the elder predicted. Believe this elder who speaks to you, children; amongst the Scetiotes there was great love, asceticism and discernment.* I have seen elders there who never ate at all, unless somebody came that way. Amongst these there was an elder named Ammonios who lived close by me. Once I realised the way he lived, I used to visit him every Saturday so that, by my intervention, he would take some food. No matter at what hour visitors arrived for the purpose of prayer, it was the practice of those fathers, once they had offered their prayers, to set the table for them and immediately to eat some food'.*

55. The life of an elder who stayed at Scêtê and concerning Abba Irenaeus

Abba Irenaeus told us that there was an elder living at Scêtê who saw the devil at night offering gardening implements <?> to the brethren. The elder said to the devil: 'What are these'? The devil replied: 'I am presenting the brothers with a distraction to make them less assiduous in glorifying God'. The same Abba Irenaeus spoke to us again saying: When barbarians came to Scêtê, I withdrew and came into the district of Gaza, where I accepted a cell for myself at the Lavra. From the abba of the Lavra I received a book of sayings of the elders.* The same day I set myself to read it and, as soon as I unrolled the book, I found a passage in which a brother visited and elder and said to him: 'Pray for me father'. The elder said: 'When you were with us I used to pray for you. Now you have gone away to your own homeland I pray for you no longer'. When I read this, I rewound the book and said to myself: 'Oh wretched Irenaeus, to have fled to your own homeland—and the fathers no longer pray for you!' I immediately gave the book <back> to the abba, left <that place> and came to The Cells.* And that, children, is why I am here.

56. The life of John, the disciple of a great elder who lived in the village of Parasêma

Ptolemaïs is a city of Phoenicia. There is a village nearby called Parasêma in which there resided a great elder. He had a disciple named John who was also great and who excelled in obedience. One day the elder sent the disciple to perform a task for him, giving him a little bread to sustain him on the way. The disciple went and completed the task and then came back, bringing the bread with him, untouched. When the elder saw the bread, he said to him: 'Why did you not eat any of the bread I gave you, my child?' Making an act of obeisance, the disciple said to the elder: 'Forgive me, father, but when you blessed me and dismissed me, you did not say I was to eat of the bread; and that is why I did not eat it'. Amazed at the disciple's discernment, the elder gave him his blessing. After the death of this elder, a vision from God appeared to the brother (who had just concluded a forty-day fast) which said to him: 'Whatever <disorder> you lay your hand on, it shall be healed'. When morning came, by the providence of God a man arrived, bringing his wife who had a cancer of the breast. The man besought <the brother> to heal his wife. The brother replied: 'I am a sinful man and unworthy of such an undertaking'. The woman's husband continued to beg him to accede to his request and to have pity on his wife. So <the brother> laid his hand <on the diseased part> and sealed <it with the sign of the cross> and she was immediately healed. From that time on God performed many signs* through him, not only in his own lifetime, but also after his death.*

57. The Death of Symeon the Stylite* and concerning Abba Julian, another stylite

Four miles from the city of Ægaion a stylite was installed whose name was Symeon. He was struck by lightening and died. Abba Julian the stylite <whose pillar was> on the Gulf <of Alexandretta?> told his disciples to burn incense, not at the accustomed time. The disciples said to him: 'Tell us why, father'. He said to them: 'Because brother Symeon of Ægaion has been struck by lightening and is dead. Behold, his soul is departing with great gladness'. They were twenty-four miles from each other.*

58. Concerning Julian again

Abba Stephan Trichinas told us this too about Abba Julian the stylite. A lion appeared in the area and destroyed many people, strangers and natives. One day the elder called his disciple to him (the man's name was Pancratios) and told him: 'Go about two miles towards the north and you will find a lion in its lair there. Say to it: "The lowly Julian says: In the name of Jesus Christ the son of the living God, withdraw from this land."' The brother went and found the lion in its lair. He delivered the elder's message, whereupon the lion immediately and without delay went away; and everybody glorified God.

59. The life of Abba Thalilaios the Cilician

Abba Peter, priest of the same lavra, told us that Abba Thalilaios the Cilician spent sixty years in the monastic life and never once stopped weeping. He would always say: 'God gave us this time for repentance; it is indeed for Him that we must seek'.

60. The Strange Deed of an Anchoress as a result of which a youth who loved her became a monk out of remorse; and concerning Julian again

When we were in Alexandria, a man who loved Christ told us a story along these lines. He said that there was an anchoress [μονάστρια] who led a solitary life in her own home, cultivating her soul with fasting, prayers, vigils and by making many charitable donations. But the devil, always at war with the human race, could not tolerate the virtuous life of the maiden. So he stirred up a cloud of trouble for her. He inflamed a young man with satanic lust for her. The youth would wait for her outside her house. When she wished to go out, to go from her home to the oratory to pray, the youth would hinder her, forcing his attentions upon her in the way lovers do. The anchoress was so besieged by the attentions of the youth that she could not even set foot outside her own house. So one day she sent her maid to the youth with this message: 'Come into the house; my mistress wants <to see> you'. The youth went in very gladly, thinking that his desires were about to be fulfilled. She was sitting at her loom. 'Sit down' she said to the youth, and seating herself, she said to him: 'Now, brother, why do you persecute me like this, sir, and why will you not even let me out of my house?' The youth answered: 'Oh mistress, I want you so badly! Whenever I see you, I am all on fire, from head to toe.' She said to him: 'What do you see in me that appeals to you so that you love me so?' The youth said: 'Your eyes. It is your eyes which have seduced me.' When the anchoress heard this, that her eyes had led the youth astray, she picked up her shuttle and pierced and cast out both her eyes <with it>. When the youth realised that it was because of him that she had put out her two eyes, he was so filled with remorse that he went away to Scêtê and distinguished himself as a monk.

61. The life of Abba Leontios the Cilician

Some fathers told us about Abba Leontios the Cilician who served devotedly on the staff of the New Church* of our Lady Mary, the holy Mother of God. For about forty years he never came out of that church; he was always deep in thought and always kept his own counsel. They also told us this about him: that if he saw an indigent coming towards him, if it was a blind man he would give him something into his hand. But if it were one who could see, Abba Leontios would put the coins before the man, perhaps on the base of a column, on a seat or maybe on the sanctuary steps and the poor man would take them from there <himself>. When an elder asked why he did not give them into the hand <of a beggar> he answered: 'Forgive me father, but it is not I who gives. It is my lady the Mother of God who provides for both me and for them.'

62. The life of Abba Stephan, priest of the Lavra of the Æliotes

One of the elders told us that once, when Abba Stephan, priest of the Lavra of the Æliotes, was sitting in his cell, the devil put evil thoughts into his mind, saying: 'Go somewhere else, for it is not good staying here'. The elder said to the devil: 'I do not accept what you say; I know who you are. You do not want to see anybody saved, but Christ, the Son of the living God, he will overthrow you!'

63. Concerning the same

They say that the same elder was once sitting in his cell when the devil appeared to him in visible form and said: 'Get away from here elder, for it is no good for you'. Then the elder said to the demon: 'To convince me that you want me to go away, make what I am sitting on start walking around'; he was sitting on a wicker-work chair. When the demon heard this, he immediately caused not only the seat, but also the whole cell to move around. When the elder perceived the craftiness of the demon, he said to him: 'Now, since you are so fierce and terrible, I will most certainly not go away'. He offered a prayer and the hostile demon disappeared.

64. Concerning the same

Three elders went to visit the same Abba Stephan the priest and whilst they remained there talking about what is beneficial to the soul he remained silent. The elders said to him: 'You are not answering us father. It was for the benefit <of your counsel> that we came to you'. Then he said to them: 'Forgive me, but I did not know what you were talking about until just now. But I can tell you what is matter with me; I can see nothing else, either by night or by day, but our Lord Jesus Christ hanging on the cross'. They went their way greatly edified.

65. CONCERNING THE SAME

Abba John, surnamed Molybas, told about this elder (I mean Abba Stephan) that when he was lying seriously ill, the doctors urged him to eat some meat. Now this blessed brother had a <blood-> brother in secular society, a very devout man who lived his life for the living God. As the brother was eating the meat, his <natural> brother who lived 'in the world' came to <visit> him—and was offended when he saw what was happening. He was distressed (he said) that at the end of so long a period of ascetic rigour and self-discipline, his brother should now partake of meat. He immediately went into a trance and saw one who spoke to him, saying: 'Why are you offended at the sight of the priest eating meat? Do you not realise that he ate it out of necessity and obedience? In truth, you ought not to be offended. If you want to know to what glory your brother has attained, then turn round and look'. He said that he turned round—and saw the priest, crucified—just as Christ was crucified; and the apparition said: 'You see to what glory he has attained? Glorify Him who glorifies those who truly love him.'

66. THE LIFE OF ABBA THEODOSIOS THE SOLITARY

Abba Anthony, superior and builder of the Lavra of the Æliotes, told us this about Abba Theodosios the solitary. He said:
Before taking up the solitary life, I went into a trance and saw a young man whose appearance was brighter than the sun. He took me by the hand and said to me: 'Come, for you must fight', and he led me into an <amphi-> theatre larger than words could describe. I could see that the theatre was full of men, those on the one side dressed in white whilst those on the other side were black-faced

ones.* As he led me to the sanded pit of the theatre I saw a black-faced man of exceedingly large stature whose head stood as high as the clouds, strong and ugly. Then the youth whom I saw in the vision said to me: 'It is with that one that you must fight'. When I saw the man, I was horror-struck; I began to quake and to be terrified. I started pleading with him who had brought me there, saying: 'What man who is merely mortal could strive with that one? [Not even the whole human race put together could withstand this fellow'. But the noble youth said to me:] 'Go in with confidence, for when you have joined in combat with him, it is I who shall decide the result and award the victor's crown.' Almost as soon as I had gone into the sanded pit and we had come to grips with each other, the noble umpire came at once, made his decision and awarded me the crown. The faction of the black-faced ones disappeared with moaning and groaning. The other faction, consisting of those who wore white, shouted their approval of the umpire and of him who had awarded me an auspicious victory.

67. Concerning the same

Concerning this Abba Theodosios the solitary, Abba Cyriacos, his disciple, told us that he spent thirty-five years as a solitary fasting two days <before he ate> and keeping completely silent, speaking to nobody. If he said anything at all, he did it by signs. I saw this man myself in the Lavra of the Æliotes mentioned above, for I stayed there ten years.

68. Concerning the same

When Abramios, higoumen of the new <Church of> Saint Mary the Mother of God, learned that Abba Theodosios had no garment to wear in the winter, he bought him a shirt. One night when <Theodosios> sat down to sleep (for he slept on a chair) some thieves came, stripped him of his monastic cloak and took it away. When this happened, the elder said nothing about it whatsoever.

69. The life of Abba Palladios and of an elder of Thessalonica, a recluse named David

Master Sophronios the sophist (before he embraced the monastic life) and I met Abba Palladios in Alexandria. He was a man who both loved and served God and he had his monastery at Lithazomenon. We pressed him to speak an edifying word to us. The elder began to say to us: 'Children, the time that remains to us is short. Let us struggle for a little <in this world> and labour, in order that we might have the enjoyment of very great things in eternity. Look at the martyrs, look at the holy men, look at the ascetics; see how courageously they persevered. We will ever wonder at the endurance of those whose remembrances have been preserved from time past. Every one who hears of them acknowledges with great astonishment the superhuman endurance of the blessed martyrs; how their eyes were plucked out; how the legs of some of them were cut off, others their hands, whilst some had their feet destroyed. How some were eliminated by raging fire whilst others were slowly roasted. How some were drowned in rivers, others at sea. How some were torn apart by carnivorous beasts like criminals whilst others were fed to birds of prey after suffering exquisite tortures. In brief, if it were possible to describe all the different tortures which were devised for their affliction, everything that the enemy, the devil, has inflicted upon the martyrs and ascetics who loved God, it would be seen how much they endured and how they have wrestled, triumphing over the weakness of the flesh by the courage of the soul. They attained to those good things for which they hoped by counting them more worthy than the trials of this earthly life. This provides a demonstration of the solid quality of their faith in two ways. On the one hand, that having endured a little, they now enjoy great benefits in eternity. On the other hand, that they so cheerfully endured the physical torments with which the adversary the devil afflicted them. If therefore we endure affliction and persevere, with the help of God, we shall be found to be friends of God indeed. And God will be with us, fighting shoulder to shoulder with us in the battle, greatly alleviating that which we must endure. My children, since we know what kind of times these are and what kind of labour is required of us, let us strive for the self-knowledge which is attained by means of the solitary life. For at this stage it is required of us that we sincerely repent, so that we may indeed be temples of God. For it will not be honour such as the world gives that we will receive in the world to come'.

Again he said: 'Let us remember Him who has nowhere to lay his head', <Mt 8:20> and again: 'Since Saint Paul says *Tribulation worketh patience,* <Rm 5:3> let us make our minds able to receive the kingdom of heaven'. And again: *'Children, let us not love the world, neither those things which are in the world'* <1 Jn 2:15.> Again the elder said: 'Let us keep a guard over our thoughts, for this is the medicine of salvation'.

We went to the same Abba Palladios with this request: 'Of your charity, tell us, father, where you came from, and how it came about that you embraced the monastic life'. He was from Thessalonica, he said, and then he told us this: 'In my home country, about three stades beyond the city wall, there was a recluse, a native of Mesopotamia whose name was David. He was a man of outstanding virtue, merciful and continent. He spent about twenty years in his place of confinement. Now at this time, because of the barbarians, the walls of the city were patrolled at night by soldiers. One night those who were on guard-duty at that stretch of the city-walls nearest to where the elder's place of confinement was located, saw fire pouring from the windows of the recluse's cell. The soldiers thought the barbarians must have set the elder's cell on fire; but when they went out in the morning, to their amazement, they found the elder unharmed and his cell unburned. Again the following night they saw fire, the same way as before, in the elder's cell—and this went on for a long time. The occurrence became known to all the city and <throughout> the countryside. Many people would come and keep vigil at the wall all night long in order to see the fire, which continued to appear until the elder died. As this phenomenon did not merely appear once or twice but was often seen, I said to myself: 'If God so glorifies his servants in *this* world, how much more so in the world to come when He shines upon their face like the sun? This, my children, is why I embraced the monastic life.'

70. THE LIFE OF A MESOPOTAMIAN MONK, ADDAS THE RECLUSE

The elder also told us this: that after Abba David, there came <to Thessalonica> another monk, also from Mesopotamia, whose name was Adolas.* He confined himself in a hollow plane tree in another part of the city. He made a little window in the tree through which he could talk with people who came to see him. When the barbarians came and laid waste all the countryside, they happened to pass by that place. One of the barbarians noticed the elder looking down at them. He drew his sword and raised his arm to strike the elder. But he remained there, rooted to the spot with his hand stuck up in the air. When the rest of the barbarians saw this, they were amazed and, falling down before him, they besought the elder [to restore their comrade]. The elder offered a prayer and healed him and thus he dismissed them in peace.

71. The Beautiful Saying of a Murderer to a Monk Who Followed Him When He Was Being Led to Execution

The same Abba, Palladios, told us of something that happened at Arsinoë, a city of the Thebaïd. A man was arrested there for murder. After suffering many tortures, he was finally condemned to be beheaded. As he was being taken to where he had committed the murder (a point about six miles outside the city), there was a monk following behind, apparently with the intention of seeing how he would be decapitated. As he passed along the way to his execution, the condemned man saw the monk who was following and said to him: 'Well now, abba, have you no cell, sir, nor any work to occupy your hands?' The monk answered: 'Of course I have a cell, brother, and also something to occupy my hands'. The man rejoined: 'Then why do you not stay in your cell and weep for your sins?' The monk replied: 'Ah, brother, I am very negligent of my soul's health—and that is precisely why I am coming to see how you die, that by this means I might come <to have some> compunction'. The condemned man said to him: 'Go your way, abba; remain in your cell, sir, and give thanks to God who saved us. It was because he was made man and died for us that man dies no more the eternal death.'

72. Abba Palladios' Story of an Old Man Who Committed Murder and Falsely Accused a Youth of the Same Crime

Abba Palladios told us that an old fellow living in the world was arrested for murder. When he was tortured by the magistrate of Alexandria he said that somebody else had been involved in the murder as his accomplice, a young fellow about twenty years old. They were both severely tortured. The old fellow said: 'You were with me when I committed the murder'. The youth denied having anything to do with the affair, nor had he been with the old fellow. When they had both been severely tortured they were condemned to be hanged. So they went out to the fifth <mile-post from the city> to where it is customary to punish such criminals. About one stade away there is a ruined temple of Kronos. When they came to the place, the populace and the soldiers wanted to hang the youth on the scaffold first. He made a profound act of obeisance before the soldiers and said: 'For the sake of the Lord, of your charity hang me towards the east so that I may look in that direction when I am hanging there alone'. The soldiers said to him: 'Why so'? He replied: 'In truth, sirs, it is only seven months since your unworthy <servant> received baptism and became a Christian'. When they heard this, the soldiers wept over the youth. The old fellow called out in great anger: 'By Serapis, hang me so I look towards Kronos!' When the soldiers heard the blasphemy of the old fellow, they left the youth aside and hung the old one. And as they were doing this, a mounted messenger arrived from the prefect and said to the soldiers: 'Do not execute the youth, bring him back'. This brought joy to all the soldiers who were there. They took him and brought him back into the praetorium, and the prefect released him. Having been rescued when he despaired <of rescue>, the young man went and became a monk. We have written this for the benefit of the many [and of ourselves, so we might be aware that the Lord knows how to deliver the godly from temptation].

73. THE LIFE OF JOHN THE SOLDIER OF ALEXANDRIA

Abba Palladios told us this too: There was a soldier at Alexandria whose name was John. This was the kind of life he led: all day long, from dawn to the ninth hour, he would stay in his monastery near the steps of Saint Peter's <church> wearing nothing but a coarse cloak and weaving baskets. He kept his peace and would say nothing to anybody. He used to stay in the oratory doing his handwork and this was all he would say with his mouth: 'Cleanse me, Oh Lord, from my secret sins <Ps 18:13> that I be not disappointed in my prayer'. When he had recited this verse he would remain silent for a good hour; then he would repeat the same thing an hour or more later. He said it seven times a day and never said any other word at all. At the ninth hour he would remove the rough cloak he was wearing and put on military uniform (in other words, his own clothes) and go on duty with his own unit. I stayed with this man for eight years and I was greatly edified by his silence and the way he lived his life.

74. A TRUE SAYING OF THE SAME ABBA, PALLADIOS, CONCERNING HERESIES

By way of injunction the elder said to us: 'Believe me children; heresies and schisms have done nothing for the holy church except to make us love God and each other very much less than before'.

75. A MIRACLE OF THE LORD FOR THE WIFE AND DAUGHTER OF ONE OF THE FAITHFUL WHO WAS ACCUSTOMED TO ENTERTAINING MONKS

On another occasion when we were visiting him, Abba Palladios told us about a Christ-loving man living in Alexandria, a man of great piety and mercy, hospitably disposed towards monks. He was married to a woman of singular piety who fasted all day long, and they had a six-year old daughter. One day this christian gentleman set out for Constantinople, for he was a merchant. He left his wife and child with one servant in the house and so departed to find a ship. As he was leaving to embark his wife said to him: 'To whom are you commending us?' The husband said: 'To our Lady, the

Mother of God'. One day as the mother was occupying herself with her tasks and the child was with her, the devil put it into the mind of the servant to murder the woman and her child, to seize all their possessions and to run away. He took a knife from the kitchen and went to the dining-room where the mistress was. But when he reached the dining-room door he was afflicted with blindness so that he was unable either to return to the kitchen or to go on into the dining-room. He spent over an hour flailing the air and making every effort to get in. Then he began to call for his mistress, saying: 'Come here'. She was surprised that the servant was standing in the doorway and did not come to her, but rather called <for her to come to him>. She said to him: 'Do you rather come here', for she did not know that he had been struck blind. The servant began to entreat her with oaths to approach him and she swore that she would not. He said to her: 'Then send the child to me', but she would not do that either, saying: 'If you want to, you come <here>.' At that, seeing that he was incapable of doing anything <to help himself> the servant turned the knife around and struck himself a mortal blow. When his mistress saw what he had done, she screamed out and the neighbours came in immediately. The police arrived too and found the servant <still> alive. They learnt everything from him and they glorified the God who showed wonders, saving both the mother and her child.

76. The Drowning of Mary

Abba Palladios also told us that he had heard a shipmaster telling a story something like this:

One day I was sailing along with passengers on board, both men and women. We came out onto the high sea and all the other ships were sailing well, some to Constantinople, some to Alexandria, others elsewhere. The wind stood well for each of them, but we alone could make no headway. We remained stuck in the same place for fifteen days, not moving at all from where we lay. We were in great distress and despair, not knowing why this should be. As I was the master of the vessel, responsible for both the boat and also for all who sailed in her, I began to pray to God about the matter. One day there came to me a voice of no visible origin saying: 'Throw Mary out and you will make good way'. As I delayed, trying to work out what this meant and who Mary might be, the voice came to me again: 'I told you: throw Mary out and you will be safe'. Then I devised the following procedure. I shouted out: 'Mary!'—for I had no idea who Mary was. She, however, was lying in her bunk; and she responded, saying: 'Why are you calling, sir?' Then I said to her: 'Would you please be so kind as to come here?' She got up and came. When she arrived, I took her aside and said to her: 'Sister Mary, you see how great my sins are and that because of me you are all going to perish?' She heaved a deep sigh and said: 'Oh Shipmaster, sir; in fact it is I who am the sinner'. I said to her: 'Woman, what sins have you committed?' She said: 'I think there is no sin which I have *not* committed; and because of my sins, everybody is going to perish'. Then (said the shipmaster) the woman said something like this to me: 'In fact, Shipmaster, wretch that I am sir, I had a husband and two children of his fathering. When one of the children was nine years old and the other five, my husband died and I was left a widow. There was a soldier living near me who wished to take me for his wife and I sent some people to <talk to> him. The soldier said he would not take a wife who had children by another man with her. When I learned that he did not want to take me on account of the children, and also because I was very much in love with him, wretch that I am, I slew the children and said to him: "See, now I have none". When he heard what I had done with the children, he said: "As the Lord lives who dwells in heaven, I will not have her". In my fear that it might become known what I had done and I lose my life, I fled'. Even when I heard this from the woman, I still did not want to throw her into the sea just like that. So I equivocated (he said) and told her: 'Look, I will get into the dinghy and if the vessel then makes way, know, woman, that it is *my* sins which are at work in this ship. Then (he said) he called for the dinghy and ordered it to be launched. But when he got into it, neither ship nor dinghy made any more headway than before. So he came back on board and said to the woman: 'You get down into the dinghy'. She did; and as soon as she set foot in the dinghy, it turned round about five times and then sank to the bottom of the deep. Then the ship sailed on and in three and a half days we completed a journey which should have taken fifteen days'.

77. The Story of Three Blind Men and of How They Became Blind

One day Master Sophronios and I went to the house of Stephan the Sophist on a business matter and it was midday. He lived at the <Church of the> holy Mother of God which was built by the blessed Pope Eulogios* and was known as Dorothea's. When we knocked at the philosopher's house, a maid peered out of an upper window and said: 'He is sleeping, but wait a while'. I said to Master Sophronios: 'Let us go to the Tetrapylon and wait there'. This place called the Tetrapylon is held in very high esteem by the citizens of Alexandria for they say that Alexander (who founded their city) took the relics of the Prophet Jeremiah from Egypt and buried them there. When we came to that place, nobody was there except three blind men, for it was noon. We quietly came to where they were, without creating any disturbance—for we had our books with us. The blind men were conversing with each other and one of them said to another: 'How in fact did you lose your sight?' This was the reply: 'As a young man I was a sailor. We set sail from Africa and on the high sea I developed ophthalmia. As I could not go and get treatment, white spots appeared in my eyes and I lost my sight'.

And he said to the other: 'Now, how did you come to be blind"? The man replied: 'I was a glass-blower by trade and both my eyes began to discharge from <exposure to> the fire. Then I became blind'. These two now said to the third: 'And you now, how did you lose your sight"? He replied: 'Well now, I will tell you. When I was a young man, I thoroughly detested work; so I became a prodigal.* When it came to the point where I had nothing to eat, I resorted to theft. One day, after I had accomplished many deeds of wickedness, I was standing in the market-place and I saw a richly decked-out corpse being taken for burial. I followed the cortège to see where they where going to bury <the body>. They went behind Saint John's Church and placed it in a sepulchre; then they went their way. When I saw that everyone had gone, I went into the sepulchre and stripped the corpse of all its clothes—except for a single shroud. As I was leaving the sepulchre (taking a considerable amount of booty with me) my evil habits said to me: "Take the shroud too; it's worth the trouble". So, wretch that I am, I turned back and removed the shroud from the corpse, leaving it naked. At which point the dead man sat up before me and stretched out his hands towards me. With his fingers he clawed my face and plucked out both my eyes. I cravenly left all behind and fled from the sepulchre, badly hurt and chilled with horror. Now I too have told you how I came to be blind.' When we had heard all this, Master Sophronios made a sign to me and we left the blind men. The he said to me: 'You know, abba, I do not think we should do any business today, sir, for we have gained much profit from what we have heard'. We had indeed benefitted <from that experience> and, having benefitted ourselves, we have written it down so that you who hear these things might benefit from them too. It is a fact that no evil-doer can escape the notice of God. We heard this story with our own ears from the very man to whom it had happened.

78. The Amazing Miracle of a Dead Girl who Detained her Despoiler and would not let him go until he Promised to Become a Monk

When we were visiting Abba John, higoumen of the Giants' Monastery at Theoupolis,* he told us a somewhat similar story: Not long ago a young man came to me saying: 'For God's sake, take me in, for I want to repent'—and he was weeping bitterly whilst he said this. I could see that he was deeply troubled and perplexed. 'Tell me how you have come to such compunction', I said, and he replied: 'Abba, I most certainly am a sinner, sir'. Again I said to him: 'Believe me child; just as there are many and different kinds of sin, so there are many cures. If you wish to be healed, tell me truthfully what deeds you have committed so that I can apply suitable penances.* One does not apply the same treatment to a fornicator and to a murderer and to a sorcerer. Greed is treated one way, [lying, anger, theft, adultery—each has its proper medication. But rather than go on listing sins for you, <let me say that> just as we see various remedies applied to different physical infirmities, so too for the sins of the soul (which are many) a variety of medicaments is available.]* He heaved a great sigh and smote himself on the breast, breaking into tears and sobbing. So great was the disturbance in his heart that he was unable to speak clearly. When I saw that he was paralysed and struck dumb by his grief and could therefore tell me nothing of his condition, I said to him: 'Listen to me, my child; take a hold of yourself and tell me what has happened. Christ our God himself will grant you his own aid. Of his unspeakable love for mankind and his immeasurable mercy he endured everything for our salvation. He consorted with publicans; he did not turn away the woman who was a sinner nor did he reject the thief; and, finally, he accepted <death on> the cross. When you repent and turn to him, he will receive you with his own hands and in great joy, for *He desires not the death of a sinner but that he should turn to Him and live* <1 Tm 2:4>. Then he made an effort to pull himself together. When his tears had abated somewhat, he said to me: 'Abba, I who am full of sin, sir, and unworthy of heaven and earth. Two days ago, I heard of the death of the maiden daughter of somebody of first rank in this city; also that she had been buried in many clothes in a sepulchre outside the city. Now I was already in the habit of doing the forbidden deed <of robbing graves>. I went to the sepulchre by night and began stripping the corpse. I stripped her of all she wore, not even leaving the innermost little garment but taking that from her too and making her as naked as the day she was born. Just before I was about to leave the tomb, she sat up before me and stretched out her left hand. She took hold of my right hand and said: "Oh, man, did you have to strip me naked? Have you no fear of God? Ought you not to have had pity on me in death? Should you not respect my sex? How can you, as a Christian, condemn me to presenting myself naked before Christ because you had so little respect for my sex? Is mine not the sex which gave you birth? Do you not outrage your own mother in so using me? Wretched man, what sort of a defence will you offer for this crime against me when you come to the terrifying judgement seat of Christ? As long as I lived, no strange man ever saw my face; and now, after death and burial, you have stripped me and looked upon my naked body. What is there to be said for humanity when it can stoop to such depths? What a heart, what hands you are going to have when you come to receive the all-holy body and blood of our Lord Jesus Christ!" When I heard and saw this, I was seized by fear and dread. Quaking, I said to her: "Let me go—and never again will I do this", but she said: "You came in here when you wanted to; but you will not go out of here as you will. This tomb shall be shared by the two of us. And do not think that you are going to die right away. Only after many days of torment will you—in evil circumstances—surrender your soul". I begged her with tears in my eyes to let me go, making great oaths by almighty God that I would never again commit that forbidden and illegal deed <of grave-robbing>. After I had implored her at great length and poured out many tears, she replied in these words: "If you wish to live and to be delivered from this anguish, give me your word that if I shall let you go, not only will you desist from your hateful and profane deeds, but also that you will, immediately and without delay, go renounce the world and become a monk—so that you can repent of your misdeeds and live in the service of Christ". I swore to her, saying: "Not only will I do all that you have said, but from this day forward I will not enter my house. Rather will I go from here immediately to a monastery". Then the maiden said to me: "Dress me as you found me". I made her fit for burial again and then she lay back down and was dead. I, the unworthy, the sinner that I am, immediately went out of the sepulchre and came here.' When I heard all this from the young man, I comforted and refreshed him by talking to him about repentance and continence. Some time later I tonsured him, clothed him in the monastic habit and shut him up in a cave in the mountain within the city, he giving thanks to God and fighting a good fight for his own soul.

79. A Tremendous and Stupendous Miracle of the Most Holy Sacrament under Dionysios, Bishop of Seleucia

When we came to Seleucia (which is not far from Antioch) we met Abba Theodore, bishop of that same city, Seleucia, and he told us this:

In the time of the blessed Dionysios who was my predecessor as bishop of this city, an event like this took place. There was a businessman who was both devout and rich; but he was a heretic of the Severite persuasion. He had a manager, however, who was in communion with the holy catholic and apostolic Church. Following the local custom, the manager received communion on Maundy Thursday, placed it in a box inlaid with mosaic and locked it up in his safe. Now it happened that after Easter the manager was sent to Constantinople on business and he inadvertently left the holy species* in his safe. But he gave the key of the safe to his master. One day the master opened the safe and found the mosaic box containing the holy species. This rather upset him, and he did not know what to do with them. He was unwilling to consume them since they originated in the catholic Church, whilst he was of the sect of Severus. So he left them in the safe, thinking that the manager would return and consume them. When it came around <again> to the great day of Maundy Thursday and the manager had still not returned, the master wanted to burn them so that they would not remain <there> for a second year. When he opened the safe he saw that all the holy portions had sprouted shoots. He was overcome with much fear and wonder at this strange and unexpected sight. He and all his household took the holy particles and, with a cry of 'Lord, have mercy', off they went at a run to the holy church <in search of> the saintly Bishop Dionysios. This great and fearful wonder which defied all reason was not seen merely by two or three persons or even by a few who could be easily counted. The whole church saw it: townsfolk and countrymen, natives and immigrants, all who travelled by land or by sea, men and women, old men and children, youths and elders, masters and slaves, rich and poor, rulers and their subjects, literate and illiterate, those dedicated to the clerical life and those who had espoused virginity and asceticism; widows and decently married people; those in and those under authority. Some cried out: 'Lord have mercy' whilst others praised <God> in different ways. Yet all gave thanks to God for his extraordinary and unspeakable marvels. Many joined the holy catholic and apostolic Church on account of their faith in this miracle.

80. The spring conferred on the brothers of the monastery in Skopelos at the prayers of Theodosios, their abbot

We came to the monastery of Abba Theodosios at Skopelos <=the rock>. There is a mountain between inland Seleucia and Rossos in Cilicia. The fathers of this monastery led us up beyond the monastery about as far as an arrow could be shot. There they showed us a spring, saying that it gave a plentiful supply of excellent water and that it was a gift of God to them. 'It is not a natural occurrence' they said, 'but was given to us by divine intervention. Our saintly father Theodosios the Great fasted at great length and poured forth tears, making many genuflexions in prayer to God that he would grant us the comfort of this water. In former times our fathers used to draw their water from the wadi. But God *who always does the will of those that fear him* <Ps 144:19> granted us the blessing of water through the prayers of our father. Two years ago some of the brethren asked the higoumen if they might construct a bath in the monastery. Our higoumen frowned on this suggestion but allowed it as a concession to the weakness of the brethren. The bath was built, but they bathed no more than the one time; for this beautiful spring which God had provided promptly faltered and failed. We tell you no less than the truth in saying that we fasted a great deal and offered up many intercessions with much tears—and still no water came from the spring. It was dry for a whole year and we were in great distress. Then our father destroyed the bath—and God gave us water again!

81. A well that filled with water when an icon of the same Abba Theodosios was let down into it

The same fathers also told us that in those days, a Christ-loving woman of the district of Apamea dug a well. She spent a great deal of money on the project and dug very deep, but she found no water. Having put so much money and effort into the project, she was very discouraged. Then one day, she had a vision of somebody saying to her: 'Send for and bring the picture of Abba Theodosios at Skopelos and by that means God will give you water'. The woman sent two men at once. They took the icon of the saint and let it down into the well and immediately water began to flow; it filled the well-shaft up to the half-way point. The men who drew the icon up out of the water brought us some of it; we drank of it and all gave thanks to God.

82. The life of John, an elder at the Skopelos monastery

We saw an elder in the same monastery whose name was John. The fathers of that place told us: 'Believe us, Christians, that is a great one and feared by the demons. Whoever comes here troubled by an unclean spirit, that elder provides a cure'.

83. Concerning the same

The fathers of that place also told us this about the same elder, John. About twenty miles from the monastery there is a market town called Leptê Akra <=the little promontory>. In that market town there was a ship-owner who had a vessel with a capacity of about 35,000 *modii* <= *ca* 750 tonnes> which he wanted to launch. He spent two weeks with many workmen on this task (he said he employed three hundred workmen each day). However he could neither get the vessel to the sea nor even move it from the spot where it lay; for the vessel was under the <spell of> men who were workers of evil. The owner of the ship was very disturbed and at a loss what to do next. By the providence of God, it happened that the elder came that way. When the ship-owner saw the elder, because he had some knowledge of his qualities, he said to him: 'Abba, please pray for my ship, sir. On account of enchantment, it cannot be launched'. The elder said to the shipmaster: 'Go, give me something to eat and God will come to your aid'. The elder said this so that the ship-owner would go away to his own house. The monk approached the ship alone, made three prostration before God and three times he signed the vessel with the sign of the cross, in the name of our lord Jesus Christ. The elder then came to the house of the ship-owner and said to him: 'Go now and launch your vessel'. Putting his trust in the elder, the ship-owner went with a very few men and, as soon as they took the strain, the ship was found to be in the sea. And everybody glorified God.

84. The life and death of an anchorite of the same monastery, a servant of God

The fathers of the same monastery told us this:
There was an anchorite in these mountains, a great man in the eyes of God who survived for many years on the natural vegetation which could be found there. He died in a certain small cave and we did no know, for we imagined that he had gone away to another wilderness place. One night this anchorite appeared to our present father, that good and gentle shepherd, Abba Julian, as he slept, saying to him: 'Take some men and go, take me up from the place where I am lying, up on the mountain called The Deer'. So our father took some <brethren> and went up into the mountain of which he had spoken. We sought for many hours but we did not

come across the remains of the anchorite. With the passage of time, the entrance to the cave <in which he lay> had been covered over by shrubs and snow. As we found nothing, the abba said: 'Come, children, let us go down',—and just as we were about to return, a deer approached and came to a standstill some little distance from us. She began to dig in the earth with her hooves. When our father saw this, he said to us: 'Believe me, children, that is where the servant of God is buried'. We dug there and found his relics intact. We carried him to the monastery and buried him <there>.

85. How the wheat of the same monastery germinated because the customary almsgiving had been suspended

They also told us this:

It used to be the custom for the poor and the orphans of the region to come here on Maundy Thursday to receive half a peck of grain or five loaves of blessed bread, five small coins, a pint of wine and half a pint of honey. For three years prior to this happening <which we are about to tell>, grain had been scarce and in this area it was selling at one piece of gold for two pecks. When Lent came round, some of the brethren said to the higoumen: 'Abba, do not make provision for the customary dole to the poor this year, sir, lest the monastery not have enough for the brethren—for grain is not to be found'. The abba began to say to the brethren: 'Children, let us not discontinue the charity of our father <Theodosios>. Behold, it is his commandment and it would be held against us if we disobeyed it. It is he himself who will look after us'. But the brethren continued to argue with the abba, saying: 'We cannot give the accustomed charity for we do not have anything to give'. Then the higoumen was deeply grieved <but he said to them> 'Go then and do what you will'. The customary charity therefore was not distributed <that> Maundy Thursday. But on Good Friday morning, the brother in charge of the granary opened up and found that what grain they did possess had germinated. So they ended up throwing it all into the sea. Then the abba began to say to the brethren: 'He who sets aside the commandments of his father suffers these afflictions. You are now reaping the fruits of disobedience. We were going to part with five hundred pecks <=125 bushels> <of grain> and, in doing so, to serve our father Theodosios by <our> obedience. Also to bring consolation to our brethren <the poor.> Now about five thousand pecks <=1250 bushels> of grain has gone to ruin. what good has it done us, brethren? We have twice been guilty of wrong-doing: once in that we transgressed the precept of our father; and again in that we did put our trust not in God, but in our granary. So let us learn from this <experience,> my brethren, that God watches over all humanity; and that Saint Theodosios invisibly cares for us, his children'.

86. CONCERNING ANOTHER ANCHORITE OF THE SAME MONASTERY

Thomas of Ægaion told us this: I was coming away from Ægaion after the feast and, as the winter was very severe, I came to the monastery of Abba Theodosios as Skopelos. Whilst I was there, this is what happened. There was an anchorite in that region who survived on nothing but wild vegetation. On the holy Lord's Day he would come and partake of the holy mysteries. On one occasion the anchorite came and something offended him; so, for five weeks he did not make his customary appearance at the monastery—which saddened those who lived there. Then, whilst I was there, he came one Sunday and the fathers of the monastery rejoiced at the sight of him. They made an act of obeisance to him and he did likewise to them—and thus there was peace between them. He partook of the holy body and blood of our Lord Jesus Christ, placed himself in the midst of the church and promptly died, without knowing a moment's illness.Then the fathers of the monastery realised that the anchorite had known of his impending death. It was because of this that he had come, so that he would not have anything against anybody when he went to he Lord.

87. The Finding of the Corpse of the Anchorite John the Humble

We went to an estate which was six miles from Rossos and there, two elders living in the world received us as their guests in the church on their property. This estate lay at the foot of a mountain. They showed us some grave-stones in the church and told us: 'Christians, a great anchorite lies in this tomb'. We asked them how they knew this. 'Seven years ago' they replied 'one night, we who belong to this estate saw a light which looked like a fire on the summit of the mountain. We thought it was because of the wild beasts <that a fire had been lit there> but we saw it for many days. One day we went up there but we saw no evidence; no lights or anything whatsoever that had been burnt in the woods. Again, the following night we saw the same lights and for three months after that. Then one night we took some local men armed with weapons (on account of the wild animals) and climbed up the mountain towards the light. We stayed there where the light was until dawn. At day-break we noticed a little cave where the lights had appeared and found the anchorite dead. He was wearing a hair-shirt and a tunic of sack-cloth. He was holding a gospel-book <enhanced with> a silver cross. Beside him we found writing-tablets inscribed thus: "I, the unworthy John, died in the fifteenth indiction". We calculated the time and discovered that he had been dead for seven years, yet he was as though he had died that very day. We carried him down and buried him in the church.'

88. The life of Abba Thomas, the steward of a community near Apamea and the miracle of his corpse after he died

When we were at Theoupolis <=Antioch> a priest of the church told us about the steward of a community in the district of Apamea, Abba Thomas. He came into Theoupolis to attend to the needs of the monastery. Whilst he was lingering there he died at Daphne, in the Church of Saint Euphemia. As he was a stranger, the local clergy buried him in the strangers' burial-ground. The following day they buried a woman and laid her on top of him. This was about the second hour. Around the ninth hour the earth threw her up. When the local people saw this they were amazed. They buried her again that evening in the same grave and next day they found her remains on the top of the tomb. So they took the body and buried it in another grave. A few days later they buried another woman and laid her above the monk, not realising that he would not allow a woman to be buried on top of him. When the earth threw up this woman too, then they realised the fact that the elder would not tolerate a woman being buried above him. Then they went to Domninos the patriarch <546-559>. He caused all the city to come to Daphne with candles and with the singing of psalms, to bring forth the relics of that holy man. They buried him in the cemetery where many relics of holy martyrs lie, and they built a small oratory over him.

89. The finding of an holy anchorite on Mount Amanon

One of the fathers in Theoupolis told us: We once went up into Mount Amanon for some reason or other and I found a cave. When I went in, I found and anchorite, kneeling down and with his hands stretched out to heaven. The hair of his head reached down to the floor. Thinking that he was alive, I made an act of obeisance before him saying: 'Pray for me, father'. As he made no reply, I got up and went close to him, intending to embrace him. When I touched him I found that he was dead, so I left him and went out. A little further on I saw another cave. This I entered and found an elder. He said to me: 'Welcome, brother; have you seen the other elder's cave?' 'Yes, father' I said in reply, and he said to me: 'Did you get anything there?' to which I replied 'No'. He said to me: 'Naturally brother, for the elder has been dead for fifteen years'. Yet he was as though he had died only an hour before. The monk offered a prayer for me and I went my way, glorifying God.

90. The death of two anchorites on Mount Ptergion

There were two anchorites beyond Rossos, living on Mount Ptergion <= the little wing> near the River Piapi and the monastery of Abba Theodosios at Skopelos. The elder <anchorite> died and his disciple offered a prayer and buried him on the mountain. A few days later the disciple of the anchorite came down from the mountain and approached the inhabited world *<oikoumenê>*. He came across a man working his land and said to him: 'Of your charity good fellow, take your mattock and spade and come with me'. The peasant did what the anchorite requested at once. When they came up into the mountain the anchorite showed the man who lived in the world the tomb of his elder, *<i.e.>* the grave of the anchorite and said to him: 'Dig here'. Whilst the peasant was digging, the anchorite stood in prayer. When his prayer was finished, he embraced the man from the world saying: 'Brother, pray for me, sir'. He went down into the grave, placed himself on top of the elder and surrendered his soul. The man from the world filled the grave in and gave thanks to God. When he had gone about a stone's throw down the mountain-side he said to himself: 'I really ought to have received a blessing from those holy men'. He returned but he could not find the saints' grave.

91. The life of Abba Gregory the anchorite and of Thalilaios, his disciple

Some of the fathers told us about Abba George [Gregory] the anchorite who for thirty-five years travelled around naked in the wilderness. They said that when he was in the mountains in which the monastery of Abba Theodosios (at Skopelos) is located, he had a disciple who died. As the elder had no tools with which to dig a grave in which to bury the brother's body, he went down from the mountain to the sea, and there he found a ship riding at anchor. He asked the shipmaster and the crew to come up into the mountain with him and bury the brother. They agreed willingly and, taking up the necessary tools, went up with him. They dug <a grave> and buried the brother's body. One of the sailors, whose name was Thalilaios, very impressed with the virtue of the elder, asked him if he could stay with him. The elder told him that he would not be able to support the rigour of the ascetic life. The younger man replied that he was sure he could endure it. So he remained with the elder and was there for a whole year, making a great effort in ascetic endeavour. When the year was up, brother Thalilaios prostrated himself before the elder and said: 'Pray for me father, for, thanks to your prayers, God has relieved me of suffering and I am no longer afflicted by discomfort, nor does this intemperate weather trouble me. I neither faint with the heat nor shiver with the cold; I am in great comfort'. The elder blessed him and brother Thelalaios remained with him for two and a half years; then he perceived that his end was near. He begged the elder: 'Take me to Jerusalem so I can venerate the Holy Cross and the Holy Sepulchre of Christ our God; for these are the days in which the Lord will take me to himself'. The elder therefore took him and went to the

Holy City. They worshipped at the holy and venerable places, then they went down to the holy Jordan and were baptised. Three days later, brother Thalilaios died. The elder buried him in the Copratha lavra. Some time later, Abba George the anchorite himself departed <this life> and the fathers of the same lavra at Copratha buried him in their own church.

92. THE LIFE OF BROTHER GEORGE THE CAPPADOCIAN AND THE FINDING OF THE BODY OF PETER THE SOLITARY OF THE HOLY JORDAN

Our holy father, Abba George, archimandrite of the monastery of our holy father Theodosios which lies in the wilderness of the Holy City of Christ our God, told this to me and to brother Sophronios the Sophist:

I had a brother here known as George the Cappadocian. He used to do manual work at Phasaelis. One day when the brothers were making loaves of bread, brother George was heating the oven. But when he had heated the oven he could not find the implement for wiping it out—because the brethren had hidden it to put him to the test. So he went in <to the oven>* and wiped it out with his garment. And he came out again not in the least harmed by the fire. When I heard of this I reproved the brethren for putting him to the test.

The same abba, our father George, also told us this about the same brother George:

One day he was pasturing swine in Phasaelis when two lions came to seize a pig. He took up his staff and chased them as far as the holy Jordan.

Again this same father of ours spoke to us saying:

When I was about to build the Church of Saint Kerykos at Phasaelis, they dug the foundations of the church and a monk, very much an ascetic, appeared to me in my sleep. He wore a tunic of sack-cloth and on his shoulders he had an over-garment made of rushes. In a gentle voice he said to me: 'Tell me, Abba George, did it really seem just to you, sir, that after so many labours and so much endurance, I should be left outside the church you are building?' Out of respect for the worth of the elder, I said to him: 'Who in fact are you, sir'? He said: 'I am Peter the grazer of the holy Jordan.' I arose at dawn and enlarged the plan of the church. As I dug, I found his corpse lying there, just as I had seen him in my sleep. When the oratory was built, I constructed a handsome monument in the right-hand aisle, and there I interred him.

93. The Life of Abba Sisinios (who declined a bishopric) and of his disciple

This same man, our father Abba George, told us:
One day I went to Abba Sisinios the anchorite. This was an elder who abandoned his own bishopric for the sake of God and had come to lead the life of a solitary near the village called Bethabara, about six miles away from the holy Jordan. When we went to visit him, after much knocking, the door was finally opened to us by his disciple who said to me: 'Abba, the elder is sick unto death sir, and he has prayed to God not to be taken out of this life until he heard that you had come to this land',—for I had been in Constantinople on monastic business, at <the court of> the most pious Emperor Tiberius. The disciple went up to the elder and told him about me. When he came back down some considerable time later, he said to us: 'He is at your service'. We went up and found the elder already dead. So I realised that when he heard that it was I who was knocking, it was then that he went to the Lord. As I embraced him, the dead man meekly said to me: 'My abba is welcome!'—and he fell asleep again. Then I let it be known to the household that they could come and bury the elder. They came and, as they were

digging the grave, the disciple of the elder said to the grave-diggers: 'Of your charity dig it a little wider so that it can accommodate both of us', and whilst they were still digging, he lay down on a mat of reeds and died. They buried the two of them together, the elder and the disciple.

94. THE LIFE OF ABBA JULIAN, THE BISHOP OF BOSTRA

This same father of ours, George the archimandrite, also told us about Abba Julian who became bishop of Bostra: that after he left the community and became bishop of Bostra, certain affluent citizens who were enemies of Christ wanted to do away with him by poison. They corrupted his butler with money and gave him some poison to drop into the cup when he poured out a drink for the metropolitan <bishop>. The servant did as they told him. When he had given the poisoned cup to the godly Julian, the bishop received it but, by divine inspiration, he knew of the conspiracy and of those who had perpetrated it. So he took the cup and set it down in front of himself without saying a word to the servant. He sent and summoned all the chief citizens, amongst whom were those who had engineered this conspiracy against him. Now the godly Julian did not wish to make a public disgrace of the guilty ones. He said to them all in a gentle voice: 'If you thought you could destroy the humble Julian with poisons, look; I will drink this in full view of you all'. He made the sign <of the cross> three times over the cup with his finger and with the words, 'I drink this cup in the name of the Father and of the Son and of the Holy Ghost', he drank it down before them all—and remained unharmed. When they saw this, they cast themselves down before him in an act of repentance.

95. The life of Patrick, an elder at the at the Monastery of Skopelos

There was an elder living in the monastery of our holy father, Theodosios, who was an native of Sebasteia in Armenia, and his name was Patrick. He was a very great age, claiming to be one hundred and thirteen, very humble and given to silence. The fathers of that place told us that this virtuous elder had once been higoumen of the community at Abazan: he had abandoned that position for fear of the judgement. It was for great men to shepherd the spiritual sheep, he said; so he came here and put himself under obedience. He thought this would be more beneficial to his soul.

96. Concerning the same <father> and also Julian, the blind Arab

They also told us this about the same <father>: There was another elder there, an Arab by race. His name was Julian and he was blind. This Abba Julian once took offence at Macarios, Archbishop of Jerusalem, and ceased to be in communion with him. One day Abba Julian said to Abba Symeon <the Stylite, d. 459>* on the Wonderful Mountain (which is about nine miles <west> from Antioch)* 'I am blind and I cannot go anywhere by myself, nor do I have anyone to lead me—and I refuse to be in communion with Macarios. But tell me, father, what I ought to do about the brother who was a fornicator and the one who swore an oath to him?' Abba Symeon said to Abba Julian: 'Do not withdraw from the monastery, nor should you distance yourself from the holy church. By the grace of our Lord Jesus Christ, the Son of God, there is no evil there. But this you must know, brother: that whoever celebrates the eucharist in your community, you have an elder there named Patrick. This elder stands outside the sanctuary, in the lowest place of all, close by the west wall of the church. This man says the eucharistic prayer for everybody and the holy sacrifice is reckoned to be his.*

97. THE LIFE AND DEATH OF TWO BROTHERS WHO SWORE NEVER TO BE SEPARATED FROM EACH OTHER

Abba John the anchorite, 'John the Red' as he was called, said: I have heard Abba Stephan the Moabite say that when he was in the Community of Saint Theodosios, the great superior of the community, two brothers were there who had sworn an oath to each other that they would never be separated from each other, either in life or in death. Whilst they were in the community and a source of edification for all, one of the brothers was attacked by a yearning for fornication. Unable to withstand this attack, he said to his brother: 'Release me, brother, for I am driven towards fornication and I want to go back to the world'. The other brother began to beg and entreat him, saying: 'Oh, brother, do not destroy all you have endured'. He replied: 'Either come with me so that I can do the deed, or release me to go my own way'. The brother did not want to release him—so he went into the city with him. The afflicted brother went into the house of fornication whilst the other brother stood outside. Taking up dust from the ground he threw it on his own head, reproaching himself. When the brother who had gone into the brothel came out again, having done the deed, the other brother said to him: 'My brother, what have you gained by this sin, and what have you not lost by it? Let us go back to our place'. The other replied: 'I cannot go back into the wilderness again. You go: I am staying in the world'. When the first brother had done all he could and still failed to persuade the other to follow him into the wilderness, he too remained in the world with his brother. They both worked as labourers to support themselves.

It was about this time that Abba Abraham (who had already founded the so-called 'Monastery of the Abrahamites' at

Constantinople, he who later became Archbishop of Ephesos, a good and gentle shepherd), it was about this same that he built his own monastery, the one known as 'The Monastery of the Byzantines' <at Olivet, west of Jerusalem>. The two brothers came there and worked as labourers, for which they received wages. The one who had fallen prey to fornication would take both their wages and go off to the city each week where he would squander <their earnings> in riotous living. The other brother would fast all day long, performing his work in profound silence, not speaking to anybody. When the workmen noticed that he neither ate nor spoke each day but was always deep in thought, they told the saintly Abraham about him and his way of life. Then the great Abraham summoned the workman to his cell and asked him: 'Where are you from, brother, and what kind of work so you do?' The brother confessed all to him. 'It is because of my brother that I put up with all this, in the hope that God will look upon my affliction and save my brother'. When the godly Abraham heard this, he said to the brother: 'The Lord has granted you the soul of your brother too'. Abba Abraham dismissed the brother, who left his cell and, behold! there was his brother, crying: 'My brother, take me into the wilderness so I can be saved'. He immediately took him and went to a cave near to the holy Jordan where he locked him up [in which they shut themselves]. After a little while, the sinful brother, having made great spiritual progress in the things that are God's, departed this life. The other brother, faithful to the oath, remained in the cave and eventually he too died there.

98. Concerning the surviving brother

Whilst this brother was staying by the holy Jordan after his brother's death, an elder came from the Lavra of Calamôn and said to him: 'Tell me, brother: what good has it done you <persevering> so long in silent recollection and self-denial?' The brother said: 'Go away and come back in ten days' time and I will tell you'. The elder came back after ten days and found the brother dead. He found there a piece of broken pottery with this written on it: 'Forgive me, father, but I have never let my mind remain earth-bound whilst performing my spiritual duties'.*

99. The life of Anthony, an elder at the Monastery of Skopelos*

The fathers of the same monastery told us that in former times there was an elder living there named Ianthos. He spent his whole life going off to Coutila.* Once while he was in the wilderness some Saracens came into those parts. When they saw the elder, one of them drew his sword and approached him, intending to kill him. When the elder saw the Saracen coming towards him, he raised his eyes to heaven and said: 'Lord Jesus Christ, thy will be done'. Immediately the earth opened and swallowed up the Saracen. The monk was saved and he went into the monastery, glorifying God.

100. The life of Peter, the monk of Pontus

Again the fathers of the same place told us that there had been a priest there whose name was Peter, a native of Pontus, who did many great and wondrous deeds. Theodore (who became Bishop of Rossos) told us something about this elder:

One day he came up to me at the Jordan, in the Pyrgia Lavra where I was staying, and said to me: 'Brother Theodore, of your charity, come up into Mount Sinaï with me, for I have a prayer <to offer>.' Not wishing to deny him, I said to him: 'Let us go'. When we had crossed the holy Jordan, the elder said to me: 'Brother Theodore, let us offer this as an act of penitence: that neither of us will eat anything until we come to Mount Sinaï'. I said to him: 'Truly, father, that is more than I am capable of', so the elder made his

<own> resolution—and ate nothing until we came to Sinaï. At Sinaï he partook of the holy mysteries and then ate some food. In the same way, from Sinaï to Saint Menas* at Alexandria, he ate no food. There too he received holy communion and then ate. From Saint Menas we went to the Holy City and he tasted nothing whatsoever along the way. He made his communion at the <Church of> the Holy Resurrection of Christ our God and then took some food. In all that long journeying the elder only ate three times: once at Mount Sinaï, once at Saint Menas and once in the Holy City.

101. The life of Pardos, the Roman monk

The fathers of that same monastery told us about another elder who had been there and had recently died. His name was Abba Paul* and he came from Rome. [As a young man he had been a muleteer.] One day he set out [for Jericho] with some mules. There was a small child at the inn whom (at the instigation of the devil and without the knowledge of Abba Paul) a mule had trampled and killed. Deeply troubled by this, Abba Paul fled into the wilderness and arrived at Arona, where he became an anchorite. He continually lamented the death of the child, saying: 'I put that child to death and it is as a murderer that I will have to stand at the judgement'. There was a lion nearby and, each day, Abba Paul would go into its den, teasing and provoking it to jump up and devour him—but the lion did him no harm whatsoever. When he realised that he was not succeeding, Abba Paul said to himself: 'I will lie down on the lion's path; then, when he comes on his way down to drink at the river, he will devour me'. He lay there and, after a little while, the lion came by. And, as though it were a human, it very carefully stepped over the elder without even touching him. Then the elder knew that God had forgiven him his sin. He came back to his monastery where he led an exemplary life (which greatly benefitted and edified everybody) until the day of his falling asleep in God.

102. THE STORY OF SOPHRONIOS THE SOPHIST ABOUT WHAT HAPPENED TO HIM ON THE ROAD

When my brother Abba Sophronios was about to make his final profession,* I stood by him together with Abba <John> the Scholasticos, Abba Kêrikos and some other fathers. He said to us: 'I set out on my way and a company of young women danced before me saying: "Welcome Sophronios; Sophronios has been crowned"!'

103. THE LIFE AND QUALITIES OF ABBA STRATEGIOS

The fathers of that same monastery said of Abba Strategios, higoumen of the same monastery of our saintly father, Theodosios, that he exceeded every monk of that generation in three virtues: in much fasting, in many vigils and in hard labour.

104. THE LIFE OF ABBA NONNOS THE PRIEST

At the community of our saintly father Theodosios, Abba Theodosios, who subsequently became bishop of Capitolias, told us about Abba Nonnos. 'One night', he said, 'before the wood<-en signal was struck> for the night office, I was lying in my bunk and I heard someone saying: "Lord have mercy", in a humble, quiet voice. After counting five hundred repetitions of "Lord, have mercy", I wanted to know who it was that was speaking. I looked towards the church from the window of my cell and saw the elder, down on his knees. There was a bright star above his head, showing me which elder it was'.

Another of the elders of the same community told us this about the same Abba Nonnos: 'One <night> before the striking of the wood<-en signal> I left my cell and went to the church. I saw the elder standing before the church with his hands stretched out to heaven in prayer. His hands shone like lamps of fire; I withdrew in fear'.

105. The life of a holy elder named Christopher, a Roman

When we were in Alexandria, we visited Abba Theodoulos who was at <the Church of> Saint Sophia <= 'holy wisdom'> by the Lighthouse. He told us:

It was in the community of our saintly father Theodosios (which is in the wilderness of the city of Christ our God) that I renounced the world. There I met a great elder named Christopher, a Roman by race. One day I prostrated myself before him and said: 'Of your charity, abba, tell me how you have spent your life from youth up'. As I persisted in my request and because he knew I was making it for the benefit of my soul, he told me, saying: When I renounced the world, child, I was full of ardour for the monastic way of life. By day I would carefully observe the rule of prayer; and at night I would go to pray in the cave where the saintly Theodosios and the other holy fathers were buried. As I went down into the cave, I would make a hundred prostrations to God at each step: there were eighteen steps. Having gone down all the steps, I would stay there until they struck the wood<-en signal> <for matins,> at which time I would come back up for the regular office. After ten years spent in that way, with fastings and continence and physical labour, one night I came as usual to go down into the cave. After I had performed my prostrations on each step, as I was about to set foot on the floor of the cave, I fell into a trance. I saw the entire floor of the cave covered with lamps, some of which were lit and some were not. I also saw two men, wearing mantles and clothed in white, who tended those lamps. I asked them why they had set those lamps out in such a way that we could not go down and pray. They replied: 'These are the lamps of the fathers'. I spoke to them again: 'Why are some of them lit while others are not'? Again they answered me: 'Those who wished to do so lit their own lamps'. Then I said to them: 'Of your charity, <tell me:> is my lamp lit or not?' 'Pray', they said, 'and we will light it'. 'Pray?' I immediately retorted, 'and what have I been doing until now?' With these words I returned to my senses and, when I turned round, there was not a person to be seen. Then I said to myself: 'Christopher, if you want to be saved, then yet greater effort is required'. At dawn I left the monastery and went to Mount Sinaï. I had nothing with me but the clothes I stood up in. After I had spent fifty years of monastic endeavour there, a voice came to me saying: 'Christopher, Christopher, go back to your community in which you fought the good fight, so that you may die with your fathers'. And a little while after he told me this, his holy soul went joyfully to rest in the Lord.

Again, the same Abba Theodoulos told us about this Abba Christopher. According to him, the elder said: 'One day I went up from the monastery to the Holy City to venerate the Holy Cross. After I had performed my devotions, as I was coming out of the ante-chamber of the Holy Cross, I saw a brother <standing> at the door, neither going in nor coming out. I also saw two ugly crows flying in his face and brushing their wings against his eyes, effectively preventing him from entering the shrine. Knowing them to be demons, I said to him: "Tell me, brother, why do you hesitate in the doorway itself and not go in"? He said: "Forgive me, abba; I have conflicting emotions, sir. One urges me to enter and to venerate the honourable Cross, but the other says: "No; make an excuse and make your devotions some other time'". When I heard this, I took him by the hand and led him into the shrine; the crows immediately fled from him. I got him to venerate the Holy Cross and the Holy Sepulchre* of Christ our God, then I dismissed him in peace. The elder told me these things (he explained) because he could see that

I was much distracted by my duties and he perceived that I was neglecting my prayers.

106. Abba Theodore's story of the Syrian monk, Severian

This same Abba Theodoulos spoke to us again, saying:
There is a hostel here, near the lighthouse, between the Church of Saint Sophia and the Church of Saint Faustus, with a guest-master <in charge>. One day this man invited me to go up to the hostel to replace him for a few days. When I got there, I found a monk staying there as a guest, a Syrian by race. His only possessions were a hair shirt, a cloak and a few loaves of bread. He stood there, in a corner, all the time: night and day, uttering verses <of the psalms> and greeting nobody. When the holy day of the Lord came around I went to him and said: 'Brother, will you not come to the Church of Saint Sophia, sir, to partake of the holy and venerable mysteries?' He said he would not, so I asked him why not. He replied that he was a partisan of Severus and was not in communion with the Church. When I heard that he was not in communion with the holy catholic and apostolic Church—and yet I had seen his excellent behaviour and his blameless way of life, I went to my cell in tears. I closed the door and threw myself on my face before God. For three days I prayed to him with many tears, saying: 'Oh Master, Christ our God, who of your ineffable and inestimable love for mankind did *bend the heavens and come down* <Ps 104:2> for our salvation and was incarnate of our Lady, the holy Mother of God, the ever-virgin Mary: reveal to me who are the right and proper believers; we, who are of the Church, or those who are followers of Severus'. On the third day, a voice with no visible source came to me, saying: 'Theodoulos, go and behold his faith'. So the next day I went and sat down before <the Syrian>, expecting to see something, in view of what the voice had said. I remained

sitting there for an hour, looking at him; and he stood there, uttering verses in Syriac. 'And then, children,—the Lord is my witness! I saw a dove, blackened with soot, hovering above his head. It looked as though it had been in a kitchen, for it was plucked and ugly. I realised that this blackened and disgusting dove which had appeared to me was his faith.' His blessed soul told us this in all truth, with many sighs and tears.

107. THE LIFE OF ABBA GERASIMOS

About a mile from the holy River of Jordan there is a place which is known as the Lavra of the holy Abba Gerasimos. When we were there, the residents told us that this Saint <Gerasimos> was walking one day by the banks of the holy Jordan when he met a lion, roaring mightily with <pain in> its paw. The point of a reed was deeply embedded in it, causing inflammation and suppuration. When the lion saw the elder, it came to him and showed him the foot, wounded by the point embedded in it, whimpering and begging some healing of him. When the elder saw <the lion> in such distress, he sat down and, taking the paw, he lanced it. The point was removed, and also much puss. He cleansed the wound well, bound it up and dismissed <the beast>. But the healed lion would not leave the elder. It followed him like a noble disciple wherever he went. The elder was amazed at the gentle disposition of the beast and, from then on, he began feeding it, throwing it bread and boiled vegetables.

Now the lavra had an ass which was used to fetch water for the needs of the elders, for they drink the water of the holy Jordan; the river is about a mile from the lavra. The fathers used to hand the ass over to the lion, to pasture it on the banks of the Jordan. One day when the ass was being pastured by the lion, it went away some distance from <its keeper>. Some camel-drivers on their way from Arabia found the ass and took it away to their country. Having lost the ass, the lion came back to the lavra and approached Abba Gerasimos, very downcast and dismayed. The abba thought that the lion had devoured the ass. He said to it: 'Where is the ass'? The beast stood silent, hanging its head, very much like a man. The elder said to it: 'Have you eaten it? Blessed be God! From henceforth you are going to perform whatever duties the ass performed'. From that time on, at the elder's command, the lion used to carry the saddle-pack containing four earthenware vessels and bring water.

One day an officer came to ask the elder for his prayers; and he saw the lion bringing water. When he heard the explanation, he had pity on the beast. He took out three pieces of gold and gave them to the elders, so that they could purchase an ass to ensure their water supply, and that the lion might be relieved of this menial service. Sometime after the release of the lion, the camel-driver who had taken the ass came back to the Holy City to sell grain and he had the ass with him. Having crossed the holy Jordan, he chanced to find himself face to face with the lion. When he saw <the beast>, he left his camels and took to his heels. Recognising the ass, the lion ran to it, seized its leading rein in its mouth (as it had been accustomed to do) and led away, not only the ass, but also the three camels. It brought then to the elder, rejoicing and roaring at having found the ass which it had lost. The elder had thought that the lion had eaten the ass, but now he realised that the lion had been falsely accused. He named the beast Jordanes and it lived with the elder in the lavra, never leaving his side, for five years.

When Abba Gerasimos departed to the Lord and was buried by the fathers, by the providence of God, the lion could nowhere be found in the lavra. A little later, the lion came, and searched for the elder. The elder's disciple, Abba Sabbatios [the Cilician,] saw it and said to it: 'Jordanes, our elder has left us orphans, for he has departed to the Lord; but come here, eat something.'* The lion, however, would not eat, but continually turned his eyes this way and that, hoping to see its elder. It roared mightily, unable to tolerate this bereavement. When Abba Sabbatios and the rest of the fathers saw it, they stroked its mane and said to it: 'The elder has gone away to the Lord and left us', yet even by saying this they did not succeed in silencing its cries and lamentations. The more they tried to mollify and to comfort it by their words, the more it roared. The louder were its cries by which it expressed its grief; for it showed by its voice, its countenance and by its eyes the sorrow which it felt at not being able to see the elder. Then Abba Sabbatios said to it: 'Since you do not believe us, come with me and I will show you where our elder lies'. He took <the lion> and led it to where the had buried <the elder>. The spot was about half a mile from the church. Abba Sabbatios stood above the grave of Abba Gerasimos and said to the lion: 'See, <this is where> our elder is', and he knelt down. When the lion saw how he prostrated himself, it began beating its head against the ground and roaring, then it promptly died; there, on top of the elder's grave.

This did not take place because the lion had a rational soul, but because it is the will of God to glorify those who glorify him—and to show how the beasts were in subjection to Adam before he disobeyed the commandment and fell from the comfort of paradise.*

108. The life of a virgin priest and of his wife, who was also a virgin

When we were on the island of Samos, we went to the community named Charizenos where we met the higoumen, Abba Isidore, a man of distinguished virtue with a great love for all humanity, adorned with simplicity and infinite humility; later he became bishop of the same city on Samos.* He told us this story:
About eight miles from the city <of Samos> there is an estate on which there is a church. It had a priest who was a very remarkable man. His parents had forced him to marry against his will. Not only did this man not let himself be led into the temptation of delight

(even though he was young and legally married to the woman), he even persuaded his wife to live with him in purity and continence. They both learnt the psalter and they used to sing the psalms together in church, both preserving their virginity into old age. Now it happened that a false accusation was made before the bishop against this priest. As the bishop was unaware of the true state of affairs, he sent and brought the priest from the estate and put him in the prison where it was customary to guard and detain clergy who had gone astray. Whilst he was in the prison, as the holy day of the Lord was dawning but whilst it was still night, there appeared to him an extremely handsome young man who said to him: 'Priest, arise: be off to your church and celebrate the eucharist'. The priest said to him: 'I cannot, for I am a prisoner'. The apparition said to him: 'I will open the prison. Come, follow me.' He opened the door of the prison and led the way out. When he was out, he accompanied the priest to within a mile of the estate. After the break of day, the jailor went in search of the prisoner and, when he could not find him, he went to the bishop, saying: 'He has run away from me and I had the key!' Thinking that he had indeed run away, the bishop sent one of the episcopal servants, saying: 'Go and see if that priest is on his estate—but do not take any further action against him'. The servant went and found the priest in the church, celebrating the eucharist. He returned and said to the bishop: 'He is there, and I saw him celebrating the eucharist'. The bishop became even more angry with the priest and swore to bring him back in dishonourable custody next day.

The night preceding Monday, the vision he had seen earlier appeared again to the priest, saying to him: 'Come along, we must return to that place in the city into which the bishop cast you'. He took the priest and led him back again, replacing him in the prison without the knowledge of the man who was charged with responsibility for it. At daybreak on Monday the bishop learned from this man that (without his knowing how it had come about) he had found the priest back in gaol. The bishop sent for the priest and demanded of him how he had got out of the prison and then come in again without the knowledge of the gaoler. This was the priest's reply: 'A very handsome young servant, beautifully dressed, who said he was of the episcopal retinue—he opened up for me and led me to within a mile of the estate on Saturday night. He came to me again last night and brought me back'. The bishop brought forward all the episcopal servants but the priest did not recognise one of them. Then the bishop realised that it was an angel of God who had done this deed, so that the virtue of the priest should not be entirely concealed—but that all might learn of it and glorify the God who glorifies his servants. He dismissed the priest in peace whilst complaining bitterly against those who had falsely accused him.

109. THE LIFE OF ABBA GEORGE WHO WAS NEVER PERTURBED

This story was told to us concerning Abba George, higoumen of the monastery of Abba Theodosios, by his disciple—that good, gentle and humble Abba Theodosios who became Bishop of Capitolias. He spent twelve years watching the elder to see if he was ever even once upset and he *never* saw him upset; and that was in these present times when there is so much negligence and insubordination in vogue. 'Who ever kept his eyes so firmly riveted to the ground as our saintly father George?' said his disciple. 'Who ever so shut the doors of his ears as this blessed one? Who was there who kept his tongue a prisoner as did our father? What ray of the sun ever shone on the earth so brightly as this, our father, illuminated the hearts of us all?'

110. VARIOUS SAYINGS OF AN EGYPTIAN ELDER

I took my lord Sophronios and we went in search of a particularly distinguished elder, an Egyptian, at the lavra which is located eighteen miles from Alexandria. I said to the elder: 'Abba, say something to us, sir, about the way in which we ought to live with each other, for my lord the sophist here has a desire to renounce the world'. The elder said: 'Well done indeed, my child, if you renounce the world and save your soul. Settle yourselves in a cell. Where does not matter: only that you live there in sobriety and recollection, praying unceasingly. And have a good hope in God, my child, that he will send you knowledge of himself to illuminate your minds.'

Again he said: 'Children, if you wish to be saved, flee from people. Today there is no end of our knocking on doors, our travelling around all the cities and countryside, to see if there is anywhere we can snap up some gratification for our avarice and vain-glory and fill our souls with vanity'.

Again the elder said: 'Let us flee, children, for the time draws nigh'.

Another time, he said: 'Ah, me! How we shall weep and repent for those things of which we do not repent now'!

And again: 'We do not retain the virtue of humility when we are praised to the skies, nor are we able to tolerate criticism. The one increases our vain-glory, the other brings grief to us poor, miserable creatures. No good thing is to be found where there is grief and vain-glory.'

Again: 'Our fathers, who were great and wondrous, were the pastors of many. I, on the other hand, cannot even direct one sheep, but am always failing prey to wild beasts.'

Again: 'This is the way the demons work; after causing a soul to fall into sin, then they cast us into despair to destroy us completely. The demons are always saying to the soul: *When will his name die and be destroyed?* <Ps 40:6> If the soul is one of sobriety, it will answer them and say: *I shall not die but live, and declare the works of the Lord* <Ps 117:17>. Yet since the demons are very impudent, they will turn back on you, saying: *Flee as a sparrow unto the hill* <Ps 10:2>. We must answer them: *God himself is my saviour and my helper, I shall not be removed* <Ps 61:7>.

Again he said: 'Do you be the door-keeper of your heart. And so that no alien may enter therein, say: "Are you on our side or the adversary's"?'

111. The Deed of a Bald Man Dressed in Sack-Cloth

When I and my companion were in Alexandria, one day we went to the Church of <Saint> Theodosios. A bald man accosted us who was wearing sack-cloth down to his knees. He seemed to be insane. Abba Sophronios said to me: 'Give me a coin and you shall see the virtue of this man who is approaching us'. I gave him five coppers *<pholeis>* which he took and gave to the one who seemed to be insane, who received them without a word. Keeping ourselves out of sight, we followed him. When he had turned the street-corner, he stretched out his right hand (in which he held the coins) towards heaven, held it up high, and then prostrated himself before God—and went his way, leaving the coins on the ground.

112. The Life and Death of Leo, a Cappadocian Monk

In the reign of the Emperor and most faithful Caesar, Tiberius,* we went to <the Great> Oasis and when we were there, we saw a monk, a Cappadocian by race, who was great in the eyes of God. Many people told us a multitude of wondrous stories about this monk. When we made contact with him and gained some experience of him, we reaped considerable benefits; especially from the humility, the recollection, the poverty and the charity which he showed to all.* This ever-memorable elder said to us: 'Believe me, children, I am going to reign'. We said to him: 'Believe us, abba, nobody from Cappadocia ever reigned;* this is an ill-suited thought you are harbouring'. But he said again: 'It is a fact, children, that I am going to reign', and nobody could persuade him to put the idea away from him.

When the Maziques* came and overran all that region, they came to <the Great> Oasis and slew many monks, while many others were taken prisoner. Among those taken prisoner at the Lavra <of the Great Oasis?> were Abba John, formerly lector at the Great Church in Constantinople, Abba Eustathios the Roman, and Abba Theodore, all three of whom were sick. When they had been captured, Abba John said to the barbarians: 'Take me to the city and I will have the bishop give you twenty-four pieces of gold'. So one of the barbarians led him off and brought him near to the city. Abba John went in to the bishop. Abba Leo was in the city at that time and so were some others of the fathers; that is why they were not captured. Abba John went in and began to implore the bishop to give the barbarian the twenty-four pieces of gold, but the bishop could only find eight. He was willing to give these to the barbarian, but he would not take them. 'Either give me twenty-four pieces of gold or the monk', he said. The men of the fortress had no choice but to hand over Abba John (who wept and groaned) to the barbarian; they took him away to their tents. Three days later, Abba Leo took the eight pieces of gold and went out into the wilderness to where the barbarians were camped. He pleaded with them in these words: 'Take me and these eight pieces of gold, and let those <three monks> go. For, as they are sick and cannot work for you, you will only have to kill them. But as for me, I am in good health and I can work for you'. Then the barbarians took both him and the eight pieces of gold of which he spoke, letting the other three <monks> go free. Abba Leo went off somewhere with them and when he was exhausted [and could go no further], they beheaded him. And Abba Leo fulfilled that which is spoken in the scriptures: *Greater love hath no man than this, that a man lay down his life for his friends* <Jn 15:13>. Then we knew what he was talking about when he used to say: 'I am going to reign', for reign he did, having laid down his life for his friends.

113. An injunction of Abba John of Petra

Together with my colleague, Sophronios, I approached Abba John of Petra and asked him to speak a saying for us. The elder said: 'Love poverty and continence.* I tell you that when I was at Scêtê as a young man, one of the fathers had a disorder of the spleen. They tried to find some vinegar in the four lavras of Scêtê and not a drop was there to be found, so great were the poverty and the continence of those who lived there.* There were about three thousand five hundred fathers there'.

114. The life of Abba Daniel, the Egyptian

On another occasion, the same elder told us this about Abba Daniel the Egyptian:

One day, this elder went up to Terenuthis to sell what he had made with his hands. A young man entreated the elder, saying: 'For the love of God, come into my house, good elder, and offer a prayer over my wife, for she is sterile'. The elder let himself be persuaded by the young man and went off into his house with him. He offered a prayer over the woman and (as it was the will of God that she should do so,) she became pregnant. Some men who did not fear God began to defame the elder and to say: 'The truth of the matter is that the young man is sterile. It is by Abba Daniel that the woman is pregnant.' This rumour came to the ears of the elder and he told the woman's husband to let him know when she had her child. So when she had given birth, the young man informed him saying: 'Through <the grace> of God and your prayers, father, she has given birth'. Then Abba Daniel went and said to the young man: 'Prepare a meal, and invite your neighbours and friends'. When they had eaten, the elder took the baby in his arms and said to is (with everybody watching:) 'Who is your father'? The child said: 'That man', and with the finger of his hand he pointed to the young man. The child was twenty-two days old. Everybody praised the God who is the guardian of truth for those who seek him with their whole hearts.

115. Injunctions of Abba John, the Cilician

Abba John the Cilician, higoumen of Raïthou, said to his brethren: 'Brethren: as we fled from the world, so let us flee from the desires of the flesh'.

Again: 'Let us be imitators of our fathers who lived here in such hardship *<sklêragôgia>* and recollection'.

Again: 'Children, let us not defile this place which our fathers cleansed of demons'.

Again: 'This is a place for ascetics, not for businessmen'.

Again: 'I have come across elders who lived for seventy years and never ate anything but grass and dates'.

Again: 'Seventy-six years I have lived in this place, suffering many awful and wicked things from the demons'.

116. The brother who was falsely accused of taking a piece of gold

Abba Andrew of Messenia* told us:

When I was a young man, my abba and I withdrew from Raïthou and came to Palestine where we stayed with an elder. The elder who was our host possessed one piece of gold; but he forgot where he had put it and began to suspect that I, young man that I was, had stolen it. The elder said to the fathers of the place: 'Brother Andrew took the piece of gold'. My abba heard this. He called me and said: 'Tell me, Brother Andrew, have you taken the elder's piece of gold?' I said: 'Spare me, abba; I took nothing'. I had a cloak however, so I sold it for one piece of gold. I took the coin, went to the elder and prostrated myself before him, saying: 'Abba, forgive me, sir. Satan led me astray and I took your piece of gold'. There was a worldling there and the elder said: 'Go away child; I have lost nothing'. Again I prostrated myself before him and said: 'For the Lord's sake, take the piece of gold (here, this is it) and pray for me; because Satan deceived me into stealing and causing you trouble'. The elder said: 'Child, I lost nothing at all'. Because he could not convince me, the worldling said to me: 'Of a truth, brother, when I came yesterday, sir, I found the elder in tears, prostrating himself in great affliction. When I saw him in so great tribulation, I said to him: "Of your charity, tell me what is matter with you". He said to me: "I wrongly accused the brother of taking my piece of gold and, look! I have found it where I put it". Then the elder was encouraged by the fact that, although I had not taken the piece of gold, I still brought it back to him, saying: "Take you piece of gold, for it was I who took it."'

117. A BROTHER WITH A DEMON, CURED BY ABBA ANDREW

A brother possessed of a demon went to Abba Symeon the Stylite on the Wonderful Mountain to have a prayer offered for him to be rid of the demon. Abba Symeon said to him: 'Where do you live?' The elder answered: 'At Raïthou'. The elder answered him: 'I am surprised at what toil you have endured, what a journey undertaken to come to me, to a mere sinful man, when you have such great fathers in your own lavra. Go, prostrate yourself before Abba

Andrew, asking him to pray for you, and he will heal you at once.' The brother went back to Raïthou and prostrated himself before Abba Andrew, as Abba Symeon had instructed him, saying: 'Pray for me, abba'. Abba Andrew said to him: 'Abba Symeon has obtained the gift of this healing'. He offered a prayer and the brother was immediately cleansed: and he gave thanks to God.

118. The life of Menas the Deacon, a monk of Raïthou

Abba Sergios of Raïthou told us this about a brother from there called Menas, who became a deacon:

He went out into the world to perform his ministry and what became of him we do not know, except that he put aside the monastic habit and returned to the world. A long time afterwards he went off to Theoupolis <=Antioch> and, as he was returning from Seleucia, he saw the monastery of the saintly Abba Symeon in the distance. He said to himself: 'I will go up to see Symeon the Great', (for he had never seen him). So up he went and came near to the column. When Abba Symeon saw him, he knew him for a monk, and as one who had been ordained a deacon. He called his servant, saying: 'Bring the shears here', then he said to the man who brought them: 'Blessed be the Lord! Tonsure that man there',—and with his very own finger he singled him out, for there were many people around the column. <Menas> was astonished at these words and he was seized by mighty dread. He patiently submitted without speaking, for he realised that God must have revealed the truth about him to the elder. Abba Symeon said to him: 'Say the deacon's prayer', and when the prayer had been recited, the saint said to him: 'Begone to Raïthou whence you came', but Menas said he was ashamed and could not endure disgrace in the sight of men. The saint spoke to him again: 'Believe me, child, you do not have to feel disgrace for this. The fathers will receive you with smiling faces and gladness at your return. Know this also: that God is going to put a sign on you that you might know that his gentle kindness has pardoned this sin.' When he came to Raïthou the fathers received him with open arms and put him in the sanctuary <*hierateion*>. One Sunday, as he was carrying the holy and life-giving blood of the great God and our Saviour Jesus Christ, one of his eyes suddenly came out. By this sign they knew that God had forgiven him his sin, just as the righteous Symeon had foretold.*

119. The demon disguised as a monk which came at the call of an elder at Raïthou

When we met Abba Eusebios, priest of the lavra at Raïthou, he told that a demon once arrived at an elder's cell disguised as a monk. He knocked at the door: the elder opened up to him and said: 'Pray'. The demon said: 'Now and for ever and unto the ages of ages, amen'. Three times the elder said: 'Pray', and each time the demon said: 'Now and for ever and unto the ages of ages, amen'. The elder then said: 'You are welcome if when you pray you say: "Glory be to the Father and to the Son and to the Holy Ghost, as it was in the beginning, is now and ever shall be, now and for ever and unto the ages of ages, amen", and when the elder said this, the demon disappeared as though it were pursued by fire'.

120. Three dead monks found by fishermen at Paran

Some fishermen of Paran* told us this:

Once we went to Bouchri, at the other side of the Red Sea. We took a good catch and made our way back. We anchored off Pteleos, wanting to sail on to Raïthou, but we were detained by contrary winds. A heavy sea held us up for ninety days. Venturing into that great wilderness, we found three anchorites dead under one stone.*

[They wore habits of palm-fibre and their cloaks were lying beside them. We brought the three corpses to the ship and at once the stormy sea subsided. The winds shifted into a favourable direction. We sailed with a following wind and came to Raïthou. The fathers buried them, together with the elders of former times.]

121. The life and death of Gregory, the Byzantine, and of another Gregory, his disciple, from Paran

[The fathers of the same place told us concerning Abba Gregory of Byzantium and his disciple, Abba Gregory from Paran, that they stayed on an island in the Red Sea. Now there was no water on that island: they used to bring the water to supply their needs from the mainland. They had a boat in which they would set out and bring back water. One day they put the boat in the water and tied it to a stone. That night a great wave came and broke the rope, sending the boat to the bottom. Now the fathers were left with no way of providing themselves with water. Eight months later, some monks came from Raïthou and found them both dead. They also found a tortoise-shell with this written on it: 'Abba Gregory of Pharon died after going twenty-eight days without drinking water, but I have gone thirty-seven days without a drink'. We found both the corpses intact: we took them back and buried them at Raïthou.*]

122. Concerning two monks who went naked into church to make their communion and were not seen by anybody, except by Abba Stephan

[We went to see Abba Stephan the Cappadocian on Mount Sinaï and this is what he told us:

When I was at Mount Sinaï some years ago, I was in church on Maundy Thursday. When the holy sacrifice was being offered and all the fathers were present, I looked and saw two anchorites enter the church. They were naked, yet not another of the fathers perceived that they were naked, except me. When they had received the communion of the body and blood of the Lord, they left the church and went away. I went out with them and when we were outside, I prostrated myself before them, saying: 'Of your charity, take me with you', for they knew that I had perceived that they were naked. They said to me: 'You are well installed here: stay where you are'. Again I asked them to take me with them. Then they said to me: 'It is not possible for you to be with us; stay here: this is the place for you'. They offered a prayer on my behalf and then, before my very eyes, they went onto the water of the Red Sea on foot and departed across the sea.]

123. The Life of Abba Zosimos the Cilician

When I was staying at Mount Sinaï I met Abba Zosimos the Cilician there. This elder renounced episcopal office and returned to his cell; he was greatly advanced in asceticism, and this is what he told me:

When I was a young man, I left Mount Sinaï and went to Ammoniac to stay there, in a cell. There I found an elder dressed in a short-sleeved shirt of palm-fibre. When the elder saw me, before greeting me, he said: 'Why have you come here, Zosimos? Get away from here: you cannot stay in this place.' I thought he knew me; I made a prostration before him saying: 'Of your charity, elder, whence do you know me?' He said to me: 'Two days ago, a being appeared to me who said: "A monk is coming to you whose name is Zosimos. Do not allow him to stay here; it is my will to entrust him with the church of the Egyptian Babylon <=Cairo."'> He fell silent and left me, going about a stone's throw from me. There he spent some two hours in prayer. Then he came back to me and kissed me on the forehead, saying: 'Naturally, child, you are welcome, for God has brought you here to bury my body'. I asked him: 'How many years have you been here, abba?' 'I am completing my forty-fifth year'; he replied. It looked to me as though his face were of fire. He said to me: 'Peace be with you, child; pray for me'. And with that, the servant of the Lord lay down and fell asleep. I dug a grave and buried him. Two days later I went my way, glorifying God.

124. A STORY OF THE SAME <ELDER>

The elder told us this too:
Twenty years ago I came to Porphyreôn intending to settle there; I took my disciple, John, along with me. When we arrived, we found two anchorites there and we settled near them. One of them was from Melitene, a man named Theodore; the other was from Galatia, Paul by name. Theodore was from the Monastery of Abba Euthymios. They wore shirts made from antelope skins. I stayed there for approximately two years; we were about two stades from each other. One day when my disciple, John, was sitting down, a serpent struck him and he died immediately with blood flowing from all his members. In my great distress, I went to the anchorites. When they saw me, distraught and distressed, before I could open my mouth, they said to me: 'What is the matter, Abba Zosimos? Is the brother dead'? I replied that he was. They came with me: they looked at him, stretched out there on the ground, then they said to me: 'Do not be sorrowful, Abba Zosimos; God is helping'. They called the brother, saying: 'Brother John, arise; the elder has need of you'. The brother got up from the ground at once. They looked for the snake, caught it, and cut it into two before our eyes. Then they said to me: 'Abba Zosimos, go to Sinaï; it is the will of God to entrust you with the church of Babylon'. We immediately left those parts; and a few

days after we had come to Sinaï, the Abbot *<abbas>* of Sinaï sent me and two others to Alexandria. The Pope of Alexandria, the most blessed Apollinarios, kept us there and made all three of us bishops: one for Heliopolis, one for Leontopolis, and me for Babylon <=Cairo>.

125. The beautiful deed of Abba Sergios the anchorite

Some of the fathers of Sinaï told us this about Abba Sergios the anchorite: When he was living at Sinaï, the steward put him in charge of the mules. One day, as he went his way, there was a lion lying in his path. When the mules and the muleteer saw the lion, they were stricken with fear—and they took to their heels. Then Abba Sergios took a holy bread-ration *<eulogia>** out of his pack and went up to the lion, saying to it: 'Take the ration of the fathers and get out of the way, so that we can pass by'. The lion took the ration and went away.

126. The unusual response of Abba Orentês of Mount Sinaï

The same holy fathers told us about Abba Orentês—that one Sunday he went into church with his garment turned inside out, so that the hair was on the outside. As he stood in choir, those who were in authority said to him: 'Good elder, why have you come in like that, making us a laughing stock before strangers?' The elder said to them: 'You have turned Sinaï inside out and nobody said anything to you; why do you reproach me for turning my garment? Get on with you! [Restore what you have overturned] and I will regularise what I have altered'.

127. The Life of Abba George of the Holy Mountain of Sinaï and of Another Person, One from Phrygian Galatia

This story was told to us by Amma Damiana the solitary, the mother of Abba Athenogenes, Bishop of Petra:

There was a higoumen at Mount Sinaï who was truly great, and an ascetic; George by name. As he was sitting in his cell one Holy Saturday, this Abba George conceived a desire to celebrate the holy resurrection in the Holy City and to partake of the holy mysteries in the Church of the Holy Resurrection of Christ our God. All day long the elder continued in prayer meditating upon the validity of these thoughts. With evening, his disciple came and said: 'Father, give the word for us to proceed to the canonical service'. The elder replied: 'You go, and when it is time for holy communion, return <home and I will> come too. Then the elder stayed in his cell. When it came to the time for holy communion at the <Church of the> Holy Resurrection, the elder was found near the blessed Bishop Peter and he, together with the priests, was given communion by <the bishop>. When the patriarch saw him, he said to his syncellos,* Menas: 'When did the abbot *<abbas>** of Sinaï come here'? The syncellos replied: 'With all due respect, my lord, I had not seen him until only this very instant'. Then the patriarch said to the syncellos: 'Tell him not to go away; I want him to take food with me'. The syncellos went and said this to the elder, who responded: 'The will of God be done'. When the elder had left the service and venerated the holy sepulchre, he found himself back in his cell again, and there was his disciple knocking at the door and saying: 'Father, if you please, come and communicate'. The elder went to the church with his disciple and partook of the holy mysteries. Archbishop Peter was saddened that <the elder> should have disobeyed him. After the feast, he sent him a letter; likewise to

Abba Photios, Bishop of Paran, and to the father of Sinaï, telling them to bring the abba to him. When the carrier of the letters arrived and had delivered them, <the abba> sent three priests to the patriarch: Abba Stephan the Cappadocian, 'the great'; Abba Zosimos of whom we have spoken above; and Abba Dulcitius, a Roman. The elder sought to justify himself by writing: 'My most holy lord; God forbid that I should disregard your holy messenger'. Then he wrote this: 'I would have your blessedness know that, six months from now, we are going to meet each other in the presence of the Lord Christ our God; and there, I will make an act of obeisance to you'. The priests went their way and gave the letter to the patriarch. They said it was many years since the elder had come up to Palestine. They showed him a letter from the Bishop of Paran certifying that for about seventy years the elder had not departed from the holy Mount Sinaï. The godly and gentle Peter <accepted as> witnesses the bishops who were there and the clergy, who said: 'We saw the elder and we all greeted him with a holy kiss'. Six months later, both the elder and the patriarch died, as the elder had foretold.

The same Amma Damiana told us this too:
On a <Good-> Friday before I was enclosed, I went to <the Church of> Saints Cosmas and Damian and spent the whole night there. In the evening, there came an old woman, a native of Phrygian Galatia, and she gave two lepta to everybody who was in the church. I knew her because she had often given me <alms>. One day a kinswoman of mine (and of the most faithful Emperor Maurice* came to pray at the Holy City and stayed there for a year. Taking her with me, I went to Saints Cosmas and Damian. While we were in the oratory, I said to my kinswoman: 'Look, my lady; when an old woman comes distributing two coins to each person, please swallow your pride and accept them'. With obvious distaste, she said: 'Do I have to accept them?' 'Yes', I said: 'Take them, for the woman is great in the eyes of God. [She fasts all week long; and

whatever she is able to gain by this discipline] she distributes it among those who are found in the church. She is a widow of about eighty years of age; take <the coins> she offers you and give them to somebody else. Do not refuse the sacrifice of this old woman.' As we were speaking in this way, the old woman came in and began her almsgiving. In silence and with serenity she came and gave me <some coins>. She gave some to my kinswoman too, saying: 'Take these, and eat'. When she had gone, we realised that God had revealed to her that I had said: 'Take them and give them a poor person'. <My kinswoman> therefore sent a servant of hers to get vegetables with the two coins. These she ate, and she affirmed before God that they were as sweet as honey. This both astonished her, and led her to give thanks to God who endows his servants with grace.

128. The Life of Adelphios, Bishop of Arabessos and concerning the blessed John Chrysostom

We visited Abba Athanasios at the lavra of our saintly father, Sabas, and he told us a story which he had heard from Abba Athenogenes, Bishop of Petra, the son of Amma Damiana. It was something like this:

My grandmother, Joanna, had a brother called Adelphios who was bishop of Arabessi. She also had a sister who was higoumenê of the women's monastery. One day the bishop went to the monastery to visit his sister. As he was entering the inner court of the monastery, he saw one of the sisters, afflicted by a demon, stretched out on the ground. The bishop called his sister and said to her: 'Does it please you that the sister is afflicted and troubled by the demon? Do you not realise that, as higoumenê, you are responsible for all the sisters?' She said to him: 'And what have the demon and I to do with each other?' The bishop spoke to her again: 'What have you been doing here all these years?' He offered a prayer and cleansed the sister <of the demon>.

The same Athanasios also told us this concerning the same Bishop Adelphios, which he had heard from Amma Joanna, his sister:

When John Chrysostom, Bishop of Constantinople, was exiled to Coucouson, he stayed at our house; from which we drew much boldness and love towards God. My brother, Adelphios, said that when the blessed John died in exile, it was an unbearable pain to him that such a man, the universal teacher of christendom who made glad the church of God with his words, should have fallen asleep away from his <episcopal> seat. I prayed to God with many tears to show me his present state of existence and whether he was ranged among the patriarchs. I prayed like that for a long time and then, one day, I fell into a trance and saw a very fine-looking man. Taking me by the right hand, he led me into a bright and glorious place where he showed me the proclaimers of piety and the doctors of the church. For my part, I looked around for him whom I so greatly desired to see, the great John, my beloved. He showed me them all and spoke the name of each one of them; then he took my hand again, and led me out. I followed, lamenting that I had not seen the saintly John among the fathers. As we were coming out, he who stood at the door said to me: 'Nobody who comes here goes forth sorrowing'. Then I said to him: 'This grief is upon me because I have not seen my most dear John, Bishop of Constantinople, among the other doctors'. Again he spoke to me: 'Do you mean John [the prince] of repentance? A man in the flesh cannot see him, for he stands in the presence of the Lord's throne.'

129. The life of a stylite

The same Abba Athanasios said that he had heard Abba Athenogenes, Bishop of Petra, say that in his territory there was a stylite. Everybody who came to him would stand down below to speak to him, for there was no ladder. Whenever a brother said to him: 'I wish to tell you a <private> thought', the stylite would reply in a gentle voice: 'Come to the base of the column', and he would himself move to the other side of the plinth. Thus placed, they would converse: the stylite on high, the brother down below. And none of the others who were standing there could hear what was being said.

According to Abba Athanasios, the bishop also told how there were two grazers who were very attached to each other. They visited the above-mentioned stylite over a period of many years, both together; the one never came without the other. But one day, one of them came to visit the stylite without the other knowing about it. He knocked at the gate for a long time, but the elder would not allow it to be opened for him. He wearied of knocking and went away. On the return journey he was met by his friend, who was himself going to see the stylite. So the first grazer returned with the second one so that they could both come to the elder at the same time. When he knocked at the gate the elder let it be known that the second grazer was to enter alone. When this one came in, he began begging the elder to let the other one enter too. The elder said he would not receive that one. When the first one continued pleading with him, the elder told him: 'God rejects him, child, and I cannot receive him'. They went back to their own parts and, two days later, the first one died.

130. Admonitions of Abba Athanasios and his wondrous vision

This same Abba Athanasios said: 'Our fathers maintained self-discipline and indifference to worldly goods,* but we have lined well both our bellies and our purses'.

Again: 'In our fathers' time it was very important to avoid distractions. Now our cooking pot and our handwork rule us'.

He also told us this:

One day, this thought came into my mind: what difference does it make whether we fight the fight *<agônizein>* or not? I fell as though into a trance and one came who said to me: 'Follow me'. He led me into a place filled with light and stood me before a door, the beauty of which was beyond description. We were hearing what sounded like an innumerable multitude within, praising God. We knocked and somebody inside heard us and cried: 'What do you want?' My guide replied: 'We want to come in'. The other answered, saying to me: 'Nobody comes in here who lives negligently *<en ameleiai>*. If you want to come in, go and fight the fight, holding nothing to be of any account in the vain world'.

131. The life of Abba Zachaios of Holy Sion

Procopios the lawyer,* who came from Porphyreôn, told us this about Abba Zachaios:

There was a deadly plague in Caesarea and I was very worried that my children might die. I did not know what to do. Should I send and bring them home? No man can flee from the wrath of God. Should I leave them there? They might die without me seeing them. Not knowing what was best to be done, I said: 'I will go to Abba Zachaios and whatever he says, that will I do'. So I went to Holy Sion (which is where he was always to be found), but I did not find him. I came into the inner court [of the Church of Saint Mary the

Mother of God and there I found him, standing in a corner of the court]. I told him about my sons. When he heard this, he turned towards the east and continued reaching up towards heaven for about two hours without saying a word. Than he turned towards me and said: 'Take heart and do not be distraught: your children shall not die in the plague. In fact, two days from now, the plague shall abate in Caesarea', [and it came about as the elder foretold. As I said, this is what Procopios the lawyer told us.]

132. CONCERNING THE SAME <ELDER>

Abba Cyprian, whose surname was Cuculas and whose monastery is outside the gate of Caesar<ea> told us this when we went to see him:

When that savage and horrendous plague ravaged this city, I shut myself in my cell and prayed the clemency of God to have mercy on us, to turn aside the wrath which threatened us. A voice came to me, saying: 'Abba Zachaios has obtained this favour'.

133. THE HOLY MONK WHO IMMOBILISED A SARACEN HUNTER FOR TWO DAYS

A pagan Saracen* told this to the inhabitants of Clisma <=Suez> and to us:

I went to the mountain of Abba Anthony to hunt. As I went along, I saw a monk on the mountain holding a book and reading. I went up to him intending to rob him; perhaps to slay him too. As I approached him, he stretched out his right hand towards me saying: 'Stay'! And for two nights and two days I was unable to move from that spot. Then I said to him: 'For the love of the God whom you worship, let me go'! He said: 'Go in peace', and thus I was able to leave the place where I was.

134. The life of Theodore the anchorite

[When we met Abba John at the Lavra of the Æliotes, he told us this story:]*

There was an anchorite in the region of the holy Jordan whose name was Theodore. He came to my cell and said: 'Of your charity, brother John, find me a book which contains all the New Testament'. I made enquiries and discovered that Abba Peter, who became Bishop of Chalcedon, possessed such a book. I went and spoke with him and he showed me <a copy of the New Testament> written on extremely fine skins. I asked him how much it was and he told me: 'Three pieces of gold'. But then he added: 'Is it you yourself who wants to buy it, or somebody else?' I said: 'believe me, father, it is an anchorite who wants it'. Then Abba Peter said to me: 'If the anchorite wants it, take it to him *gratis.* Here too are three pieces of gold. If he does not like <the book>, there are the three pieces of gold; buy him what he wants'. I took up the book and brought it to the anchorite. He took it and went off into the wilderness. Two months later the anchorite returned and came to my cell saying: 'You know, Abba John, the thought troubles me that I got the book for nothing'. I told him not to worry; that Abba Peter was rich and good and that he was pleased to have done what he had done. But the anchorite replied: 'I will get no rest until I have given him the price'. I asked him if he had anything to pay with and he answered: 'No, nothing at all, but give me a rough tunic to wear' (for he was naked). I gave him the tunic and an old cloak and he went and worked on the reservoir which the Patriarch of Jerusalem (whose name was John) was constructing at Sinaï. He received five copper coins *<pholleis>* a day so he came <and stayed?> near me at the Lavra of the Æliotes. He ate no more than ten lupin seeds a day and yet he worked all the day long. When he had saved up three pieces of gold out of the coppers he earned, he said to me: 'Take the money and give it to him. If he will not accept it, give him back the book.' I went off and told this to Abba Peter, but he would accept neither the book nor the price of it. I did, however, prevail on him to accept the price and not to disdain the anchorite's labour. He took the money, whilst I went back and gave the book to the anchorite—who went off into the wilderness rejoicing.

135. Five virgins who wanted to leave the monastery and were possessed by demons

When Brother Sophronios and I visited the Monastery of the Eunuchs* by the holy Jordan, Abba Nicholas, the priest of the monastery, told us this:

In my country (he was from Lycia) there is a monastery of virgins housing about forty persons. Five of the virgins in that monastery conspired to run away from the monastery and to find themselves husbands. So one night, when all the nuns were asleep, as they were trying to get into their clothes to run away, all five of them suddenly became possessed by demons. This having happened, they never went out of the monastery again; they were always giving thanks to God and confessing their sins, saying: 'We give thanks to God, the great giver of gifts, who has inflicted this chastisement on us to save our souls from perdition'.

136. The love of Abba Sisinios for a Saracen woman

Abba John, priest of the Monastery of the Eunuchs, told us that he had heard Abba Sisinios the anchorite say:

One day I was in my cave near the holy Jordan and, as I was singing the third <hour>, a Saracen woman came that way and entered my cave. She sat herself down before me and took off her clothes. I was not distracted; I quietly completed the appointed office in the fear of God. Then, when I had finished, I said to her (in Hebrew): 'Sit up and let me talk to you—and I will do whatever you wish'. She sat up and then I said to her: 'Are you christian or pagan'? She said she was christian. 'Do you not know that those who play the harlot go away <into perdition>?' I asked, and she said she did. 'Then why do you play the harlot?' I asked. 'Because I am hungry', she replied. Then I said to her: 'Stop playing the harlot and come here each day'—and I began giving her some of the food that God provided for me to eat, until I left those parts.

137. Abba John's story about Abba Calinicos

The same Abba John said:
When I was a young man I had a longing to go to the great and famous elders, to receive their blessing and to be edified by them. I heard of Abba Calinicos the Great, the recluse at the Monastery of Abba Sabas. I asked one of them who knew him to bring me to him. The elder who had brought me sat down at the window and spoke with the elder through the window for a long time. I told myself that, since the elder had never seen me, he was not going to be inclined to receive me. The elder just mentioned withdrew <from the window>, bidding me to enter; to greet the elder and to be blessed by him. And he said to him: 'Father, pray for this, your servant, for it was one of his dearest wishes to come here'. The elder said: 'But of course, my child; I know him. Twenty days ago I went down to the holy Jordan and he met me on the road and said to me: "Pray for me", and I asked him: "What is your name?" He answered: "John". I have known him since then.' When I heard this I knew that when I had conceived the desire of coming to him, God had revealed to him my name and who I was.

138. ABBA SERGIOS THE ANCHORITE AND A GENTLE MONK WHO WAS BAPTISED

The elder told us this too:
When Abba Sergios was an anchorite at Rouba, after he had withdrawn from Sinaï, he sent a young monk from there to the monastery to be baptised. When we asked why he had not been baptised, the attendant* of Abba Sergios (<also named> Abba Sergios) said: 'When this man came wanting to stay with us in the wilderness, I, as attendant, received him and greatly exhorted him not to <commit> himself to this way of life without a period of probation. Having perceived his determination, the next day I took him to the elder. As soon as the elder saw him, before I had said a word, he said to me privately; "What does the brother want?" I said: "He is asking to become one of us". Then the elder said to me: "Believe me, brother, he has not been baptised. But take him to the Monastery of the Eunuchs and they will have him baptised in the holy Jordan."' In my amazement at what was said, I asked the brother who he was and where he was from. He said he was from the west and that his parents were pagans. He did not know whether he was baptised or not. We therefore catechised him and had him baptised in the holy Jordan. He stayed in the monastery, giving thanks to God.

139. ABBA SERGIOS' PROPHECY CONCERNING GREGORY, HIGOUMEN OF THE MONASTERY OF PARAN

Concerning this Abba Sergios the anchorite, his attendant, Abba Sergios the Armenian, told us that Abba Gregory,* higoumen of the lavra at Paran, was very insistent that he should be taken to the elder. 'So one day', <said the attendant>, 'I took him to the elder who, in those days, was in the region of the Dead Sea. When the elder saw him, he greeted him with great gladness and, bringing water, washed his feet. All day long he spoke with him about what is beneficial to the soul. The next day he dismissed him. When Abba Gregory had departed, I said to the elder: 'You know, father, you have rather offended me. Of all the bishops and priests and other people whom I have brought to you, not one of them has ever had his feet washed by you except Abba Gregory and him alone.' Then the elder said to me: 'Child, as for Abba Gregory, I do not know who he is. This thing alone I know: that I have received a patriarch in my cave. I saw him wearing the *omophorion* and carrying the holy gospel'. And that is what came to pass. Six years later God raised up Abba Gregory to the dignity of the patriarchate of Theoupolis <=Antioch,> as the elder had foreseen.*

140. The life of the same Gregory, Patriarch of Theoupolis

Some of the fathers said that Abba Gregory, Patriarch of Theoupolis, excelled in these virtues: almsgiving, forgiveness and tears. He also had great compassion for sinners. 'We certainly had many occasions to put these virtues to the test', they added.

141. The judicious reply of Abba Olympios

A brother visited Abba Olympios at the Lavra of Abba Gerasimos near the holy Jordan and said to him: 'How can you stay in this place with its burning heat and so many insects'? The elder answered him: 'I put up with the insects to escape from *the worm that sleeps not.* <Mk 9:44> Likewise, I endure the burning heat for fear of the eternal fire. The one is temporary, but of the other there is no end'.

142. ANOTHER JUDICIOUS REPLY FROM ABBA ALEXANDER

Another brother visited Abba Alexander, the higoumen at the lavra of Abba Gerasimos, and said to him: 'Abba, I want to leave the place where I am settled because I am badly afflicted by accidie'. Abba Alexander replied: 'Child, this is surely a sign that you have neither eternal punishment nor the kingdom of heaven before your eyes. If you had, you would not be in accidie.'

143. DAVID, THE ROBBER-CHIEF, WHO LATER BECAME A MONK

We came to the Thebaïd and at the city of Antinoë we visited Phoebamon the Sophist for the benefit <of his words>. He told us that in the district around Hermopolis there had been a brigand whose name was David. He had rendered many people destitute, murdered many and committed every kind of evil deed; more so than any other man, one might say. One day, whilst he was still engaged in brigandage on the mountain, together with a band of more than thirty, he came to his senses, conscience-stricken by his evil deeds. He left all those who were with him and went to a monastery. He knocked at the monastery gate; the porter came out and asked him what he wanted. The robber-chief replied that he wanted to become a monk, so the porter went inside and told the abbot about him. The abbot came out and, when he saw that the man was advanced in age, he said to him: 'You cannot stay here, for the brethren labour very hard. They practice great austerity. Your temperament is different from ours and you could not tolerate the rule of the monastery.' But the brigand insisted that he could tolerate these things, if only the abbot would accept him. But the abbot was persistent in his conviction that the man would not be able. Then the robber-chief said to him: 'Know, then, that I am

David, the robber-chief; and the reason why I came here was that I might weep for my sins. If you do not accept me, I swear to you and before him who dwells in heaven that I will return to my former way of life. I will bring those who were with me, kill you all and even destroy your monastery.' When the abbot heard this, he received him into the monastery, tonsured him and gave him the holy habit. Thus he began the spiritual combat and he exceeded all the other members of the monastery in self-control, obedience and humility. There were about seventy persons in that monastery; he benefitted them all, providing them with an example.

One day when he was sitting in his cell, an angel of the Lord appeared to him, saying: 'David, David; the Lord has pardoned your sins and, from this time on, you shall perform wonders *<sêmeia>.'* David replied to the angel: 'I cannot believe that in so short a time God has forgiven me all my sins, which are heavier than the sand of the sea'. The angel said to him: 'I did not spare Zacharaiah the priest when he refused to believe me concerning his son. <Lk 1:20> I imprisoned his tongue to teach him not to doubt what I said; how then should I now spare you? You shall be totally incapable of speech from this time onwards.' Abba David prostrated himself before the angel and said: 'When I was in the world, committing abominable acts and shedding blood, I had the gift of speech. Will you deprive me of it by imprisoning my tongue, now that I wish to serve God and offer up hymns to him?' The angel replied: 'You will only be able to speak during the services. At all other times you shall be completely silent'—and that is how it was. He sang the psalms, but he could say no other word, big or little. The one who told us these things said: 'I saw him many times and I glorified God'.

144. Injunctions of one of the elders who were at The Cells

One of the elders said to the brethren at The Cells: 'Let us not enslave ourselves to the pleasures of Egypt which <deliver us into the hands of> the wicked tyrant, Pharaoh'.

Again: 'If only people would care as much for good things as they care about that which is bad. If only they would transfer to a yearning for piety all the attention they lavish on spectacles, magnificent festivals, on avarice, vain-glory and injustice. We are not ignorant of how highly God values us, nor are we powerless against the demons.'

Again: 'Nothing is greater than God; nothing is equal to him; nothing is only a little inferior to him. What then is stronger or more blessed than someone who has the help of God?'

Again: 'God is everywhere. He draws near to those who live devoutly and fight the spiritual battle; to those whose religion goes further than mere pronouncements, but who are distinguished by their deeds. Where God is present, who would wish to hatch conspiracies? Who would be strong enough to inflict any hurt?'

Again: 'The strength of man does not lie in his physical constitution, for that is subject to change. It lies rather in his intention, assisted by God. Let us therefore care for our souls as we do for our bodies, children.'

Again: 'Let us gather together the cures of the soul: piety, righteousness, humility, submission. The greatest physician of souls, Christ our God, is near to us and is willing to heal us; let us not under-estimate him.'

Again: 'The Lord teaches us to be sober but, wretches that we are, by soft-living we become yet more addicted to the delights <of the flesh>.'

Again: 'Let us offer ourselves to God, as Saint Paul says, *as living men returned from the dead* <Rm 6:13>, neither looking back or remembering what has gone before, but *pressing toward the mark for the prize of the high calling* <Ph 3:14>.

A brother asked the elder: 'Why am I always sitting in judgment on my brothers?' The elder replied: 'Because you do not yet know yourself. Someone who knows himself does not see the <short-comings> of his brothers.'

145. THE LIFE OF THE BLESSED GENNADIOS, PATRIARCH OF CONSTANTINOPLE, AND OF HIS READER, CHARISIOS

We visited the Community of Salama, <nine miles out of> Alexandria, and there we found two elders who said they were priests of the church of Constantinople. [They spoke to us about Gennadios, the blessed Patriarch of Constantinople saying, that he was very gentle, pure of body and very much in control of himself.] And they told us this about him: that he was troubled by many <people complaining> about a cleric who was leading a very dissolute life, a man named Charisios. The patriarch sent for him and tried to correct him by exhortation, but when nothing was achieved by this, he proceeded to chastise and discipline him after the manner of a father and a churchman. The patriarch realised that this was doing the cleric no good, for now he was indulging in murder and dabbling in witchcraft. So he sent one of the agents in his service, ordering him to say to the holy martyr Eleutherios (in whose oratory Charisios served as lector): 'Saint Eleutherios, your officer is a great sinner. Either reform him, or get rid of him.' So the agent came to the oratory of the holy martyr Eleutherios and, standing before the altar, turning towards the apse, he stretched out his hand and said to the martyr: 'Holy martyr of Christ, the Patriarch Gennadios declares to you, through me, sinner though I be, that your officer is deeply in sin. You are either to reform him or get rid of him.' Next day, that worker of evil deeds was found dead. All were amazed, and glorified God.

146. The vision of Eulogios, Patriarch of Alexandria

When we were at the Community of Tougara, nine miles outside Alexandria, Abba Menas who ruled that community,* told us this concerning the saintly Pope Eulogios:

One night when he was performing the office alone in the chapel of the episcopal residence, he saw the Archdeacon Julian standing before him. When he saw him he was disturbed that the man should have dared to enter unannounced, but he said nothing. At the end of the psalm, he prostrated himself; and so too did the one who had appeared to him in the form of the archdeacon. When the pope got up and offered the prayer, the other one remained prostrate on the ground. The pope turned to him and said: 'How long will it be before you stand up?' The other said: 'Unless you offer me your hand and raise me, I cannot stand up'. Then the abba put out his hand, took hold of him and raised him up. Then he took up the psalm again; but when he turned round, he no longer saw anybody. When he had completed the dawn office, he called for his chamberlain and said to him: 'Why did you not announce the entry of the archdeacon, but let him come to me unannounced, and that in the night-time?' The chamberlain said neither had he seen anybody nor had anybody come in. The pope was not convinced. 'Call the porter here,' he cried, and when the porter arrived he said to him: 'Did the Archdeacon Julian not come in here?' The porter asserted with an oath that the archdeacon had neither come in nor gone out. Then the pope kept his peace. When day dawned, Archdeacon Julian came in to pray. The pope said to him: 'Why did you break the rule by coming in to me unannounced last night, Archdeacon Julian?' He replied: 'By the prayers of my lord, I did not come in here last night, nor did I leave my own house until this very hour'. Then the great Eulogios realised that it was Julian the Martyr he had seen, urging him to <re>build his church which had been dilapidated for some time and antiquated, threatening to fall down. The godly Eulogios, the friend of martyrs, set his hand to the task with determination. By rebuilding the martyr's temple from its foundations and distinguishing it with a variety of decoration, he provided a shrine worthy of a holy martyr.

147. THE WONDROUS CORRECTION OF A LETTER WRITTEN BY THE BLESSED ROMAN PONTIFF TO FLAVIAN*

Abba Menas, ruler of the same community,* also told us that he had heard this from the same Abba Eulogios, Pope of Alexandria: When I went to Constantinople, [I was a guest in the house of] master Gregory the Archdeacon of Rome, a man of distinguished virtue. He told me of a written tradition preserved in the Roman church concerning the most blessed Leo, Pope of Rome. It tells how, when he had written to Flavian, the saintly patriarch of Constantinople, condemning those impious men, Eutyches and Nestorios, he laid the letter on the tomb of Peter, the Prince of the Apostles. He gave himself to prayer and fasting, lying on the ground, invoking the chief of the disciples in these words: 'If I, a mere man, have done anything amiss, do you, to whom the church and the throne are entrusted by our Lord God and Saviour Jesus Christ, set it to rights'. Forty days later, the apostle appeared to him as he was praying and said: 'I have read it and I have corrected it'. The pope took the letter from Saint Peter's tomb, unrolled it and found it corrected in the apostle's hand.

148. THE VISION OF THEODORE, BISHOP OF DARA, CONCERNING THE SAME MOST BLESSED LEO

Theodore, the most holy bishop of the city of Dara in Libya, told us this:

When I was syncellos to the saintly Pope Eulogios, in my sleep I saw a tall, impressive looking man who said to me: 'Announce me to Pope Eulogios'. I asked him: 'Who are you, my lord? How do you wish to be announced?' He replied: 'I am Leo, Pope of Rome', so I went in and announced: 'The most holy and most blessed Leo, Primate of the Church of the Romans, wishes to pay you his respects'. As soon as Pope Eulogios heard, he got up and came running to meet him. They embraced each other, offered a prayer and sat down. Then the truly godly and divinely-inspired Leo said to Pope Eulogios: 'Do you know why I have come to you'? The other said he did not. 'I have come to thank you', he said, 'because you have defended so well, and so intelligently, the letter which I wrote to our brother, Flavian, Patriarch of Constantinople. You have declared my meaning and sealed up the mouths of the heretics. And know, brother, that it is not only me whom you have gratified by this labour of yours, but also Peter, the chief of the apostles; and, above all, the very Truth which is proclaimed by us, which is Christ our God.' I saw this, not only once, but three times. Convinced by the third apparition. I told it to the saintly Pope Eulogios. He wept when he heard it and, stretching out his hands to heaven, he gave thanks to God, saying: 'I give you thanks, Lord Christ, our God, that you have made my unworthiness become a proclaimer of the truth, and that, by the prayers of your servants Peter and Leo, your Goodness has received our feeble endeavour <as you did receive> the widow's two mites.'

149. The amazing tale of Amos, Patriarch of Jerusalem concerning the most sacred Leo, the Roman Pontiff

When Abba Amos went down to Jerusalem and was consecrated patriarch, all the higoumens of all the monasteries went up to do homage to him and, amongst them, I also went up, together with my higoumen. The patriarch started saying to the fathers: 'Pray for me, fathers, for I have been handed a great and difficult burden and I am more than a little terrified at the prospect of the patriarchal office. Peter and Paul and Moses, men of their stature are adequate shepherds of the rational sheep, but I am a person of little worth. Most of all, I fear the burden of ordinations.* I have found it written that the blessed Leo who became primate of the church of the Romans, remained at the tomb of the Apostle Peter for forty days, exercising himself in fasting and prayer, invoking the Apostle Peter to intercede with God for him, that his faults might be pardoned. When forty days were fulfilled, the apostle appeared to him, saying: 'I prayed for you, and all your sins are forgiven, except for those of ordinations. This alone will be asked of you: whether you did well, or not, in ordaining those whom you ordained'.

150. The life and holiness of the Bishop of Romilla*

Abba Theodore told us that thirty miles from Rome there is a small town called Romilla. In that town there was a very great and virtuous bishop. One day some of the people of Romilla came in to the most blessed Agapetos, Pope of Rome, and made charges against their own bishop to the pope, saying that he ate from a consecrated paten. The pope was shocked when he heard this. He sent two clerics to bring the bishop, bound, to Rome, on foot; and he threw him into prison when he arrived. When the bishop had been in prison three days, Sunday came around. Whilst the pope was sleeping, as dawn broke on the Sunday morning, he saw in his sleep one who <stood beside him and> said: 'You are not to celebrate the eucharist this Sunday, neither you nor any other of the clergy and bishops who are in this city, except the bishop whom you are holding in prison. I want him to celebrate the eucharist this day. When the pope awoke, he said to himself concerning the vision he had seen: 'I have received such a complaint against him, and *he* is to celebrate the eucharist?' A second time the voice came to him in his sleep, saying: 'I told you: that bishop; who is in prison, *he* shall celebrate the eucharist'. Likewise a third time the figure appeared to him as he was grappling with the problem and said the same thing to him. When the pope awoke, he sent to the prison and had the bishop brought out. Then he questioned him: 'What is your way of life *<ergasia>?* But the bishop would answer nothing other than: 'I am a sinner'. As he could not persuade the bishop to say anything else, he said to him: 'Today you shall celebrate the eucharist'. When he stood at the holy altar with the pope beside him and the deacons in a circle around the altar, the bishop began the prayer of consecration; but before adding the conclusion, he began the prayer of consecration all over again for a second, a third, and a fourth time. Everybody was astonished at such repetition and the pope said to him: 'What is this then, that you are starting the holy prayer for a fourth time and do not bring it to a conclusion?' Then the bishop replied: 'Forgive me, holy pope, but I do not perceive the coming of the Holy Ghost *<epiphoitêsis>* as is usually the case; that is why I do not conclude <the prayer>. However, my sacred lord, would you send that deacon holding the fan *<rhipidion>** away from the altar, for I do not dare to tell him to go.' Then the godly Agapetos gave the order and the deacon went away. Straightaway the bishop and the pope saw the presence *<parousia>* of the Holy Ghost; but the curtain which was above the altar moved of its own volition and overshadowed the pope, the bishop, all the deacons who were in attendance and even the holy altar itself, for three hours. Then the godly Agapetos realised that this was a great bishop who had been falsely accused. And so great was his distress at having wronged him that he resolved never again to make any hasty decision, but to act with much thought and great patience.*

151. John the Persian's story of the most blessed Gregory, Bishop of the City of Rome

We encountered Abba John the Persian at <the Lavra of> Monidia and he told us this about Gregory the Great, the most blessed Bishop of Rome:

I went to Rome to pray at the tombs of the most blessed Apostles, Peter and Paul. One day as I was standing in the city-centre I saw that Pope Gregory was going to pass by. I had it in mind to prostrate myself before him. The attendants <of the pope> began saying to me, one by one, 'Abba, do not prostrate yourself', but I could not understand why they had said that to me; certainly it seemed improper for me not to prostrate myself. When the pope came near and perceived that I was about to prostrate myself—the Lord is my witness brethren—he prostrated himself down to the ground and refused to rise until I had got up. He embraced me with great humility, handed me three pieces of gold and ordered me to be given a monastic cloak, <stipulating that> all my needs were to be taken care of. So I glorified God who had given him such humility towards everybody, such generosity <with alms> and such love.

152. The Life and Sayings of Marcellus the Scetiote, Abba of the Monastery of Monidia

At the Lavra of Monidia we encountered Abba Marcellus the Scetiote. Wishing to edify us somewhat, he told us this:
When I was in my homeland (he was from Apameia,) there was a charioteer there whose name was Philerêmos <='lover of the wilderness>. One day, when he failed to take the prize, his supporters rose up, shouting: 'Philerêmos takes no prize in the city'. After I came to Scêtê, whenever I was tempted by my thoughts to go to the city, I would say to myself: 'Marcellus, Philerêmos takes no victor's crown in the city', and, by the grace of Christ, that thought kept me from leaving Scêtê for thirty-five years, down to the time when the barbarians came, sold me <into slavery> and devastated Scêtê.

This same Abba Marcellus told us this as though it were about another elder who lived at Scêtê, but it was in reality himself: On a certain night he got up to perform the office and, as the service was beginning, he heard a sound like that which is made by a military trumpet. The elder was troubled by this and wondered to himself from where this sound could be coming. No soldiers were there, nor was there any fighting in the district. As he was pondering in this way, behold—a demon approached him and said: 'Yes, there is war. If you wish neither to fight nor to be attacked, go to sleep; then you shall not be attacked.'

Again the elder said: 'Believe me, children, there is nothing which troubles, incites, irritates, wounds, destroys, distresses and excites the demons and the supremely evil Satan himself against us, as the constant study of the psalms. The entire holy Scripture is beneficial to us and not a little offensive to the demons, but none of it distresses them more than the psalter. In public affairs, when one party sings the praises of the emperor, the other party is not distressed, nor does it move to attack the first party. But if that party begins reviling the emperor, then other will turn on it. Thus it is that the demons are not so much troubled and distressed by the rest of holy Scripture as they are by the psalms. For when we meditate upon the psalms, on the one hand, we are praying on our own account, while, on the other hand, we are bringing down curses on the demons. Thus, when we say *Have mercy upon me O God after your great goodness: and according to the multitude of your tender mercies, do away with my transgressions* <Ps 50:1> and again: *Cast me not away from your presence: and take not your holy spirit from me* <Ps 50:11> and *Cast me not away in the time of age: forsake me not when my strength fails me* <Ps 70:9>, we are praying for ourselves. But then we bring down curses on the demons when, for instance, we say: *Let God arise and let his enemies be scattered: let them also that hate him flee before him* <Ps 61:1>, and again: *Let him scatter the people that delight in war* <Ps 67:31>, and: *I myself have seen the ungodly in great power and flourishing like a green bay-tree: I went by and lo, he was gone; I sought him, but his place could nowhere be found* <Ps 36:35-36>, and *Their sword shall go through their own heart* <Ps 36:15>, and *He has excavated and dug up a pit, and is fallen himself into the destruction which he made for an other* <Ps 7:16-17). *His travail shall come upon his own head and his wickedness shall fall on his own pate'.*

Again the elder said: 'Believe me, children, when I say to you that it is a highly praiseworthy and a very glorious thing, a kingdom in itself, for a man to take vows and become a monk, for spiritual pursuits are eminently preferable to the quest for what gratifies the senses. Therefore, great is the disgrace and the dishonour of a monk who lays aside his habit, even if it be to become emperor.'

Again: 'In the beginning, man was in the likeness of God. But, when he fell away, he became like the wild beasts'.

Again: 'Nature raises up the physical desires, brethren; but the intensification of asceticism extinguishes them'.

Again: 'You must have personal experience of the good life, and not be frightened as though it were impossible'.

Again: 'Do not be amazed that, though you are an earthling, you can become an angel; for a glory like that of the angels lies before you, and he who presides over the games promises <that glory> to those who run the race'.

Again: 'There is nothing which draws monks to God so much as good, decent, godly purity, *which is conducive to a graceful and constant fidelity to the Lord* <1 Co 7:35>. The all-holy Spirit bears witness to this through the godly Paul.'

Again: 'Brethren, let us leave marriage and the raising of children to those whose eyes are towards earth, who long for the things of the present and take no thought for that which is to come; who do not strive to possess the good things of eternity, and are unable to disentangle themselves from the ephemera of this world'.

Again: 'Let us make haste to depart from the life of the body, even as Israel hurried to escape from slavery in Egypt'.

Again: 'We have the splendid and delicious rewards of God ahead of us, brethren, in exchange for the bitter delights of this world'.

Again, the elder said: 'Let us flee from avarice, which is the mother of all evils' <*cf* 1 Tm 6:10>.

153. The answer of a monk of the monastery of Raïthou to a secular brother

There were two brothers living in the world, at Constantinople, who were very devout and much given to fasting. One of them came to Raïthou where he renounced the world and became a monk. Some time later, his brother (who still lived in the world) came to Raïthou to see his brother, now become a monk. Whilst he was staying there, the worldly brother saw the monastic brother taking refreshment at the ninth hour. He was offended and said to his brother: 'Brother, when you were in the world, you never took refreshment before sun-set'. Then the monk said to him: 'In truth, brother, when I was in the world I received sustenance through my ears; for vainglory and the praise of men sustained me in no small way and eased the discomfort of the austerity'.

154. THE LIFE OF THEODORE WHO LIVED IN THE WORLD, A MAN OF GOD

Abba Jordanes the grazer said:
Three of us anchorites went to Abba Nicholas at the Wadi Betasimos. He lived in a cave between Saint Elpidios and the monastery known as 'the Strangers'. We found a stranger close by him and, as we were speaking about the salvation of the soul, Abba Nicholas said to him: '*You* say something to us too'. He replied: 'What could I say that would do you any good, I who am a man of the world? Would that I could even do myself some good!' The abba said to him: 'Indeed, you shall say something <to us>.' Then the man of the world said: 'For twenty years, Saturdays and Sundays excepted, the sun never saw me eating. I am the hired servant on the estate of a rich man who is unjust and greedy. I was with him for fifteen years, toiling night and day, and he would not pay me my wages, but treated me with considerable harshness. I said to myself: "Theodore, if you endure this man, he is going to obtain the kingdom of heaven for you instead of the wages he owes you". So I kept my body free of contact with women until this day.' When we heard this, we were greatly edified.

155. Abba Jordanes' story of the Saracens who killed each other

Abba Jordanes also told us that Abba Nicholas said to him:
In the reign of the most faithful Emperor Maurice, when the Saracen leader Naaman was making his raids, as I was travelling around Annon and Aïdon, I saw three Saracens. They had as their prisoner a very handsome-looking young man, about twenty years old. When he saw me, he began crying to me to take him away from them. So I started begging the Saracens to let him go. One of the Saracens answered me in Greek: 'We are not letting him go'. I said to them: 'Take me and let him go, for he cannot endure servitude'. The same Saracen replied: 'We are not letting him go'. Then I said to them for the third time: 'Will you let him go for a ransom? Hand him over to me and I will go seek and bring whatever you demand'. The Saracen replied: 'We cannot give him to you because we promised our priest that if we took a good-looking prisoner, we would bring him to the priest to be offered as a sacrifice. Now be off with you, or we will cause your head to roll on the ground'. Then I prostrated myself before God and said: 'O Lord God, our Saviour, save your servant'. The three Saracens immediately became possessed of demons. They drew their swords and cut each other to pieces. I took the young man to my cave and he no longer wished to leave me. He renounced the world—and after completing seven years in the monastic life, went to his rest. He was from Tyre.

156. The reply of an elder to two philosophers

Two philosophers came to an elder and asked him to say something beneficial to them. The elder remained silent. Again the philosophers spoke: 'Will you not answer us, father?' The elder said to them: 'That you are skilled in the use of words *<philologoi>* I am fully aware, but I do testify to you that you are not truly lovers of wisdom <*philosophoi*>. How long will you cultivate the art of speech, you who have no understanding of what it is to speak? Let the object of your philosophy be always to contemplate death, possessing yourselves in silence and tranquillity.'*

157. THE STORY OF TWO MONKS OF THE SYRIANS' MONASTERY AT SOUBIBA ABOUT A DOG WHO SHOWED A BROTHER THE WAY

At the Lavra of Calamôn, near the holy Jordan, Sophronios the Sophist and I met Abba Alexander. There were two monks with him from the Syrians' monastery at Soubiba.* This is what they told us:

Ten days ago, an elder from afar arrived. He came to the monastery of the Besoi at Soubiba and made an offering. He asked the abba of the monastery of his charity to send someone to the neighbouring monastery of the Syrians so that they too could come and receive a donation; and he wanted them to pass on the invitation to the monastery of Chôrembê, so that those who lived there would come too. So the abba sent a brother to the higoumen of the monastery of the Syrians at Soubiba. When the brother arrived, he said to him: 'Come to the monastery of the Besoi and send a message to the monastery of Chôrembê that they should come'. The elder replied: 'I have nobody to send. But do you, of your exceeding great charity, go and tell them.' The brother said: 'I have never been there before and I do not know the way'. Then the elder said to his little dog: 'Go with the brother to the community of Chôrembê so that he can deliver his message'. The dog accompanied <the brother> until he stood before the gate of the monastery. Those who told us this story showed us the dog, for they had it with them.

158. An ass in the service of the monastery called Mardes

There is a mountain by the Dead Sea called Mardes* and it is very high. There are anchorites living in that mountain. They have a garden about six miles away from where they live, near the edge of the Sea, almost on its banks. One of the anchorites is stationed there to tend the garden. At whatever hour the anchorites wish to send to the garden for vegetables, they put a pack-saddle on the ass and say to it: ‘Go to the one who tends the garden and bring us some vegetables’. It goes off alone to find the gardener; when it stands before the door, it knocks with its head. The gardener loads it up with vegetables and sends it away. You can see the ass returning alone each time, but it only serves those elders; it supplies the needs of nobody else.

159. The life of abba Sophronios the solitary and some injunctions of Menas

Abba Menas, higoumen of the monastery of Abba Severian, said this about Abba Sophronios the grazer: ‘He grazed around the Dead Sea. For seventy years he went naked, eating wild plants and nothing else whatsoever.’ <Abba Menas> also said he had heard <Abba Sophronios> say: ‘I prayed to the Lord that the demons would not come near my cave. I saw them coming to within three stades of the cave, but they were unable to come any nearer.’ Abba Menas said to the brothers who were in the community: ‘My little children, let us avoid communications with those of the world for these can be hurtful, especially to younger monks’. He also said: ‘Persons of every age, both young and old, need to repent in order to enjoy eternal life in the future with praise and great glory. Young men need to repent because in the full flood of carnal desire they have bent their necks beneath the yoke; old men, that they might change their propensity for evil which has been reinforced by long habitude.'

160. How a demon appeared to an elder in the form of a very black boy

Abba Paul, higoumen of the monastery of Abba Theognias told us that a certain ascetic elder had said:

One day I was sitting in my cell doing my handwork (I was plaiting baskets actually, and singing psalms) and see! What looked like a Saracen youth wearing a bread-basket came in through the window. He stood before me and began to dance. As I continued singing psalms, he said to me: 'Elder, do I dance well?' I answered not a word. He spoke again: 'Do you like the way I dance, elder?' As I answered him no word whatsoever, he said to me: 'Oh, wicked old man; why do you imagine you are doing something important? I tell you, you made a mistake in the sixty-fifth, the sixty-sixth and the sixty-seventh psalms.' Then I stood up and prostrated myself before God: he disappeared at once.

161. The life of Abba Isaac of Thebes and how a demon appeared to him in the form of a youth

There is a city in the Thebaïd called Lycos. Six miles from it there is a mountain on which there are monks living: some in caves, others in cells. When we went there we met Abba Isaac the Theban, who said:

Fifty-two years I was working at my handwork (I was making a large mosquito net) and I made a mistake. I was very upset about that mistake because I could not find it. I spent the whole day in distress and did not know what to do. Whilst I was so distraught, a youth came in through the window and said to me: 'You have made a mistake. Give the work to me and I will put it right.' I said to him: 'Get out of here, you, and may it never be that I should do such a thing!' He answered me: 'But it will be pain and grief to you if you have done it badly'. I said to him: 'There is no need for you to worry yourself about that'. 'But I am sorry for you', he rejoined, 'because of your wasted effort', and I said: 'Neither you nor those who brought you are welcome here.' But he replied: 'Actually, it was you who compelled me to come here and you are mine'. I asked him how he could say that. 'Because three Sundays running you have received holy communion whilst being at daggers-drawn with your neighbour', he said—and I told him he was lying. But he said: 'Are you not harbouring a grudge against him because of a plate of lentils? I am the one who is in charge of grudges and, from now on, you are mine.' When I heard that, I left my cell, went to the brother <in question> and prostrated myself before him in order to become reconciled with him. When I returned, I found that my visitor had burned the mosquito net and that mat on which I had prostrated myself, because he was so consumed with jealousy for our love.

162. The response of Abba Theodore of Pentapolis to the question of abstaining from wine

Twenty miles from Alexandria, there is a lavra called Calamôn, between the eighteenth mile-post and Maphora. There we met Abba Theodore (Sophronios the Sophist was with us) and we asked him if it were permissible to break the rule of abstaining from wine when we were visiting somebody, or when somebody paid us a visit. He said it was not: so we asked him why it was that the fathers of old time would set aside that rule. The elder replied: 'The fathers of old time were truly great and highly disciplined men who could loosen the rule and then bind it again. This present generation is not strong enough to loosen the rule and then to bind it again. If we once loosen the rule, we no longer maintain our ascetic way of life.'

163. THE LIFE OF ABBA PAUL THE GREEK

Abba Alexander of the Lavra of Calamôn by the holy Jordan said: One day when I was with Abba Paul the Greek at his cave, somebody came and knocked at the door. The elder went out and opened to him. Then he took out and set before him bread and soaked <peas>, which he wolfed down. I thought it must be some stranger; I looked through the window and saw that it was a lion. I said to the elder: 'Good elder, why do you feed that animal? Explain to me'. He said: 'I have required of it that it harm neither man nor beast; and I have told it to come here each day and I will give it its food. It has come twice a day now for seven months—and I feed it.' Some days later I met him again, when I wanted to buy some bottles for he occupied his hands by making bottles. I said to him: 'How are things, good elder? How is the lion?' He answered: 'Badly', and I asked: 'How so?' He told me: 'It came here to be fed yesterday and I noticed that its muzzle was all stained with blood. I said to it: "What is this? You have disobeyed me and eaten flesh. Blessed Lord! Never again will I feed you the food of the fathers, carnivore! Get away from here." He would not go away, so I took a rope, folded it up into three and struck it three blows with it. Then it went away.'

164. THE REPLY OF ABBA VICTOR THE SOLITARY TO A FAINT-HEARTED MONK

A brother visited Abba Victor the solitary at the lavra of Eleousa* and said to him: 'What shall I do, father, for I am in the grips of the spiritual disease of faint-heartedness?' The elder replied: 'This is a disease of the soul. Just as those who suffer from ophthalmia have the impression of seeing more light (when their disease is acute) than do those whose eyes are healthy, so too do the faint-hearted quickly take offence at some small neglect and think that neglect to be something of great moment. It is just the opposite with those who are healthy in soul, for they rejoice in their trials.'

165. THE LIFE OF A ROBBER NAMED CYRIACOS

The <same?> friend of Christ* told us about a robber named Cyriacos whose thefts were committed in the area around Emäus, known also as Nicopolis. He became so cruel and inhuman that they called him 'the wolf'. There were other robbers with him; not only Christians, but also Judaeans and Samaritans too. One day—it was in holy week—some people from an estate in the region of Nicopolis came up to the Holy City to baptise their children. When <the children> had been baptised, they were returning to their own estate to celebrate Easter Day there. But they were confronted by the robbers on the way (the chieftain was not present). The men took to their heels. Casting aside the newly baptised <children>, the Hebrews and Samaritans seized the women and took possession of them. As the men fled, they ran into the chieftain of the robbers who asked them: 'Why are you running away?' They told him what had happened to them. He took them with him and went in search of his companions; he found the children stretched out on the ground. When he discovered who had perpetrated this atrocity, he beheaded the guilty ones. He had the men take up the little ones (because the women were unwilling to do so on account of their defilement <by the robbers>) and then he conducted them all safely to their own estate. A little while later, the robber-chief was arrested. For ten years he languished in gaol and no ruler had him executed; finally, he was released. He would say over and over again: 'It is thanks to those babes that I escaped bitter death. I used to see them in my dreams, saying to me: "Do not be afraid; we are putting forward the case for your defence"'. We met this man, I and Abba John, priest of the Lavra of the Eunuchs. He told us all this—and we glorified God.

166. The Life of a Robber Who Became a Monk and Was Later Beheaded in Lay Clothes

Abba Sabbatios said: When I was living at the lavra of Abba Firminos,* a robber came to Abba Zosimos the Cilician and begged him: 'Of your charity, for God's sake, make me a monk, for I am the author of many murders. Make me a monk so that for the rest of my life I may desist from my evil doings.' The elder gave him instruction, made him a monk, and provided him with the holy habit. A few days later, the elder said to the new monk: 'Believe me, my child, you cannot stay here. If the governor hears about you, he will arrest you. Or maybe your enemies shall pass this way and kill you. But pay heed to me; I will take you to a community some distance from here.' He took him to the community of Abba Dorotheos,* near to Gaza and to Maïouma.* He spent nine years there, learning the entire psalter and all the conventions of monastic observance. The he went back to the lavra of Abba Firminos and said to the elder: 'Abba, have pity on me, sir; give me back my worldly clothes and take the monastic habit from me'. Distressed by these words, the elder said to him: 'Whatever for, child?' The other answered: 'See now, father; as you know, I have been nine years in the community. I have fasted to the full extent of my ability; I have practised self-discipline; I have lived under obedience with complete serenity and in the fear of God. I believe that, of his goodness, <God> has pardoned my many evil deeds. Yet every day I see an infant which says to me: "Why did you slay me?" I see him in church, I see him in the refectory, always saying the same thing to me. The vision never leaves me untroubled for an hour at a time. This is why I want to go away, father. I must die for that infant, for

I killed it without reason.' He took his clothes, put them on, and went out of the lavra. He went to Diospolis. The following day he was arrested and beheaded.

167. The life and death of Abba Poemên, the solitary

Abba Agathonicos, higoumen of the community of our holy father Sabas at Castellium,* said:

One day I went down to Rouba to visit Abba Poemên the grazer. When I found him, I told him the thoughts which troubled me. When night fell, he left me in a cave. It was winter and that night it got very cold indeed; I was freezing. When the elder came at dawn, he said to me: 'What is matter, child?' I said: 'Forgive me, father; I had a very bad night because of the cold'. He said to me: 'Indeed, child? I did not feel the cold.' This amazed me, for he was naked. I asked him of his charity to tell me how he did not feel the cold. He said: 'A lion came down and lay beside me; he kept me warm. But I tell you, brother: I shall be devoured by wild beasts.' I asked him why, and he told me: 'Because when I was in our homeland'—we were both from Galatia—'I was a shepherd. I was hostile to a stranger who came by and my dogs devoured him. I could have saved him, but I did not. I left him to his fate and the dogs killed him. I know that I too must die in that way.' Three years later that elder was devoured by wild beasts, as he himself had foretold.

168. Sayings of Abba Alexander the elder

Abba Alexander, the elder of Abba Vincent, said to the brethren: 'Our fathers sought out the wilderness and affliction; we seek for cities and comfort'.

Again: 'In the days of our fathers, the virtues of poverty and humility flourished; these days, avarice and pride are in fashion'.

Again: 'Our fathers never used to wash their faces; but we indulge ourselves at the public baths'.

Again: 'Alas, children, we have eliminated the angelic way of life'.

Abba Vincent, his disciple, said to him: 'We are indeed sickly, father'. The elder rejoined: 'What do you mean, Vincent, by "We are sickly?" Believe me child: we are fit in body as Olympic athletes, but we are sick indeed in the soul.'

Again: 'We are able to eat and drink a great deal and to wear fine clothing; but we are incapable of mastering our passions or our pride.'

Again the elder said: 'Oh. Alexander, Alexander! How you are going to be put to shame when others receive the crown!'

169. The life of a blind elder at the Monastery of Abba Sisoës

There was a blind elder at Scêtê in the lavra of Abba Sisoës; his cell was located about half a mile from the well. He would never allow anyone else to fetch water for him. He made a rope and attached one end of it to the well, the other to his cell; the rope lay on the ground. When he went to fetch water, he walked along the rope. The elder did this so that he could find the well that way. When the wind blew the sand so that it covered the rope, he would take it up in his hand, shake it and put it back down on the ground and walk along it. When a brother offered to fetch water for him, the elder replied: 'Truly brother, for twenty-two years I have fetched my own water; so you wish to deprive me of my labour?'

170. The Life of a Holy Woman Who Died in the Wilderness

<About twenty miles> from Jerusalem there is a monastery called Sampson,* from which two fathers went up to Sinaï to pray. When they returned to the monastery, they told us:

After we had performed our devotions at the holy mountain, on our way back we got lost in the wilderness. For many days we were borne along in the wilderness as though we were on the high sea. One day, we saw a little cave in the distance and we made our way towards it. When we came near to the cave, we saw a very small spring with some vegetation around it, and there were human footprints. We said to each other: 'Indeed, there is a servant of God here'. When we entered the cave, we could not see anybody, but we could hear somebody breathing. We carefully searched the place and we found something rather like a manger with somebody lying in it. We came near to that servant of God and begged him to speak to us. When there was no answer, we touched him. The body was still warm, but his soul had gone to the Lord. Then we realised that he had departed this life as we entered the cave. So we took his body from where it lay and dug a grave for him there in the cave. One of us took of the pallium he was wearing and wrapped the elder's body in it; and we buried him in it. But we discovered that it was a woman—and we glorified God. We performed the office over her and buried her.

171. The Life of Two Remarkable Men, Theodore the Philosopher and Zoïlos the Reader

In Alexandria there were two wondrously virtuous men, Abba Theodore the philosopher and Zoïlos the reader; we were well acquainted with both of them, the one from his lectures, the other because we shared the same homeland and up-bringing. Abba Theodore had no possessions whatsoever, except for a philosopher's cloak and a few books. He slept on a bench whenever he came across a church. He finally renounced the world at the Community of Salama and there he ended his days. As for Zoïlos the reader, he too was equally indifferent to possessions. He too had nothing but a philosopher's cloak, a very old suit and a few books. Calligraphy was his occupation. When he died in the Lord, he was buried at Lithazomenos, in the monastery of Abba Palladios.

Some fathers went to Master Cosmas the lawyer and asked him about Abba Theodore the philosopher and Zoïlos the reader: which of the two had progressed farther in the practice of asceticism? He replied: 'They both had the same kind of clothing, the same kind of bed and the same kind of food. They both rejected anything that was in excess of basic necessities. They were equal in humility, poverty and self-discipline. But Abba Theodore, who went bare-foot and suffered greatly with his eyes, had learnt both the Old and the New Testaments by heart. But he had also the consolation of the company of the brethren, contact with friends; a not inconsiderable distraction when he was active and when he was teaching. In the case of Zoïlos the reader, not only is his isolation from the world <*xeniteia*> praiseworthy, but so is his solitude <*erêmia*>, his immense toil, the way he keeps his tongue on a leash. He had no friend, nothing to call his own, no-one to talk to; he engaged in no worldly activity; allowed himself no relief, nor would he accept the smallest service from anybody. He did his own cooking and washing; he allowed himself no pleasure from reading. He was ready to be of service to others; neither cold nor heat nor bodily sickness was of any account with him. He shunned laughter, sadness, inactivity, relaxation. For all the exiguity of his clothing he was constantly devoured by lice. Yet this man, in comparison with the first one, had no small consolation from his freedom of movement, for he was entirely free to go wherever he would, by night or by day. Yet even this freedom was of no avail because so heavy was his toil, that he never made use of it. Thus he appeared studiously to avoid over-much contact with the world. Each one of them shall receive his own reward, consonant with his toil, and the progress he made; with his spiritual and mental purity, his fear of God, his charity, his worship, his compunction *<katanuxis>,* his constancy in psalm-singing and prayer, his persistent faith—and the good pleasure of God, which is hidden and concealed from people.

172. THE LIFE OF THE ABOVE-MENTIONED COSMAS, THE LAWYER

Concerning this master Cosmas the lawyer, many people told us many things; some one thing, others another. But most people told us a great deal. We shall write down what we saw with our own eyes and what we have carefully examined, for the benefit of those who chance to read it. He was a humble man, merciful, continent, a virgin, serene, cool-tempered, friendly, hospitable, and kind to the poor. This wondrous man greatly benefitted us, not only by letting us see him and by teaching us, but also because he had more books than anybody else in Alexandria and would willingly supply them to those who wished. Yet he was a man of no possessions. Throughout his house there was nothing to be seen but books, a bed and a table. Any man could go in and ask for what would benefit him—and read it. Each day I would go in to him and I never entered without finding him either reading or writing against the Jews. It was his fervent desire to convert the Hebrews to the truth. For this reason he would often send me to some Hebrews to discuss some point of Scripture with them, for he would not readily leave the house himself.

One day I went to the house of Master Cosmas the lawyer and, as I was quite familiar with him, I said to him: 'Of your charity, how long have you been leading the solitary life? *<hêsuchazôn>*' He kept his silence and gave no answer, so I asked again: 'For the sake of the Lord, tell me'. He remained silent a little longer, then he told me: 'For thirty-three years'. When I heard this, I glorified God.

Another time I came to him and asked him: 'Of your extreme charity, and in full knowledge that it is for the benefit of my soul that I ask you this; will you tell me what you have accomplished in so long a period of solitude and continence *<hêsuchia...egkrateia>*?' He heaved a great sigh from the depths of his heart and said to me: 'What shall a man living in the world accomplish, especially a man who stays in his own house?' Yet I begged him to tell me; for the Lord's sake, and for the good of my soul. Finally, coerced by my persistence, he said: 'Forgive me; there are three things I know of which I have accomplished: not to laugh, not to swear and not to lie'.

173. THE WONDROUS DEED OF THEODORE THE ANCHORITE WHO MADE FRESH WATER AT SEA BY HIS PRAYER

There was an anchorite in the area of the holy Jordan, Theodore by name, who was a eunuch. He was obliged for some reason or other to go to Constantinople so he boarded a ship. The vessel was delayed so long on the high sea that they ran out of water. Sailors and passengers alike were greatly afflicted by anxiety and despair. The anchorite stood up and stretched out his hands to heaven, to the God who saves our souls from death. He offered a prayer and sealed the sea with the sign of the cross. Then he said to the sailors: 'Blessed be the Lord! Draw as much water as you need'. They filled every receptacle with fresh water out of the sea and everybody glorified God.

174. THE DEED OF A RELIGIOUS SHIP-MASTER WHO PRAYED TO THE LORD FOR RAIN

Abba Gregory the anchorite told us:
I was returning from Byzantium by ship and a scribe came aboard with his wife; he had to go pray at the Holy City. The ship-master was a very devout man, given to fasting. As we sailed along, the scribe's attendants were prodigal in their use of water. When we came into the midst of the high sea, we ran out of water and we were in great distress. It was a pitiful sight: women and children and infants perishing from thirst, lying there like corpses. We were in this distressing condition for three days and abandoned hope of survival. Unable to tolerate such affliction, the scribe drew his sword, intending to kill the ship-master and the sailors. He said: 'It is their fault that we are to be lost, for they did not take sufficient water on board for our needs'. I interceded with the scribe, saying: 'Do not do that; but rather, let us pray to our Lord Jesus Christ, our true God, *who does great and wonderful things which cannot be counted* <Jb 34:26>. Behold, this is now the third day that the ship-master has occupied himself with fasting and prayer.' The scribe quietened down and, on the fourth day, about the sixth hour, the ship-master got up and cried in a loud voice: 'Glory to thee, Christ our God'!—and that in such a way that we were all astonished at his cry. And he said to the sailors: 'Stretch out the skins', and whilst they were unfolding them, look! A cloud came over the ship and it rained enough water to satisfy all our needs. It was a great and fearful wonder, for as the ship was borne along by the wind, the cloud followed us; but it did not rain beyond the ship.

175. A story about the Emperor Zeno who was much given to almsgiving

Concerning the Emperor Zeno <474-491> one of the fathers told us this: that he wronged a woman by wronging her daughter. She frequented the Church of our all-holy Lady Mary, the Mother of God, beseeching her and saying with tears: 'Defend my cause against the Emperor Zeno'. When she had continued this for many days, the all-holy Mother of God appeared to her saying: 'Believe me, woman, I frequently tried to get satisfaction for you, but his right hand prevents me',—for he was a very good almsgiver.

176. The beautiful story of Abba Andrew about ten travellers, of whom one was a Hebrew

Abba Palladios told us he had heard one of the fathers whose name was Andrew (whom we also met) say:

When we were in Alexandria, Abba Andrew at the eighteenth <mile post> told us, saying:*

As a young man I was very undisciplined. A war broke out and confusion reigned so, together with nine others, I fled to Palestine. One of the nine was a fellow with initiative and another was a Hebrew. When we came into the wilderness, the Hebrew became mortally sick, so we were in great distress, for we did not know what to do for him. But we did not abandon him. Each of us carried him as far as he was able. We wanted to get him to a city or to a market-town so that he should not die in the wilderness. But when the young man was completely worn out and was brought to the point of death by hunger and a burning fever, by utter exhaustion and a raging thirst from the heat (in fact he was about to expire), he could no longer bear to be carried. With many tears, we decided to abandon him in the wilderness and go our way. We could see death from thirst lying in store for us. We were in tears when we set him down on the sand. When he saw that we were going to leave him, he began to adjure us, saying: 'By the God who is going to judge both the quick and the dead, leave me to die not as a Jew, but as a Christian. Have mercy on me and baptise me so that I too may depart this life as a Christian and go to the Lord.' We said to him: 'Truly, brother, it is impossible for us to do anything of the sort. We are laymen and baptising is bishops' work and priests'. Besides, there is no water here.' But he continued to adjure us in the same terms and with tears, saying: 'Oh, Christians, please do not deprive me of this benefit'. While we were most unsure what to do next, the fellow with initiative* among us, inspired by God, said to us: 'Stand him up and take off his clothes'. We got him to his feet with great difficulty and stripped him. The one with initiative filled both his hands with sand and poured it three times over the sick man's head saying: 'Theodore is baptised in the name of the Father and of the Son and of the Holy Spirit', and we all answered *amen* to each of the names of the holy, consubstantial and worshipful Trinity. The Lord is my witness, brethren, that Christ, the Son of the living God, thus cured and re-invigorated him so that not a trace of illness remained in him. In health and vigour he ran before us during the rest of our journey through the wilderness. When we observed so great and so sudden a transformation, we all praised and glorified the ineffable majesty and loving kindness of Christ our God. When we arrived at Ascalon, we took this matter to the blessed and saintly Dionysios, who was bishop there, and told him what had happened to the brother on the journey. When the truly holy Dionysios heard of these things, he was stupefied by so extraordinary a miracle. He assembled all the clergy and put to them the question of whether he should reckon the effusion of sand as baptism or not. Some said that, in view of the extraordinary miracle, he should allow it as a valid baptism; others said he should not. Gregory the Theologian enumerates all the kinds of baptism.* He speaks of the Mosaic baptism, baptism in water, that is, but before that of baptism in a cloud and in the sea. 'The baptism of John was no longer Judaic baptism, for it was not only a baptism in water, but also unto repentance. Jesus also baptised, but in the Spirit, and this is perfection. I know also a fourth baptism: that of martyrdom and of blood. And I know a fifth: the baptism of tears.' 'Which of these baptisms did he undergo', asked some, 'so that we might pronounce on its validity? For indeed the Lord said to Nicodemos: *Except a man be born again of water and of the spirit, he shall not enter into the kingdom of heaven* <Jn 3:5.>' Others objected to this: 'How so? Since it is not written concerning the apostles that they were baptised, shall they not enter the kingdom of heaven?' To this, others replied: 'But indeed they were baptised, as Clement, the author of *Stromatês,* testifies in the fifth book of *Hypotyposes.** In commenting on the saying of the Apostle Paul, he opines: *I thank God that I baptised none of you* <1 Co 1:14> that Jesus is said to have baptised none but Peter; Peter to have baptised Andrew; Andrew, James and John, and they the others'. When they had said all this and much more beside, it seemed good to the blessed Bishop Dionysios to send the brother to the holy Jordan and for him to be baptised there. The fellow with initiative he ordained deacon.

177. The bad death of an Egyptian monk who wanted to occupy the cell of Evagrios, the heretic*

Abba John the Cilician told us that while they were staying at the ninth mile-post from Alexandria, an Egyptian monk visited us and said: 'A brother from foreign parts came to the Lavra of The Cells and wanted to stay there. He prostrated himself before the priest *<presbyteros>* and requested that he might stay the night at the cell of Evagrios. The priest told him that he could not stay there. The brother said: 'If I may not stay there, I will go away'. The priest said to him: 'My child, the fact of the matter is that a cruel demon inhabits that place. It led Evagrios astray, alienating him from the true faith, and it filled his mind with abominable teachings'. The brother persisted, saying: 'If I am to remain here, that is where I am going to stay'. Then the priest said: 'On your own head be it: go and stay there'. The brother went and stayed there for a week and, when the holy day of the Lord came round, he came to the church. The priest was relieved to see him. The following Sunday he did not come to the church, so the priest summoned two brothers to go and find out why he was not present in church. They went to the cell and found that the brother had put a rope around his neck and strangled himself.

178. The life of an elder of the Community of the Scolarii, a simple man

Abba Gregory, priest of the Community of the Scholarii, told us that at Monidia there lived a monk who was an exceedingly hard worker, but somewhat indiscriminating in matters of faith. He would receive holy communion indiscriminately, in whatever church he happened to be. One day an angel of God appeared to him and said: 'Tell me elder, when you die, how do you want us to bury you? The way the Egyptian monks bury <the dead>, or after the custom of Jerusalem?' The elder said he did not know, and the angel replied: 'Think about it. I will come to you three weeks from now and you shall tell me.' The elder went to a colleague and told him what he had heard from the angel. The <second> elder was utterly amazed at what he heard. He stared at the man for a long time; then, inspired by God, he said to him: 'Where do you partake of the holy mysteries?' The other replied: 'Wherever I happen to be'. The elder said to him: 'Never again should you communicate outside the holy catholic and apostolic Church in which the four holy councils are named: the council of the three hundred and eighteen fathers at Nicaea, that of the one hundred and fifty fathers at Constantinople, the first Council of Ephesos of two hundred, and that of the six hundred and thirty fathers at Chalcedon. And when the angel comes, say to him: "I wish to be buried according to the custom of Jerusalem."'

Three weeks later, the angel came and said to him: 'Which is it to be, elder? Have you given thought to the matter?' The elder replied that he wished to be buried according to the Jerusalem custom. The angel replied: 'Very well, very well', and the elder immediately surrendered his soul. This was done so that the elder would not lose his labour and be condemned as a heretic.

179. The Life of a Woman Religious *<sanctimonialis feminae>* who was from the Holy City

We visited John the anchorite, known as 'the red', and he told us that he had heard Abba John the Moabite say that there was in the Holy City a nun *<monastria>* who was very devout, progressing in the service of God. The devil resented this virgin, so he implanted a satanic desire <for her> in the heart of a certain young man. That wondrous virgin perceived the demon's subterfuge and <foresaw> the young man's destruction. So she put some <beans> soaked in water into a basket and went into the wilderness. By her withdrawal she brought peace and serenity to the young man whilst she herself attained the security which is borne of solitude. A long time afterwards, by the providence of God, so that her virtuous conduct should not remain unknown, an anchorite saw her in the wilderness of the holy Jordan and he said to her: 'Amma, what are you doing in this wilderness?' Not wishing to reveal herself to the anchorite, she said to him: 'Forgive me; the fact is that I have lost my way. But of your charity, father, and for the sake of the Lord, show me my path.' By divine inspiration he knew all about her. He said to her: 'Believe me, amma, you have neither lost your way nor are you looking for the path. You know that lies are of the devil; so tell me the real reason why you came here'. Then the virgin said to him: 'Forgive me abba; a young man was in danger of falling into sin on my account and, for that reason, I came into the wilderness. I thought it was better to die here than to be an occasion of stumbling to somebody as the Apostle <Paul, 2 Co 6:3> says.' The elder asked: 'How long have you been here?' 'Seventeen years, by the grace of Christ', she replied. 'What do you eat?' asked the elder. She produced the basket containing steeped <beans> and said to the anchorite: 'I brought this basket away from the city with me containing these few steeped <beans> and so great has been the providence of God to me that I have been able to eat of them all this time and they have not decreased. And this too you should know, father: that his goodness has so sheltered me that in all these seventeen years no man ever laid eyes on me until you did today. Yet for my part, I could see all of them.' When the anchorite learned this, he glorified God.

180. The life of John the Anchorite* who lived in a cave on the Socho estate

The most holy Dionysios, priest and sacristan of the most holy church of Ascalon, said to us concerning Abba John the Anchorite: 'This was a man who, in our own generation, was truly great in the eyes of God', and as a demonstration of the extent to which he was pleasing to God, he related this miracle attributed to him:

This elder lived in a cave in the district of the Socho estate, almost twenty miles from Jerusalem. In the cave he had an icon of our all-holy and spotless Lady, the Mother of God and ever-virgin Mary, holding our God in her arms. Sometimes this elder would decide to go somewhere on a journey; maybe a great distance into the wilderness, or to Jerusalem to reverence the Holy Cross and the Holy Places, or to pray at Mount Sinaï, or to visit martyrs <shrines> many a long day's travel from Jerusalem. He was greatly devoted to the martyrs, this elder. Now he would visit Saint John at Ephesos; another time, Saint Theodore at Euchaïta or Saint Thecla the Isaurian at Seleucia or Saint Sergios at Saphas. Sometimes he would go to visit this saint, sometimes another. Yet whenever he was about to set out, it was his custom to prepare and light a lamp. He would stand in prayer, beseeching God to make straight the way which lay before him; running towards her icon, he would say to the Lady: 'Holy Lady, Mother of God: since I am about to undertake a long journey of many days' duration, watch over your lamp and keep it from going out, as I intend that it should not. For I am setting out with your help as my travelling-companion.' Having said this to the icon, he would set off <on his journey>. When he returned from his proposed trip, maybe a month or two months or three months later, even sometimes after five or six months, he would find the lamp well cared for and alight, just as he had left it when he set out on his journey. He never saw it go out of its own accord; not when he awakened from sleep or when he returned to his cave from a journey or from the wilderness.

181. Concerning the same

This Dionysios the priest also told us this about the same man: One day the elder was out walking in the environs of the Sochas estate, which is where his cave was located. As he walked along, he saw a large lion approaching in the opposite direction and getting very near. The path along which he was travelling was very narrow and there was a hedge on either side of it; the kind of hedge that farmers use to fence their fields and which they plant with thorn-bushes. The thorns made the path so narrow that it was only just possible for one person (provided he were not carrying anything) to walk through it and through which a person walking would certainly not pass unscathed. As they drew nearer to each other, the elder and the lion, the elder would not turn back and yield the right of way to the lion, whilst the lion *could* not turn round because the passage was so narrow. And it was impossible for them both to pass by. When the lion saw that the servant of God intended to go straight forwards and that he would under no circumstances retrace his steps, it stood up on its rear paws. When it was upright, it leaned against the hedge to the left of the elder. With its weight and its physical strength it widened the passage a little and this allowed the righteous man to continue his journey without interruption. Thus the elder came through, brushing against the lion's back. After he had passed by, the lion got down from the hedge and went its own way.

A brother visited Abba John and found nothing in the cave. He asked him: 'How can you stay here, father, with no provision for you needs'? The elder replied: 'This cave is a wrestling-ring; it is a matter of give and take'.

182. THE LIFE OF ABBA ALEXANDER THE CILICIAN WHO WAS BESIEGED BY A DEMON WHEN HE WAS NEAR TO DEATH

The Monastery of Saint Sergios (also known as Xeropotamos) is near to holy Bethlehem, about two miles away. The higoumen there was a very devout man, Abba Eugenios, who later became bishop of Hermopolis in Egypt, which is on the border of the first Thebaïd. When we visited that monastery, he told us that when Abba Alexander the Cilician reached old age in the caves of the holy Jordan, he took him into his own monastery. For three months, at the end of his life, he was confined to bed. Ten days before he went to the Lord, he fell into the clutches of a malicious demon. The elder began saying to the demon: 'Wretch, you have come at evening time. That is no great deed, for I am bed-ridden and immobilised. Without intending to, you have shown me your weakness, fool! If you were able and strong, you should have come to me fifty or sixty years ago. Then, by Christ who lends me strength, I would have shown you your weakness. I would have beaten down your pride and bowed your stiff neck. This weakness which afflicts me is not of my own making, but something which weighs me down. However, I give thanks to God, to whom I am going, and to whom I shall make known the injustice which you inflict upon me by your merciless attacks upon me at the end of my life, after so many years spent in rigorous asceticism.' He would say this, and much more besides, each day. Then, on the tenth day, he surrendered his spirit to the Lord Jesus Christ in utter serenity and at peace.

183. The wondrous deed of David, the Egyptian

Abba Theodore the Cilician said:

When I was staying at Scêtê, there was an elder there called David. One day he went out with some other monks to reap. The Scetiotes have this custom, that they go out to the estates and reap. The elder went to an estate and offered himself for hire an a day-to-day basis. A farmer hired him and as the elder was reaping <...> about the sixth hour it was very hot, so the elder entered a shack and sat down. When the farmer came and saw him sitting there, he said to him angrily: 'Elder, why are you not reaping? Do you not realise that I am paying you?' He said: 'Yes, but the heat is so intense that the grains of wheat are falling out of the husks. I am waiting a little for the heat to abate so that you suffer no loss.' The farmer said to him: 'Get up and work, even if everything bursts into flames'. The elder said to him: 'Do you want it all to burn?' The farmer angrily rejoined: 'Isn't that what I said?' The elder stood up, and suddenly the field began to burn. Then, in fear, the farmer came to the other part of the field where the other elders were reaping. He begged them to come and intercede with the elder for him, to pray that the fire might cease. They came and made an act of obeisance to the elder, who said: 'But he himself said that it should burn'. Yet they were able to convince him. He went and stood between that part of the field which was burning and that which remained unscathed. He offered a prayer and immediately the fire in the field was extinguished. The rest of the crop was saved. Everybody was amazed and glorified God.

184. The life of Abba John the Eunuch and of a young man who resolved never to drink and of another elder greatly given to prayer

When we were at the ninth mile-post from Alexandria, we visited the monastery of Abba John the Eunuch for the benefit <of our souls>. There we found a very old man who had been at the monastery for about eighty years. He had more compassion than anybody we ever saw, not only for men, but also for animals. What did this elder do? No other work but this: he would rise early and feed all the dogs at the lavra. He would give flour to the small ants, grain to the bigger ones. He would dampen biscuits and throw them up on the roof-tops for the birds to eat. Living like this, he left nothing to the monastery <when he died>, neither door nor window nor spy-hole not lamp nor table. In brief (not to say it all and make the story too long), he left nothing whatsoever of the world's goods behind. Not even for one hour did he ever possess books, money or clothing. He gave everything to those in need, investing his entire concern in those things which were to come.

Those who wished to make known his pity and compassion told us this about him:

One day a farmer came and asked the elder to give him a piece of gold. As the monk had nothing to give (for he never did have gold in his possession) he sent and borrowed a piece of gold from the monastery and gave it to the farmer—who said he would repay it a month later. When, after two years, the gold had still not been returned (for the farmer did not have the wherewithal to pay), Abba John sent for his and said: 'Give me the piece of gold, brother'. He answered: 'As God knows well, I do not have it.' 'Then I have found a way in which you can repay me for it', was the elder's reply. The <farmer>, thinking that he was to be given some task to perform, said: 'Tell me, and I will do it'. Then Abba John said: 'When you have time to spare and no work to do, come and make thirty prostrations and I will pay you one *keration'*, and he gave the man something to eat and drink. So it was agreed with the man that, when he was free to do so, he would come, and when he had performed his prostrations, the elder would give him his reward, that is, one *keration.* He also gave him something to eat and drink and hard-tack enough for the five persons of his household. When he had saved up twenty-four *keratia,* which is equal to one piece of gold, the elder received that sum from him and sent him on his way with his blessing.

The same John, the Eunuch, told us:

I came up into the Thebaïd, the community of Abba Apollo, and there I saw a young brother whose father in the flesh was also a monk. The young man had made it rule for himself to drink neither water nor wine nor any other liquid as long as he lived. So he ate chicory and bitter herbs and those vegetables which had the ability of assuaging his thirst. His task was to put the loaves in the oven. After three years he fell ill and eventually went to the Lord. As he burned with fever and terrible thirst, everybody pressed him to drink a little, but the brother would not hear of it. The abba of the community summoned a doctor to do what could be done for the dying man; but when he arrived and saw the brother in such a miserable condition, he too pressed him to take a little drink—but without success. So he said to the abba: 'Get me a large vessel'. He poured four measures of tepid water into it and then had the brother put into it up to his thighs and made to stay there for about an hour. The godly elder <John the Eunuch> assured us (for he said he was present when they took the brother out of the water) that when the doctor measured the water, he found it to have been reduced by one measure. This is the sort of thing the ascetics endured in gaining complete self-mastery, ill-treating themselves for the sake of God, in order to attain to the good things of eternity.

The same elder told us:

I went to the cell of a certain elder in that community and I noticed that, where he used to prostrate himself, there was a slab; it was on that he would prostrate himself. Where his hands and knees touched, the slab was hollowed out to a depth of more than four fingers, so often did he prostrate himself.

185. The Life of a Faithful Woman Who, with Wondrous Wisdom, Converted Her Gentile Husband to the Faith

On the island of Samos, Mary, the friend of both God and the poor, the mother of Master Paul, the military official attached to the court *<kandidatos>,* told us that there was a christian woman in Nisbis whose husband was a pagan *<Hellên>*. They possessed fifty *miliarisia.* One day, the husband said to his wife: 'Let us lend out that money and get some advantage from it, for in drawing on it a little at a time, we are going to spend it all'. The wife answered: 'If you insist on lending this money, come: lend it to the God of the Christians'. He said to her: 'Well, where is this God of the Christians, so we can lend it to him'? She said: 'I will show you. Not only shall you not lose your money, but it shall even earn interest for you and the capital shall be doubled.' He said to her: 'Come on then; show me him and we will lend to him'. She took her husband and led him to the most holy church. Now the church at Nisbis has five large doorways. As she brought him to the entrance, there where the great porches are, she showed him the poor and said: 'If you give to these <persons>, the God of the Christians receives it, for these are all his'. Immediately, and with gladness, he gave the fifty *miliarisia* to the poor, and went back to his house. Three months later, their expenses exceeded their ability to pay. The man said to his wife: 'Sister, the God if the Christians is not going to pay us back anything of that debt and, here we are, in need'. In reply, the woman said: 'Yes, he will <repay>. Go to where you handed over the money and he will return it to you right away.' He went off to the holy church at a run. When he came to the spot where he had given the *miliarisia* to the poor, he went all around the church, expecting to find somebody who would give back to him what was owing to him. But all he found was the poor, still sitting there. While he was trying to decide to which of them to speak or whom he should ask, he saw at his feet, on the marble <floor>, one large *miliarision* lying there, one of those which he himself had distributed to his brothers <the poor>. Bending down, he picked it up and went to his house. Then he said to his spouse: 'Look, I just went to your church and, believe me, woman, I did not see the God of the Christians as you said I would. And he certainly did not give me anything, except that I found this *miliarision* lying there where I gave fifty of them away.' Then that wondrous woman said to him: 'It is he who invisibly provided <that *miliarision*>, for he is invisible and he operates the universe with invisible power and an unseen hand. Now, go, sir; buy us something so we can eat today, and he will provide you with something else.' Off he went and bought bread, wine and fish for them. He came back and gave <his purchases> to his wife. She took the fish and began to clean it. When she cut it open, she found within a stone so magnificent that she was struck with wonder at it. She had no idea what it was, but she kept it nevertheless. When her husband came, she showed him whilst they were eating the stone she had found and said: 'Look, I found this stone inside the fish'. When he saw it, he too was amazed at its beauty, but he did not know what it really was. When they had finished eating, he said to her: 'Give it to me; I will go and sell it, if I can find a way of getting anything for it'. As I said, he did not know what it was, for he was a simple man. He took the stone and went to the money-changer; he was also a silver-smith. It was time for the smith to go home (for it was evening,) but the man said to him: 'Would you like to buy this stone?' When the money-changer saw it, he said: 'How much do you want for it?' The man said: 'Give me what you will'. The other replied: 'Take five *miliarisia* for it then'. Thinking that the merchant was making fun of him, the man said: 'Would you give that much for it?' The merchant thought the man was being sarcastic, so he said: 'Well, take ten *miliarisia* for it then'. Still thinking that the merchant was making fun of him, the man remained silent, at which the other said: 'Then take twenty *miliarisia* for it'. As the man still kept silent and made no response, the merchant raised his offer to thirty, and then to fifty *miliarisia,* swearing that he would indeed pay that much. The seller of the stone realised that it must be very valuable if the merchant were prepared to pay fifty *miliarisia* for it. Little by little the merchant raised his offer until it reached three hundred large *miliarisia.* This sum the man accepted. He handed over the stone and went home to his wife with a glad heart. When she saw him, she asked him how much he had sold it for, expecting him to say five or ten *pholleis.* He took out the three-hundred *miliarisia* and handed them to her, saying that for so much he had sold the stone. Filled with wonder at the goodness of God, she said to him: 'Oh husband, see how good and generous and affluent is the God of the Christians! Look how he has not merely returned to you the fifty *miliarisia* you lent him together with interest, but in only a few days has given you the capital multiplied by six! Know therefore that there is no other God, neither on earth nor in heaven, but him alone.' Convinced by this miracle and learning the truth by experience, he immediately became a Christian and glorified our God and Saviour, Jesus Christ, with the Father and the Holy Spirit, gratefully acknowledging the intelligence of his wife by which it had been granted to him to know God in very truth.

186. THE LIFE OF MOSCHOS, THE MERCHANT OF TYRE

At the community of the Cave of Saint Sabas, we visited Abba Eustathios, the higoumen. He told us:

There was a merchant at Tyre called Moschos. This is what he told us when we were in Tyre:

When I was engaged in commerce, late one evening I went to bathe. On the way I came across a woman standing in the shadows. I went up and greeted her; she agreed to follow me. I was so diabolically delighted that I did not bathe but went straight to dinner. I did my best to persuade her but she would not consent to taste <a morsel>. Finally, we got up to go to bed and, as I began to embrace her, she let out a tremendous cry and broke into tears, saying: 'What a woeful wretch I am!' I was trembling as I asked her what was the matter. She wept even more and said: 'My husband is a merchant and he has been shipwrecked. He lost both his own property and others.' Now he is in prison because of the others' losses. I am at my wits' end what to do and how to get bread for him. I decided, in great shame, to sell my body; it was to get bread. They have taken everything from us.' I said to her: 'How much is owing?' She said: 'Five pounds of gold.' <=360 pieces, or 1638 grams of gold> I took out the gold and gave it to her, saying: 'For fear of the judgement of God, I have not touched you. Go, redeem your husband with this gold, and pray for me.'

Some time later, certain slanders against me reached the ears of the emperor to the effect that I had squandered my merchandise. The emperor sent and seized all my estate, dragged me to Constantinople in my shirt and delivered me into prison. I lay there for some time in the old shirt. Everyday I heard that the emperor intended to put me to death. I despaired of my life; it was in tears and lamentation that I went to sleep. I seemed to see that free woman whose husband had been in prison. She said to me: 'What is the trouble, Master Moschos? Why are you imprisoned here?' I told her that I had been falsely accused and that I thought the emperor intended to put me to death. She asked me: 'Do you want me to speak to the emperor about you and have you set free?' I said to her: 'Does the emperor know you?'—and she said he did. I awoke and I was confused as to what this could be. A second and a third time she appeared to me and said: 'Have no fear; tomorrow you go free'.

At dawn they took me to the palace on the emperor's orders. When I went in and he saw me with my disreputable garment, he said to me: 'I am moved to compassion for you; go, and act correctly in the future'. I saw that woman standing at the emperor's right hand. She said to me: 'Take heart and do not be afraid'. The emperor gave orders for my property to be restored to me. He gave me many goods and re-appointed me to my former position with great honour and he made me his representative.

That very night the same woman appeared to me and said: 'Do you know who I am? It was upon me that you took pity when, for the sake of God, you respected my body. Behold, I have delivered you from danger. So you see how kindly God deals with men. That is how you dealt with me, and I have extended my mercy towards you.'

187. The teaching of Abba John of Cyzicos on how to acquire virtue

When we were going from holy Gethsemane to the Mount of Olives, we came to a monastery known as Abba Abraham's which was founded by Abraham the Great (of the New Church of the all-glorious Mother of God, the ever-virgin Mary) who became higoumen there after Eudoxios. The higoumen was Abba John of Cyzicos <when we were there>. One day we asked him how one could attain virtues. The elder replied: 'Anybody who would attain a certain virtue cannot succeed unless he first hate the vice which is the antithesis of that virtue. If you wish to attain sorrow, then you must hate laughter. Do you long for humility? Then hate haughtiness. Do you wish to be temperate *<egkratês>?* Then hate gluttony. If you want to be pure, then hate lewdness. If it is poverty you long for, then hate material possessions. If you wish to be an almsgiver, then hate the greed for money. Anybody who would live in the wilderness, let him hate cities. Anybody who wants to practise the discipline of silence must hate unrestricted speech. Anybody who would be as a stranger, let him hate ostentation. The man who desires to be free of anger must hate all communication with persons <living> in the world. He who would be forgiving must hate recrimination; he who would be undisturbed *<aperispastos>*, let him live alone. He who wants to master his tongue, let him seal his ears so that he does not hear much. He who wishes to live in unbroken fear of God, let him shun bodily rest but love affliction and distress. Thus shall he perfectly serve God.'

188. The life of two brothers who were Syrian money-dealers

Abba Theodore, higoumen of the Old Lavra,* told us that there were two brothers, Syrian money-dealers, at Constantinople. The elder brother said to the younger: 'Come, let us go down to Syria and take possession of the paternal home'. The younger said: 'Why both of us? We would have to leave the business unattended. You go, and I will stay here. Or let me go, and you stay here.' They came to an agreement that the younger should go. A little while after his departure, the brother who stayed at Constantinople saw an elder in his sleep who said to him: 'Do you know that your brother has committed adultery with the tavern-keeper's wife?'* When he got up, he was distressed. He said to himself: 'This is my fault. Why did I let him go alone?' A little later, he saw the same elder again, saying to him: 'Do you know that your brother has forced his attentions on the tavern-keeper's wife?' The brother was grieved again at this. A third time, a little later still, he saw the same elder saying: 'Do you know that your brother has destroyed an honest woman and has degraded himself with the tavern-keeper's wife?' He wrote from Constantinople to Syria to him, to leave everything and return to Byzantium at once, without delay. When the younger brother received the letter, he immediately left everything and went back to his brother. When the elder brother laid eyes on him, he took him to the Great Church* and began to reproach him with a heavy heart, saying: 'Did you do well in fornicating with the tavern-keeper's wife?' When the other heard this, he began to swear by almighty God that he did not know what his brother was talking about; that he had never had sinful intercourse, nor any intercourse at all except with his lawful wife. When the elder brother heard this, he said to him: 'Have you then done something even worse?' He denied it: 'I am not aware of having done anything irregular, except that I found monks in our village of the Severan persuasion. Not knowing whether this was a bad thing, I made my communion with them. I have not done anything else, so far as I am aware.' The elder brother realised that his brother's fornication consisted of his having left the holy catholic Church for the heresy of Severus Acephalos, a tavern-keeper indeed.

In this he had fallen into disgrace and besmirched the nobility of the true faith.

189. THE LIFE OF A WOMAN WHO REMAINED FAITHFUL TO HER HUSBAND, A MERCHANT, AND HOW GOD HELPED THEM BOTH

We came too the hospice of the Fathers at Ascalon and there Eusebios the priest said to us:

There was a merchant of our city who set sail and lost all his own goods and everything else he was carrying at sea. He alone was saved. When he came back he was seized by his creditors and thrown into prison. Everything in his house was confiscated. There was nothing left to him except what he and his wife stood up in. Although she was in great distress and anxiety, she made it a rule at least to feed her husband with bread. One day, as she was sitting eating with her husband in prison, a person of note came in to distribute some comforts to the inmates. When he saw the woman who was free to come and go sitting with her husband, he was smitten with desire for her, for she was exceedingly good-looking. He sent a message to her through the gaoler and she came to him with a light heart, expecting to receive some charity. He took her aside and said to her: 'What is the matter? Why are you here?' She told him the whole story and he said to her: 'If I discharge your debt, will you sleep with me tonight?' She, who was very beautiful and very pure-minded, said to him: 'My lord, I have heard the Apostle <Paul; 2 Co 7:1-7> say that a wife does not have authority over her own body: her husband has. Let me go and ask my husband, sir, and I shall do what he commands.' She came and told the whole matter to her husband. He was a wise man who loved his wife dearly; he did not let the prospect of freedom lead him astray. Sighing deeply and shedding tears, he said to his wife: 'Go and refuse the man, sister, and let us hope in God that he will not abandon us at the last'. She got up and sent the man away, saying: 'I told me husband and he was unwilling'.

At that time, there was a highway man who had been thrown into the inner prison. Observing all that passed between the husband and his wife, he sighed to himself and said: 'Look what a situation they are in—yet they would not surrender their honour* <*eleutheria*> neither for money, or to be set free. They held chastity to be of more worth than all riches and they despised all the things of this life. And what shall I do, wretch that I am, who have never even thought about the question of whether there is a God—and on that account, I am responsible for so many murders.' He called them over and through the window of <the cell> where he lay, he said to them: 'I was a robber and many are the evil deeds and the murders I have committed. And for that reason, when the governor comes and I appear before him, I shall die as a murderer. Yet when I saw your chastity, I was moved with compassion for you. Go to such-and-such a place by the city-wall; dig there, and take the money you find. You are to have it to discharge your debts and to make many charitable donations. Pray for me, that I might receive mercy.'

A few days later, the governor came to the city and ordered the robber to be brought out and beheaded. The day afterwards, the woman said to her husband: 'Is it your wish, sir, that I go to the place revealed by the robber and see if he was telling the truth'? He said to her: 'Do what you think best'. She got a small mattock and in the evening she went and dug at the spot he had mentioned. She found a covered pot with gold in it. She used it very prudently, giving it out a little at a time (as though she were borrowing from this one and from that one) until she had discharged all <their debts>. Then she was also able to get her husband out. The man who told us this story said: 'Behold, even as they were faithful to the law of God, so did our Lord and God multiply his mercies on them'.

190. THE MIRACLE OF SOME WOOD GIVEN TO ABBA BROCHA, THE EGYPTIAN

Athanasios the Egyptian, who was connected with the civil authority,* said that Abba Brocha found a spot in the wilderness outside the city of Seleucia near Antioch and tried to build a small cell there. As his building progressed, he wanted wood to build the roof. One day he went into the city and found Anatolios, known as 'the hunchback', a magnate of Seleucia, sitting outside his house. He went up to him and said: 'Of your charity, give me a little wood to roof my house with. The magnate replied testily: 'Look, there is wood over there; take it, and go', and he indicated a large mast which he had lying in front of his house and which he had made for a vessel of fifty-thousand bushels. Abba Brochas said: '<The Lord> bless you; I will take it'. Still in a bad humour, Anatolios said: 'Blessed be God'. <The elder> grasped the mast, lifted it from the ground all by himself and put it on his shoulders. In this way he took it away to his cell. Anatolios was so taken aback by this extraordinary miracle that he granted him as much wood as he required for his needs. With this, Abba Brocha was able not only to roof his cell of which we spoke, but to do many other things for his monastery.

191. A BRIEF LIFE OF SAINT JOHN CHRYSOSTOM, PATRIARCH OF CONSTANTINOPLE

It was said of Saint John of Constantinople, justly known as Chrysostom <=golden mouth> for the purity and the brilliance of his teaching and the splendour of his eloquence, that from the day he received the salutary sacrament of baptism, he neither swore nor required anybody else to swear, nor lied, nor spoke, nor listened to witty words.

192. THE STORY OF A MONK OF THE MONASTERY OF THE GODLY POPE GREGORY, AND OF HOW HE WAS ABSOLVED OF EXCOMMUNICATION AFTER DEATH*

A priest named Peter, coming from Rome, told us concerning the saintly Gregory, pope of that city, that when he became pope, he built a large monastery for men, and made a rule that none of the monks should have anything of his own whatsoever, not even an *obol.* There was a brother there who had a brother in the world. To him he appealed, saying: 'I have no shirt. Of your charity, buy me one.' The brother in secular life said to him: 'Here are three pieces of gold; take them and buy yourself whatever you like.' The monk took the three pieces of gold, then went and reported it to his higoumen, who, when he heard it, went and reported it to the most holy pope. When the blessed Gregory heard it, he excluded the brother from communion because he had contravened the rule of the monastery. A little while later, the excluded brother died and the pope did not learn about it. Two or three days later the higoumen came and reported to him that the brother had gone to <his> rest. The pope was grieved at this in no small way—for not having absolved the brother of the punishment of exclusion before he departed this life. So the pope wrote a prayer on a tablet and gave it to one of the archdeacons. He told him to go and read it over the brother. It was a prayer absolving the dead man from exclusion. The archdeacon went as he was commanded and read the letter containing the prayer over the brother. That same night the higoumen saw the dead brother. The higoumen said to him: 'Are you not dead, brother?' and he said: 'Yes, indeed'. Then the abba asked him again: 'Where were you until today?' The brother said to him: 'Truly, sir, I was in prison and I was not set free until yesterday'. Thus everybody knew that he was absolved of his exclusion in the very same hour at which the archdeacon said the prayer over the grave, and that his soul had been delivered from condemnation.

193. The wondrous deed of charity by the holy Abba Apollinarios, Patriarch of Alexandria, for a rich young man reduced to penury

We were told that the saintly Apollinarios, Pope of Alexandria, was outstanding for his almsgiving and compassion. To demonstrate this, they said that there was a young man whose parents were among the most prominent citizens of Alexandria. When they died, they left him their many possessions in the form of ships and gold, but he was unsuccessful in his management of this legacy and he lost everything. He was reduced to absolute poverty, not by eating and *wasting his substance in riotous living* <Lk 15:13-14> but because he suffered shipwreck and divers <other> adversities. From being one of the great ones, he became small. As the Psalmist says: *They mount up to the heavens above: they go down to the depths beneath* <Ps 106:26>, so the young man, having been exalted in his riches, suffered a yet greater fall.

When the blessed Apollinarios heard about this and saw the dejection and indigence which had befallen the young man, since he had known his parents and how well-off they had been, he wanted to do something practical to help him; to give him some small charitable donation to relieve his distress; but he was embarrassed over <how> to do so. Yet every time he saw the young man in his office he was wounded in the soul at the sight of his disreputable clothes and his sad countenance, which are the hall-marks of utter destitution. Whilst the pope was in this dilemma, one day, by the inspiration of God, he devised a wonderful plan which was suitable for his blessedness.

He sent for the legal-officer of the most holy church, took him aside and said to him: 'Can you keep a secret for me, Master Chancellor?' He replied: 'By the Son of God, I hope so, my lord. If it be your wish, I shall not tell it to anybody , nor would anyone ever learn anything you revealed to your servant from my lips.' Then Pope Apollinarios said to him: 'Go and draw up a letter of credit against the most holy church in favour of Macarios, the father of the young man, for fifty pounds of gold. Have it witnessed and make an order for repayment, then bring that document to me'.

The chancellor did what the pope had commanded immediately and without delay, then he brought the document and gave it to him. Since the father of the young man had been dead ten years or more but the paper was very new, the pope said: 'Master Chancellor, go bury this paper in wheat or oats and bring it back to me in a few days' time'. The man went away and came back again after the stated number of days, bringing the document to the pope. Then the pope said to the chancellor: 'Now go and say to the young man: "What will you give me in return for a document which is to your advantage?"—but see that you take no more than three pieces of gold from him, Master Chancellor. Then give him the document.' The chancellor replied: 'In truth, my lord, if it is your will, I will not even take as much as that'. The pope said: 'No, I want you to take three pieces of gold'. At that the chancellor went to the young man as he was commanded, and said; 'What will you give me if I provide you with something that will be of the greatest advantage to you?' The other agreed to pay whatever price was demanded. The chancellor thought for a moment, then said to the other: 'Five or six days ago I was looking for some papers in my house and I found this document. And I remembered that Macarios, your father, (who trusted me) had left it with me for a few days. When he died, its fate was to lie forgotten in my house until this day, for it escaped my memory and it never came into my mind to give it to you.' The young man said: 'How much do you want me to give you for it?'

'Three pieces of gold', was the reply. 'And do you know whether the party that is in debt to me is rich?' asked the young man. 'Oh yes, rich indeed', the chancellor replied; 'Rich and generous. You shall easily be able to recover the debt.' The young man said: 'God knows I have nothing; but if the debt is repaid, I will give you the three pieces of gold and as much more as you will'. Then the chancellor handed over the document worth fifty pounds of gold <16,380 grams>.

The young man took the document to the most holy pope, prostrated himself at his feet and gave it to him. The pope took it and read it. Then he began to make himself look troubled. He said to the man: 'Where have you been until now? Your father has been dead for more than ten years. Go away sir; I give you no response.' He said to the pope: 'Really, my lord, I did not have the document; the chancellor had it and did not know. But God was merciful to him, for he has now given it to me, saying: "While I was looking for some papers I found this"'. The pope sent him away, saying: 'I will think about it and, in the meantime, I will keep the paper here with me'. A week later the young man came back to see the pope, who again reproached him with taking so long to produce the document and again showed himself unwilling to give him anything. The young man said to him: 'My lord, God knows that I do not have enough even to support my family. If God puts it into your heart to do anything, have compassion on me'. Then, pretending that he had just acceded to the man's request, the saintly Apollinarios said to him: 'I will repay you in full; but this, sir, I beg of you, brother: not to demand any interest of the holy church'. The youth fell 76
at his feet and said: 'Whatever my lord requires of me, that will I do; and if he would like to reduce the capital, let him do so'. The pope said: 'No, I am satisfied if you forego the interest'. Then he brought out fifty pounds of gold and dismissed the young man with many expressions of gratitude for having been excused the interest (as he said). This was how the godly Apollinarios worked in secret;

this was the kind of beautiful deed he performed and the quality of his compassion. God so blessed that young man that he was able to rise up out of poverty and regain his former standing. He exceeded his parents in wealth and possessions and also greatly benefitted his soul.

194. THE EXHORTATION OF AN ELDER WHO LIVED AT SCÊTÊ TO A MONK, NOT TO ENTER TAVERNS

The was a monk living at Scêtê who went up to Alexandria to sell his handiwork and he saw a younger monk go into a tavern. This troubled the elder, so he waited outside, intending to meet the monk when he came out, which is indeed what happened. When the younger monk came out, the elder took him by the hand and led him aside, saying to him: 'Brother, do you not realise that you are wearing the holy habit, sir? Do you not know that you are a young man? Are you not aware that the snares of the devil are many? Do you not know that monks who live in cities are wounded by means of their eyes, their hearing and their clothing? You went into the tavern of your own free will; you hear things you do not want to hear and see things you would rather not see, dishonourably mingling with both men and women. Please do not do it, but flee to the wilderness where you can find the salvation you desire.' The young man answered him: 'Away with you, good elder. God requires nothing but a pure heart.' Then the elder raised his hands to heaven and said: 'Glory to you, Oh God, that I have spent fifty years at Scêtê and have not acquired a pure heart, yet this man, who frequents taverns, has attained pureness of heart'. He turned to the brother and said: 'May God save you and *not disappoint me in my hope'* <Ps 118:116>.

195. The life of Evagrios the Philosopher who was converted to the Christian faith by Synesios, Bishop of Cyrene

While we were in Alexandria, Leontios of Apamea, a devout man who loved Christ, came from Pentapolis (where he had made his home for some years at Cyrene). In <those> days of <Eulogios>, the saintly Pope of Alexandria, the future bishop> of the same town of Cyrene came <too>. And when we were all together, he told us this:

That in the time of Theophilos, the blessed Pope of Alexandria, Synesios the philosopher became Bishop of Cyrene. When he came to Cyrene, he found there a philosopher named Evagrios who had been his fellow student and had remained his good friend, even though he was strongly attached to the cult of idols. Bishop Synesios wanted to convert him. He not only wanted to, but also made great efforts and put himself to much trouble and care for the sake <of the friendship> in which he held him from the beginning. The other would neither be persuaded, nor would he in any way accept the bishop's teaching. Yet, for the sake of his great friendship for him, the bishop was unflagging in his efforts, continuing day by day to instruct, entreat and exhort his friend to believe in Christ and to come to full knowledge of him. And it had this effect: that one day the philosopher said to him: 'You know, Bishop, of all the things which you Christians say, there is this, sir, which displeases me. It is that there will be an end to this world and that, after the end, everybody who existed throughout this age shall arise in this human body and shall live for ever in that incorruptible and immortal flesh; that they shall receive their rewards; a body who has compassion on the poor lends to God; that anyone who distributes money to the poor and destitute lays up treasures in heaven and shall receive them back from Christ an hundredfold at the regeneration, together with eternal life. All this seems to me to be deception and a laughing matter; a yarn which is no more than an old wives' tale.' Bishop Synesios assured him that all the <beliefs> of the Christians were true and that there was nothing false or alien to the truth about them. He attempted to demonstrate with many examples that this was so.

A long time afterwards, the bishop succeeded in making him a Christian. He baptised the philosopher, his children and everybody in his household. A little while after his baptism, he gave the bishop three gold *denarii* for the benefit of the poor. 'Take these three *kentênaria*; give then to the poor and let me have a certificate that Christ shall give them back to me in the world to come'. The bishop took the gold and promptly made out the desired certificate. The philosopher lived for some years after his baptism, and then he fell terminally ill. At the point of death, he said to his children: 'When you prepare me for burial, put this paper in my hands and bury me with it'. When he died, they did as he had commanded and buried him together with the hand-written paper. The third day after his burial, while Bishop Synesios was lying down at night, the philosopher appeared to him and said: 'Come to the tomb where I lie and take your hand-written paper, for I have received what was owing to me. I am satisfied and I have no further claim on you. To make you quite sure, I have counter-signed the paper in my own hand.' The bishop was not aware that his hand-written certificate had been buried with the philosopher.

The next morning he sent for <the dead man's> sons and said to them: 'What did you deposit in the tomb together with the philosopher?' They thought he was speaking to them about money and they replied: 'Nothing, my lord, except the grave clothes'. 'What then', he asked; 'Did you not bury a paper with him?' Then they remembered, for they did not realise he was talking about a paper. They said: 'Yes, my lord; when he was dying, he gave us a paper and said: "When you prepare me for burial, lay me out that I am holding this paper in my hand, and nobody else is to know about it."' Then the bishop told them of the dream he had seen that night. He took the sons, the clergy and some prominent citizens and went off to the philosopher's tomb. They opened it, and they found the philosopher lying there, holding the bishop's hand-written certificate in his own hands. They took it from his hands, opened it and found this, newly written on it, in the philosopher's hand: 'From me, Evagrios the Philosopher, to you sir, the most holy Bishop Synesios, greetings. I have received what you wrote down in this promissory note. I am satisfied and I have no further claim on you in respect to the gold which I gave you; or rather, by your agency, to Christ our God and Saviour.' Great was the amazement of those who saw it. For many hours they cried out: 'Lord have mercy', glorifying God who works wonders and grants such assurance to his servants. Master Leontios assured us that the manuscript with the philosopher's signature has survived to this day and that it is lying in the treasury of the church of Cyrene. It is delivered into the safe-keeping of each man who is appointed custodian there, together with the sacred vessels. He guards it diligently and will pass it on, safe and sound, to his successors.

196. The miracle which happened to the boys of Apamea who recited the prayer of consecration in a game

This is what was told to us by George, the Governor of the Province of Africa; a man who loved Christ, the monks and the poor; one who was endowed with all the virtues which are pleasing to God:

In my homeland (he was from the district of Apamea in the second Eparchy of Syria from a town named Thorax) there is an estate called Gonagos forty miles from the city. Some children were pasturing animals about a mile away from the property. As is usually the case, these children wanted to play games the way children do. While they were playing, they said to each other: ‘Let us have a service and offer the holy sacrifice’. They all thought this was a good idea, so they chose one of their number to serve as priest and two others to be deacons. They came to a flat rock and began their game. They placed loaves on the rock which was to serve as an altar and some wine in an earthenware vessel. They took their places, the one who was to be priest and the two would-be deacons on either side of him. The <‘priest’> recited the Prayer of Oblation *<proskomidê>* while the other two fanned the air with branches. The acting-priest found that he knew the Prayer of Consecration *<anaphora>* by heart, for in those days it was the custom for children to stand before the holy sanctuary during divine worship and to be the first after the clergy to partake of the holy mysteries. As it was <also> the custom in some places for the priests to say the prayer out loud, children were found to learn it by heart from continually hearing it audibly recited. They did everything according to the custom of the church; but, before they divided the bread, fire came down from heaven and consumed all the offerings, burning up the entire stone. Not a trace remained, neither of the rock nor of what had been set upon it. When the children saw this sudden phenomenon, they all fell to the ground and lay there, half dead. They could neither raise their voices nor get up from the ground. When they failed to return to the estate at the hour at which they usually came back (for they were lying stunned on the ground) their parents went out from the estate to find out why they had not returned as usual. They searched and found them lying there but the children could recognise nobody; nor could they reply when spoken to. When the parents saw them half dead like that, each one took up his own child and carried it back to the estate. They were staggered to see the children in such a strange condition, for they could not discover the reason for it. They questioned the children about it often, all day long, but they could get no response from them. It was simply impossible to find out what had happened to them until that day had passed and the night too. Then, little by little, the children became themselves again; and then they told their parents what they had done and what had happened. Then the parents set out with the children and with the proprietors of the estate and the children pointed out the spot where that extraordinary occurrence had taken place. They also indicated some traces of the fire that had descended. This convinced those who heard the story that it was true, so they went running to the city and reported everything in detail to the bishop of the city. He was amazed to hear so tall a story. He went out to the scene of the event together with all the clergy. He saw the children and heard from them what had happened. He also saw the evidence of the fire from heaven. He sent the children to a monastery and converted the place <where the event happened> into a distinguished monastery. He built the church on the spot where the fire had descended and erected the holy altar there.

The same Master George told us that he had himself seen one of the children in that very monastery where this wonder had occurred. This is the divine and angelic wonder which was reported by George, the friend of Christ, to have happened in our own time.

197. Rufinus' anecdote of Saint Athanasios and other boys who were with him*

Rufinus, the ecclesiastical historian, reported something similar which happened a long time ago to children at play. It concerns Saint Athanasios, the great proclaimer and defender of the truth, the bishop of the great city of Alexandria, who shepherded all his charges prudently and according to the will of God. Speaking of the saint's childhood, <Rufinus> shows how his elevation to the episcopate was originally foreshadowed by a revelation to him from God. Let us trace the history of this man, the kind of life he led as a child and the manner of his up-bringing, insofar as these things have come to our ears.

The saintly Alexander succeeded Achilles as Pope of Alexandria, just as Saint Peter the martyr-archbishop foretold, he who condemned the impious Arius. One day, Alexander was looking out to sea; he saw some children playing on the shore as children usually do. They were imitating a bishop and all the ceremonies which are customary in church. Paying careful attention to what was going on, he realised that they were acting out some of the secret parts of the mysteries. This troubled him, so he immediately summoned the clergy. He showed them what was taking place and required them to go and apprehend all those children and bring them to him. When they arrived, he asked them about the nature of their game and what they were doing. Being children, they were frightened, <and at first> they denied everything. But then they told him every detail of their game: how they had baptised some catechumens by <the hand of> Athanasios—whom those children had appointed as their bishop. Then Alexander enquired diligently of them which ones they had baptised and when he discovered that everything had been performed strictly in accordance with the customs of our religion, he informed his clergy of this, decreeing that those who had been made worthy of that holy bath stood in no need of a second baptism. He sent back to their parents Athanasios and the others who served as clergy, to be brought up in the fear and nurture of the Lord; especially Athanasios, whom he very soon afterwards consecrated to God. Being better endowed with godly attributes, he was advanced to a higher rank by the then-archbishop; such was his distinction. <The archbishop> summoned the parents* of Athansios and of the other <children> whom the latter pretended to have as his priests and deacons in the game and, with God as his witness, handed them over to the church to be nourished therein.

A little time elapsed during which Athanasios was thoroughly educated by a short-hand writer and well-enough by a grammar-school teacher. Then, as a sacred trust committed to them by the Lord, he was handed back to the priest by his parents and, like a second Samuel, he was raised in the temple of God. And when Alexander went to visit <other> bishops in his old age, he would have Athansios follow him, carrying the vestment of priesthood which is called *ephod* in the Hebrew tongue.

So great were Athansios' exertions against the heretics on behalf of the Church that it might seem as though that verse were especially written for him—the one which says: I will show him what he must suffer for my name's sake. The whole world conspired to persecute him; the kings of the earth* showed him what he must suffer for my name's sake. The whole earth moved, kingdoms and an army came together against him. But he stood fast by the saying of God which says: *Though a host of men were laid against me, yet shall not my heart be afraid. And though there rose up war against me yet will I put my trust in him* <Ps 26:3.> But so many and such things are reported of him which are so important that they cannot be passed over in silence. Yet they are nevertheless so numerous that I am compelled do so in may cases. I am on the horns of a dilemma, not being able to decide what to retain and what to let go. That is why we are recording a few matters which are directly connected with the subject; the rest of them will be relayed by common report. Common report, however, can be relied on to relay less than the <whole> truth, for it has neither the ability nor anything to add to the truth.

198. The reply of Saint Athansios, Bishop of Alexandria, to <the question of> whether one can be baptised without faith

Saint Athanasios, the Pope of Alexandria, was once asked whether a person could be baptised whose beliefs were not in accordance with the faith and preaching of the Christians, and what would be the fate of—or, how would God receive—somebody who had been baptised under false pretences and had simulated belief. Athansios replied: 'You have heard from those of old how the blessed martyr, Peter, was faced with a situation in which there was a deadly plague and many were running to be baptised for no other reason than that they feared death. A figure appeared to him which had the appearance of an angel and which said to him: "How much longer are you going to send from here those purses which are duly sealed, but are altogether empty and have nothing inside them?" So far as one can tell from the saying of the angel, those who have the seal of baptism are indeed baptised since they thought they were doing a good work in receiving baptism'.

199. THE STORY OF A SIMPLE ELDER WHO USED TO SEE ANGELS WHEN HE OFFERED THE EUCHARIST

One of the fathers said that there was one of the elders who was pure and holy; who, when he was celebrating the eucharist, used to see angels standing to his right hand and to his left. He had learned the eucharistic rite from heretics but, as he was unlearned in theological matters, when he offered <the eucharist> he spoke the prayer in all simplicity and innocence, unaware that he was at fault.

By the providence of God, there came to him a brother who was skilled in theology and it happened that the elder offered the eucharist in his presence. The brother (who was a deacon) said to him: 'Father, these things which you say at the eucharist are not in accordance with the orthodox faith; they are heresy <not orthodox but *kakadox*>. Since the elder could see angels when he was celebrating, he paid no attention to what was said, and thought nothing of it. But the deacon went on saying: 'You are at fault, good elder; the Church does not allow those things to be said'.

When the elder realised that he was being accused and blamed by the deacon, the next time he saw the angels, he asked them: 'When the deacon speaks to me like this, what am I to make of it?' They said to him: 'Pay attention to him; he is giving good counsel'. The elder said to them: 'Then why did you not tell me so?' They said: 'Because God has ordained that men should be corrected by men', and from that time forth he accepted correction, giving thanks to God and to the brother.

200. HOW A YOUNG GOLDSMITH BECAME THE ADOPTED SON OF A MAN OF PATRICIAN RANK

One of the fathers told us of a gifted young man who was apprenticed to a goldsmith and became highly skilled in his craft. A person of patrician rank commissioned the goldsmith to make a jewelled cross as an offering to the church. As the youth was very gifted, the master charged him with the work. The youth thought: 'Since the patrician is offering so much wealth to Christ, why should I not add my wages to the value of the cross so that Christ will reckon this in my favour, just as he did that widow's two mites?' He worked out how much he was going to receive, borrowed that amount and disbursed it on the making of the cross. When the patrician came, he weighed the cross before the precious stones were set in it—and found that it weighed more than the mass <of gold> he had given. He began accusing the youth of having deceitfully tampered with the gold. The other replied: 'He who alone knows the secrets of our hearts is fully aware that I have done no such thing. I saw how much money you were offering to Christ and I thought I would add my wages so that I could have a share <in the offering> together with you, and that Christ would accept my offering as he did the two mites of that widow' <Mk 12:42; Lk 21:2>. The patrician was astounded at this. He said: 'Did you really think that, child?' and the youth answered that he did. 'Since you thought like that and dedicated your entire course of action to Christ in order to gain a share in my offering, from this day forward I make you my son and heir'. He took him with him and made him his heir.

201. THE LIFE OF A MOST NOBLE MAN OF CONSTANTINOPLE WHOSE FATHER, WHEN HE WAS DYING, LEFT HIM THE LORD JESUS CHRIST AS HIS GUARDIAN

One of the fathers who had gone to Constantinople to attend to some necessary business said:

Whilst I was sitting in the church, a man who was illustrious in the worldly sense but <also> a great lover of Christ came in; and when he saw me, he sat down. He then began asking about the salvation of the soul. I told him that the heavenly life is given to those who live the earthly life in a seemly way. 'You have spoken well, father', he said. 'Blessed is the man whose hope is in God and who presents himself as an offering to God. I am the son of a man who is very distinguished by the standards of the world. My father was very compassionate and distributed huge sums amongst the poor. One day he called me; showing me all his money, he said to me: "Son, which do you prefer; that I leave you my money, or that I gave you Christ as you guardian?" Grasping the point he was making, I said I would rather have Christ; for everything that is here today shall be gone tomorrow: Christ remains for ever. So from the moment he heard me say that, he gave without sparing, leaving very little for me when he died. So I was left a poor man and I lived simply, putting my hope in the God whom he bequeathed to me. There was another rich man, one of the leading citizens, who had a wife who loved Christ and feared God; and he had one daughter: his only child. The wife said to the husband: "We have only this one daughter, yet the Lord has endowed us with so many goods. What does she lack? If we seek to give her <in marriage> to somebody of our own rank whose way of life is not praiseworthy, it shall be a continual source of affliction to her. Let us rather look for a lowly man who fears God; one who will love her and cherish her according to God's holy law". He said to her: "This is good advice. Go to church and pray fervently. Sit there, and whoever comes in first, he it is whom the Lord has sent." This she did. When she had prayed, she sat down and it was I who came in at that moment. She sent a servant to call me straightaway and she began asking me where I was from. I told her that I was from this city, the son of such-and-such a man. She said: "He who was so generous to the poor? And have you a wife?" I said I had not. I told her what my father had said to me and what I had said to him. She glorified the Lord and said: "Behold, the good guardian whom you chose has sent you a bride—and riches, so that you may enjoy both in the fear of God". I pray that I might follow in my father's footsteps to the end of my days.

202. The life of the servant of God, Abibas, the son of a worldly man

One of the fathers said there was a man living in the world who had a pious son, pure and temperate in all things, who, from his childhood, had not drunk wine. It was his intention to withdraw from the world. The father wanted him to become involved in business matters but the son was reluctant. There were other brothers. but he was the oldest. As his father's wishes and his own could not be reconciled, the father was always reproaching him and casting his temperance in his teeth, saying: 'Why are you not like your brothers, and why do you not get yourself involved in business affairs?' The son endured it all in silence; everybody loved him for his piety and his moderation *<sôphrosunê>*.

When the father was dying, some of the family, together with others who friends of Abibas, for that was the son's name, came together and said: 'Perhaps the father will deny the servant of God his inheritance', for they thought that he hated his son from the way he used to revile him. They resolved to intercede with the father (who was sick) on his son's behalf. They went to him and said: 'We have a favour to ask of you'. He said to them: 'What would you ask of me'? They said: 'It concerns Master Abibas. We want to ask you not to despise him'. He said: 'You want to ask a favour of me for him?' They said they did, and he continued: 'Call him here to me'. They thought he was going to reproach him as usual. When the son came in, the father told him to come near <to him>—which he did. And then the father collapsed in tears at his feet, saying: 'Forgive me, my child, and pray to God that the wrong I have done you be not be held against me. For you were seeking for Christ and I was burying myself with worldly affairs.' He called his other sons and said to them: 'This is your master and your father. Whatever he says you may have, that you may have; and whatever he says you may not have, that you may not have'. They were all astonished. The father then died. <Abibas> gave to each brother his share of the inheritance and he took his own share too, but he gave it all to the poor, leaving nothing for himself. He built a small cell into which he could withdraw from the world and when the cell was completed, he fell ill. His end was approaching. His <monastic> brother was sitting with him, to whom the dying man said: 'Go and keep company with your household, for it is a holy day' (it was the feast of the Holy Apostles). The brother replied: 'How could I go and leave you?' The other replied: 'Go; and when the time comes, I shall call you'. When the time came, he stood at the window and knocked. The brother heard and obeyed the sick man's signal to come. As soon as he entered, the older brother surrendered his soul to the Lord. Everybody was amazed and glorified God, saying: 'His end was worthy of the love with which he loved Christ'.

203. The story of a jeweller who, by a wise decision, saved his life at sea

One of the fathers said there was a jeweller of the kind known as a gem-engraver. He had some very valuable stones and pearls when he went aboard a ship together with his servants; it was his intention to go do business elsewhere. By the providence of God, it happened that he became very fond of the member of the ship's crew who was detailed to wait upon him. This servant slept near him and ate the same food as he ate. One day this boy heard the sailors whispering to each other and deciding among themselves to throw the gem-engraver into the sea, to get their hands on the stones he had with him. It was a very disturbed servant who went in to wait on the good man* as usual. 'Why are you so subdued today, boy?' asked the jeweller, but the other kept his counsel and said nothing. He asked him again: 'Come now, tell me what is matter', at which the servant broke down into tears and sobbed out that the sailors were planning to do this and that to the jeweller, who asked: 'Is this really so?' 'Yes' was the reply; 'That is what they have decided among themselves to do to you.' Then the jeweller called his servants and said to them: 'Whatever I tell you to do, do it at once and without arguing'. Then he unfolded a linen cloth and said to them: 'Bring the inlaid chests', and they brought them. He opened them and began taking out the stones. When they were all set out, he began to say: 'Is this what life is <all about>? Is it for these that I put my life in danger and at the mercy of the sea when, in a little while, I shall die, and take nothing with me out of this world?' He said to his servants: 'Empty it all into the sea'. As soon as he spoke, they cast the riches into the sea. The sailors were amazed—and their conspiracy was frustrated.

204. HOW A RELIGIOUS WOMAN WHO FEARED GOD RESTRAINED A MONK FROM LASCIVIOUS DESIRE

Somebody said that a <brother> was bitten by a snake and went into the city to receive treatment. He was taken in by a devout woman who feared the Lord and she healed him. When he found some relief from his discomfort, the devil began sowing some libidinous thoughts about the woman in his heart. He began wanting to touch her hand, but she said to him: 'Not so, father; you have Christ to fear. Think of the sorrow and the remorse in which you shall repent, sitting in your cell. Imagine the sighs you shall utter and the tears you shall shed.' When he heard this and other similar remarks from her, the war receded from him and he wished to run away in shame—for he could not look her in the face. She, however, in the tender mercy of Christ, said to him: 'Do not let shame get the better of you. You are still in need of treatment. Those sinful thoughts did not arise from your pure soul; it was a dart of the envious devil which caused them'. Thus, without offence being either given or taken, she healed him and sent him on his way, giving him what was needed for the journey.

205. CONCERNING ANOTHER WISE WOMAN WHO, BY JUDICIOUS ADVICE, TURNED ASIDE A MONK WHO WAS HARASSING HER

Somebody told of a brother who lived in a community and who used to be sent to conduct the business of his house. There was a devout secular person in a village who used to give him hospitality as an act of faith, as often as he came in and out of the village. <This man> had a daughter who had recently been widowed after living with her husband for a year or two. As the brother came in and out of their house, he began to be troubled by thoughts of her.

As she was no fool, she realised this, and took care not to enter his presence. One day her father went into the neighbouring city on necessary business, leaving her alone in the house. The brother came, as was his custom, and finding her alone in the house, he said to her: 'Where is your father?' 'He has gone into the city', she replied. Then he began to be troubled by temptation and wanted to throw himself on her. She prudently said to him: 'Do not be troubled; my father shall not return until evening; there are <only> the two of us here. But I know you monks never do anything without prayer. Get at it, then; pray to God, and if he puts it in your heart to do something, that we will do'. This was not acceptable to him, for temptation continued to rage within. She said to him: 'Have you ever really known a woman?' He said: 'No; and that is why I want to know what it is like'. She said to him: 'That is why you are troubled by temptation, for you do not know the bad odour of wretched women'. And to cool his ardour, she added: 'I am having my period. Nobody can come near me or bear the smell of me for the stench which mars my body'. When he heard this and similar things from her, he regretted what had happened; he became himself again, and wept. When she realised that he was his normal self again, she said: 'Look, if I had listened to you and given in to you, we would already have been satisfied—and would have sinned utterly. How then could you have looked my father in the face or gone back to your monastery and heard the choir of those holy ones who sing <there>? Be sober, I beg of you; and do not be so ready to lose all the sufferings you have endured and to deprive yourself of the good things of eternity, just for the sake of a little short-lived pleasure.' When he heard what she had to say, the brother to whom it happened told it to him who now related <the story>, giving thanks to God who, by the woman's prudence and temperance, had prevented him from taking an irremediable fall.

206. A STRATAGEM BY WHICH A GREAT LADY WAS TAUGHT HUMILITY

One of the holy fathers said that a woman of senatorial rank came to worship at the Holy Places. When she came to Caesarea, it pleased her instead to stay there in solitary retirement <*hêsuchasai*>. She asked the bishop to give her a virgin who could train her in religion and teach her the fear of God. The bishop selected a modest <virgin> and gave her to <the great lady>. Sometime later the bishop encountered her and asked: 'How is the virgin I gave you?' 'She is fine', she replied, 'but not much benefit to my soul because she is so humble that she lets me go my own way. I need somebody who will stand up to me and not let me do whatever I want'. So the bishop took away the first virgin and sent another, a stern one who used to her address her as 'fool of a rich woman' and heap similar imprecations upon her. Afterwards, the bishop asked her again how she found the virgin and the lady replied: 'This one is certainly good for my soul', and she became distinguished for her humility.

207. THE LIFE OF AN ALEXANDRINE GIRL WHO WAS RECEIVED FROM THE SACRED FONT BY ANGELS

Abba Theonas and Abba Theodore said that in the time of the Patriarch Paul, there was a maiden in Alexandria who lost both her parents—and they possessed a great fortune. The girl was unbaptised at the time <of her bereavement>. One day she went apart into the garden which her parents had left her (for there are gardens in the middle of the city, in the houses of the great ones). Whilst she was in the garden, she saw a man preparing to hang himself. She rushed to him and said: 'What are you doing, good man?' He said to her: 'Look, leave me alone woman, for I am in great affliction'. The maiden said to him: 'Tell me the truth, for perhaps I may be able to help you'. He told her: 'I am heavily in debt and my creditors are putting pressure on me to repay them. I have chosen to die rather than to lead such a woeful existence.' The maiden said to him: 'I beg of you, take whatever I have and give it to them; only please do not destroy yourself'. He took what she offered and paid off his debts. Then the girl began to run into difficulties. Having no one to look after her (because she had been deprived of her parents) and being in great need, she began to prostitute herself. Some people who knew her, and knew the standing which her parents had enjoyed in society, said: 'Who knows the judgements of God or why he allows a soul to fall for some reason or other?' The some time later, the girl fell ill—and came back to her senses. Consumed with remorse, she said to her neighbours: 'For the sake of the Lord, have mercy on my soul; speak to the pope about making me a Christian'. But they all laughed at her and said: 'As if he would accept this woman who is a prostitute!' This caused her great distress. Whilst she was in this condition and very frustrated, an angel of the Lord stood by her—in the form of the man on whom she had compassion. He said to her: 'What is the trouble?' She replied: 'I desire to become a Christian and nobody will stand up for me'. He said: 'Do you really want this?' She replied: 'Yes, I beg of you'. He said to her: 'Take courage; I will get some people to take you to church'. He brought two others who were also angels and they carried her to the church. Then they transformed themselves into illustrious personages with the rank of prefect. They summoned the clergy charged with the responsibility for baptisms, and these asked: 'Your Charity will vouch for her?' They answered: 'Yes'. Then the clergy did what was called for in the service for those who are about to be baptised; then they baptised her in the name of the Father and of the Son and of the Holy Spirit, and they vested her in the garment of the neophyte. Clothed in white, she returned home carried by the angels, who set her down and promptly disappeared. When the neighbours saw her all in white, they said to her: ‘Who baptised you?’—and she told them of those who had taken her to church, how they had spoken to the clergy and how the clergy had baptised her. They asked her who those people were; to which the woman would give no answer. So they went and reported the matter to the pope. He summoned those in charge of the baptistry and said to them: ‘Did you baptise that woman?’ They admitted that they had <baptised her>, adding that she had been vouched for by so-and-so of prefectorial rank. The bishop sent for those whom they had named and enquired of them whether they had vouched for her. They said: ‘We are not aware of having done so, nor do we know anybody else who has’. Then the bishop realised that this was divine business. He summoned the woman and said: ‘Tell me, daughter, what good have you done?’ She said: ‘I am a prostitute and a poor woman too; what good could I do?’ He said to her: ‘Are you not aware of ever having done any good <deed> at all?’ She said: ‘No. Except that I once saw a man about to hang himself because he was being harassed by his creditors. I gave him my entire fortune and freed him <of his debt>.’ She said this, and fell asleep in the Lord, released from both her voluntary and her involuntary deeds of sin. Then the bishop glorified God and said: *Righteous you are O God, and upright are your judgements* <Ps 118:137.>

208. The Fine Response of an Elder to a Brother Besieged by Depression

A brother who was in the grips of depression asked an elder: ‘What am I to do; for I am assailed by doubts which say to me: “You became a monk in vain: you shall not be saved”?’ The elder replied: ‘You know, brother, even if we cannot enter the promised land, it is better for our bones to fall in the wilderness than for us to turn back to Egypt’.

209. The fine exhortation of a certain holy elder on the words of the Lord's prayer: *Lead us not into temptation*

One of the saints said:
When we pray to the Lord and say *Lead us not into temptation,* we are not saying this so that we shall not be tried; that would be impossible. We are praying not to be overcome by temptation to the extent of doing something displeasing to God. That is what it means not to enter temptation. The holy martyrs were tried by their torments but, as they were not overcome by them, they did not enter into temptation, any more than someone who fights with a beast and is not devoured by it. When he is devoured, then he has entered into temptation. So it is with every passion, so long as one is not overcome by that passion.

210. How a holy bishop overcame another one who was opposing him—by humility

One of the fathers said that there were two neighbouring bishops who had an altercation with each other. One was rich and the other was more lowly. The rich one sought to do the other a mischief. The lowly bishop heard of this and, knowing what he was going to do, said to his clergy: 'We shall triumph, by the grace of Christ'. They said to him: 'My lord, who could possibly prevail against that one?' He said to them: 'Wait, and you shall see'. He bided his time and when his fellow bishop was celebrating a feast in honour of some holy martyrs, he gathered his clergy and said to them: 'Follow me, and we shall triumph'. They said to themselves: 'What can he be going to do?' He came to the other bishop, and when he came by in the procession, the visiting bishop fell at his feet together with the clergy, saying: 'Forgive us; we are you lordship's humble servants'. The other was amazed at what he had done and a stab of remorse went through his soul. God gave him a change of heart, and *he* now grasped his colleague's feet, saying: 'It is you who are my lord and father'. From that time on, there was a strong bond of love between them. <The lowly bishop> said to his clergy: 'Did I not tell you that we should triumph, by the grace of God? When there is any ill feeling between you, do you likewise—and triumph'. The elder also said that a humble man has more glory than the emperor himself; for *he* is only praised in his presence, whereas a humble man is praised and said to be blessed both in and out of his presence.

211. CONCERNING AN ELDER OF GREAT VIRTUES WHO GOT A BROTHER WHO HAD STOLEN THINGS FROM HIM OUT OF PRISON

One of the higoumens said:
An elder was living near our community, a good man in spiritual matters. A brother lived near him. When the elder was somewhere else, the brother was incited to open his cell door, go in and take the elder's books and vessels.* When the elder came, he opened the cell door and found his equipment stolen. He went and told the brother about it and, there were his things, right there in plain view (for the brother had stowed them away). The elder did not want to put him to shame or condemn him, so he pretended that his belly was troubling him. He went out and stayed away for as long as it would take to do the necessary, long enough for the brother to stow away the vessels out of sight. Then the elder returned and began to ask about some other matter, and did not accuse the brother. Some days later, the elder's equipment was found. They arrested the brother and threw him into prison, but the elder learned nothing about it whatsoever. When he eventually heard that the brother was in prison, he did not know *why* he was in prison. 'He came to me', said the higoumen, 'for he visited us frequently, and he said to me:

"Of your charity, give me a few eggs and some white bread."' I said to him: "Obviously, you have guests today", and he said he had. He was <in fact> taking those provisions to the prison to offer some comfort to the brother. When he entered the prison, the brother fell at his feet and said: 'It is on your account that I am here, abba. It is I who stole your equipment. But look: your book is in such-and-such a place and your vestment is in such-and-such a place.' The elder said to him: 'Be assured, child, that is not why I came; neither was I in the least aware that it was because of me that you are here. But hearing that you were here, I was grieved and came to offer you some comfort. See, here is white bread and some eggs. And I will do everything I can until I get you out of prison.' He went and interceded with some important people, for he was known to them for his virtue. They sent and released the brother from prison.

212. OF TWO BROTHERS WHO EXERCISED MARVELLOUS PATIENCE IN DEALING WITH ROBBERS

One of the elders said:

An elder of great virtue visited us and we were reading the sayings of the holy fathers in <the book called> *Paradise,* for that elder was always very fond of going through <the sayings>. He inhaled them, as it were, and from that <seed> he produced the fruit of every virtue. We came to the story of that elder to whom robbers came and said: 'We have come to take everything in your cell'. When he replied: 'Take whatever you like, children', they took everything and went their way. But they had overlooked a purse which was hanging* <in the cell>. The story says that the elder took the purse and ran after the robbers, shouting and saying to them: 'Children, take this from me which you overlooked in our cell'. They were so amazed at his forbearance that they gave back to the elder everything that had been in his cell. And they repented, saying to each other: 'Truly, this is a man of God'. When we read this, the elder said to me: 'You know, abba, this saying has been very advantageous to me'. I asked him: 'How so, father"? And he said: 'I read this at a time when I was in the Jordan region, and I was filled with admiration for the elder. I said: "Lord, let me follow in his footsteps, you who have counted me worthy to embrace this way of life". While this desire was still strong within me, two days later some robbers came by. When they knocked at the door I knew they were robbers. I said to myself: "Thanks be to God; the occasion has arisen for me to show the fruit of my desire". I opened the door and welcomed them cheerfully. I lit a lamp and began showing them the things that were there, saying: "Do not worry; before the Lord, I believe that nothing shall be hidden away from you". They said to me: "Have you any gold?" "Yes", I replied: "I have three pieces of gold". I opened the chest before them; they took the gold and went their way in peace'. With a smile, I asked him if they had returned like the robbers in the saying. He replied without hesitation: 'No, God forbid! Nor did I want them to come back'.

213. Why there are signs and prodigies from God in the holy church

One of the elders spoke of the divine prodigies which happen in the Church of God even now on account of the godless heresies which used to flourish and flourish still, and most of all because of the heresy of Severus Acephalos and of the pernicious sects of the rest of them. These prodigies occur for the assurance and confirmation of weaker souls and for the conversion of the sectaries themselves, if they are so disposed. For these reasons miracles were performed daily in the catholic Church of God (as they still are) by the godly fathers and, before them, by the holy martyrs.

214. The miracle of the baptismal font in the City of Coeana

Sorouda is a village in the vicinity of the city of Coeana. There is a font there which exudes liquid on the feast of the Epiphany. It fills itself up in this way over a period of three hours and, after the baptism, it slowly empties itself again, taking three hours to do so.

215. Another miracle: of the baptistry of the village of Cedrebat

In the village of Cedrebat in the vicinity of the city of Oenoanda there is a font which consists of one single piece of stone. And at the paschal feast of the resurrection it suddenly fills up of its own accord and retains the water until Pentecost. Then suddenly, after Pentecost, the water disappears. Both these wonders are in the Province of Lycia. If anybody does not believe this, it is no burdensome journey to Lycia where he can inform himself of the truth.

216. Some good advice about neither being obdurate nor remaining obdurate

Once when I was in the Holy City a person who loved Christ came to me and said: 'There had been a small altercation between my brother and me and he will not be reconciled with me. You go speak to him and reason with him'. I received this commission joyfully. I called the brother and spoke to him of those things which tend to love and peace, and it seemed as though he was coming round to my point of view. At last, he said to me: 'I cannot be reconciled with him because I swore on the cross'. I said to him with a smile: 'Your oath was equivalent to saying: "Oh Christ, by the honourable cross, I will not keep your commandments, but I will do the will of your enemy the devil". We ought not only to put a halt to what we have set in motion, but also (and even more so) to repent and lament for what we have wrongly instigated to our own hurt. As the divinely inspired Basil says: "If Herod had repented and not kept his oath, he would not have committed that heinous sin of beheading John the Forerunner of Christ"'. Finally I brought out the opinion of Saint Basil which he took from the gospel: that when Christ wanted to wash the feet of Saint Peter, although <the apostle> obstinately refused at first, he afterwards changed his mind. <Some manuscripts add: when he heard this, he was reconciled with his brother>.

217. THE BEST ADVICE OF AN ELDER: THAT A MONK SHOULD NOT GO NEAR A WOMAN

An elder said: 'Children, salt comes from water. But if it comes back to water, it is dissolved and disappears. So the monk comes from a woman; and if he comes back to a woman, he is undone and, insofar as his being a monk is concerned, he dies'.

218. HOW ABBA SERGIOS PACIFIED A CURSING FARMER BY PATIENCE

The higoumen of the monastery of Abba Constantine, Abba Sergios, told us:

Once we were travelling with a holy elder and we lost our way. Quite without meaning to, and indeed without knowing where we were going, we found ourselves in sowed fields and we trod down some of the seedlings. The farmer was working there and he noticed what we had done. He began to upbraid us angrily in these words: 'You are monks? You fear God? If you had the fear of God before your eyes you would not have done this.' At once the holy elder said to us: 'For the Lord's sake, let nobody say anything', and he addressed the farmer: 'Well spoken, my child. If we had the fear of God, we would *not* be doing these things.' Again the farmer spoke angry and abusive words, to which the elder again responded: 'You speak the truth, child, when you say that if we were true monks we would not have done this; but, for the sake of the Lord, forgive <us>, for we have sinned'. The farmer was astonished. He came and threw himself at the feet of the elder, saying: 'I have sinned, forgive me, and for the Lord's sake, take me with you'. The blessed Sergios said: 'And in truth he followed along with us; and when he came <here> he received the monastic habit'.

219. How a brother was reconciled with a deacon who was aggrieved at him

An elder told me something like this:
Once I stayed for a short time at the Lavra of Abba Gerasimos, and there was somebody there who was very dear to me. One day as we were sitting together talking about those things which are beneficial <to the soul> I recalled this saying of Abba Poimên: that each man should always question himself on every matter. He said to me: 'Father, I have experience of those sayings, of their severity and of their strength. Once I had a beloved and dear deacon from the lavra. Somehow or other, something about me came to his ears which brought him grief and he began to treat me very cooly. When I perceived his coldness, I sought to know the reason for it. He said to me: "You have done such-and-such". Since I was not aware of having done any such thing whatsoever, I began to assure him, thus: "I am not aware of having done such a thing". He said to me: "Forgive me, but I am not convinced". I retired to my cell and began to search my heart to see whether any such deed had been done by me and I found nothing. Seeing him holding the holy chalice and distributing <holy communion> I swore to him on the

chalice that I had no knowledge of having done such a thing, but he was not convinced. Then I became myself again and thought of these words of the holy fathers <that each man should always question himself on every matter>. I put my trust in them and changed my line of reasoning a little. I said to myself: "The kindly deacon loves me and, prompted by his love for me, he has confided to me that which was in his heart concerning me to put me on my guard. I will make sure that I do not do that deed in future. But, oh, wretched soul! While you say you have not done *that* deed, are there not thousands of misdeeds done by you which you have forgotten? Where are the things you did yesterday or the day before that or ten days ago? Can you recall them? Is it not possible that you have done this deed as lightly as you did the others, and have forgotten it as readily as you forgot them?" And so I disposed my thoughts to accept the possibility that I had in truth committed that deed, but had forgotten it—just as I had forgotten my other misdeeds. Then I began to give thanks to God and to the deacon, because, through him, God had made me worthy to acknowledge my fault and to repent of it. With these thoughts in my mind, I got up to go and apologise to the deacon and to thank him, because through him I had acknowledged my fault. I knocked at the door; he opened it and immediately fell at my feet, saying: "Forgive me; I was deceived by demons into thinking that of you. But in truth, God has informed me that you are not guilty of anything." He said that he would not allow me to offer my assurance, for there was no need. I was greatly edified by this experience and I glorified the Father, the Son and the Holy Spirit; to whom be the power and the magnificence, for ever and ever. Amen.'

SUPPLEMENTARY TALES

edited by Theodor Nissen and/or Elpidio Mioni

220. NISSEN 1* *BHG* 1442b

At the beginning of the reign of the Emperor Tiberius, the most faithful Caesar, we came to the oasis which lies to the west of the innermost Thebaïd, in the wilderness. Rumour has it that Nestorios was exiled to the eastern regions for having blasphemed against the all-holy Mary, the true Mother of God, and against the eternal Word of God who was incarnate without sin and born of her. A letter of recall was sent to him by the emperor at the behest of persons of consequence who shared his opinion. Late in the evening, <Nestorios> went to the privy before going to bed and, while he was there, he is said to have exclaimed within the hearing of those who were standing outside: 'I showed you, Mary: you bore a man, and no God'! Having heard him speak like that, they withdrew, for they were under orders to let no one into the apartment until he invited them to do so from within. Immediately, whilst the blasphemous words were still on his lips, an angel of wrath sent by God smote him as he was sitting in the privy and his bowels gushed out. Thus the wretch suffered just retribution for his evil counsel and blasphemy.

At dawn, the bearer of the imperial letters arrived in haste, saying he had to meet a dead-line and could not wait. Since Nestorios did not call in accordance with the instructions they had received, and the officer *<magistrianos>* was standing there waiting, they forced their way into the apartment. Coming to the chamber in which <Nestorios> was accustomed to sleep, they knocked, but received no reply. As the doors were fastened from within, they broke them from their hinges, and so gained entrance. When they did not find him there, they sought him in the privy and found him sitting there, dead. When those who served him were asked whether some indisposition had befallen him to bring him to this pass, they replied, saying: 'Late in the evening, he dismissed us with joy and happiness. He fastened the doors (as you found them), went to the privy and sat down. Just as we were about to go, each one of is to his place of rest, we heard him talking to himself and saying: "I showed you, Mary: you bore a man, and no God."'

Then all those who heard this perceived that he had undergone that lamentable death so that the saying of the great prophet Jeremiah might thereby be fulfilled, the one that says: *Woe to that man! They will not weep for him, Oh Lord, neither let them say: 'Oh brother, Oh sir'! He will be buried in the grave of an ass, he will be dragged along and cast out beyond the gates* <Jer 22:18-19 approx.>. Such was the end of the impious Nestorios, when he was about to succeed to eternal outer darkness and had already beheld the fore-court thereof. The wretch brought upon himself a just retribution for his evil counsel and blasphemy.

221. NISSEN 2 *BHG* 1442c

A brother gave all his goods away when he became a monk, but retained one fine piece of land. A distinguished layman longed to possess that land and he frequently asked the monk either to sell it to him or to take another <piece of land> in exchange for it; but neither alternative was acceptable. Now the layman became governor of that region and be brought pressure to bear on the monk to give up that land. He threatened him often, and put his own cattle on the other's land. When the monk perceived the extent of the danger he was in and his inability to frustrate the governor, in the end he went off to an elder who led a solitary life in those parts, a virtuous and celebrated man. The brother was in the habit of coming to him; the elder would encourage him and send him back to his cell. Realising that the governor was determined to have the land, he came yet again to the elder and said to him: 'Help me, for the Lord's sake! Write to him, or send somebody to him'. When the brother continued to trouble him with this request, the elder wrote a letter to the governor which went like this: 'The person who lives the life of a monk does so in order to be rid of possessions on account of which he might be wronged'. Having written thus, he gave the letter to the brother to take to the governor—and brother was unaware of what the writing said. He went and gave it to the governor, who received it with great honour; he reverenced it, opened it and read it. Then he asked the brother: 'Do you know what he wrote?' 'That you should desist from encroaching on that land <of mine>,' said the other. In his amazement at the virtue of the elder <the governor> did desist from encroaching on the land. From this <example>, let us wonder at the goodness of God and the nature of virtue, for the elder wrote a letter which contained nothing haughty or threatening, and yet it constrained the archôn to have pity on the one who requested it.

222. NISSEN 3 Nau 342

Some philosophers once visited an elder, and after he had offered a prayer he remained silent, braiding cord and paying no attention <to them>. They besought him, saying: 'Say something to us, father', but he held his peace. They said to him: 'This is what we came for: to hear you say something and to benefit <from it>.' The elder said to them: 'You spend your money to learn how to speak: I left the world to learn how to keep silent'. They were filled with amazement on hearing this and went their way edified.

223. Nissen 4 *BHG* 1440r

One of the fathers said that in Thessalonica there was a monastery of virgins. One of them was coerced by the operation of the evil one into going out of the monastery. She went out and fell into lechery <πορνεία> by the <machinations> of the demon who scoffed at her until she left <the monastery>. Once she had fallen, she remained some time in sin then finally, undergoing a change of heart by the cooperation of God the good, she came to repentance. <Re>entering her community in order to repent, she fell before the gateway of the monastery—and died. Her death was revealed to one of the holy bishops. He saw holy angels coming to receive her soul and demons in attendance; he witnessed a dialogue taking place between them. The angels were saying: 'She came in repentance', but the demons said: 'She has served us so long a time that she is ours'. Their altercation lasted some time and then the demons, those who obstruct the good, said: 'She did not get as far as entering the monastery; how can you say she repented?' In answer <to this> the holy angels said: 'Insofar as God saw her intention tending in that direction, he accepted her repentance. And she was mistress of repentance by virtue of the goal she set before herself: the Lord of life and the Master of all'. Put to shame by these <words>, the demons withdrew. The holy bishop who witnessed this revelation told it to some people from whom we heard it—and told it to you. In knowledge of this, brethren, let us secure ourselves against giving in to any kind of sinful thoughts. Let us rather resist and fight, especially against <the temptation> to go out of one's monastery, lest we unwittingly fall well and truly into the snares and nooses of our enemy.

224. Nissen 5 *BHG* 1440q

One of the fathers said:

When I was in Alexandria, I went into a martyr's shrine to pray, and I saw a Christ-loving woman wearing (it seemed) widow's weeds. She had some <serving> boys and girls with her. This is how she spoke to the holy martyr as she firmly grasped the railing <of his tomb>: 'You have abandoned me, Lord; have mercy upon me, Master, lover of humanity!' Such were her cries and tears that I broke off from my prayers and paid attention to her, mightily affected by her cries and tears. I supposed it likely that, being a widow, she was being oppressed by somebody. Since I was acquainted with the deputy prefect <? πρὸς τὸν σύνεδρον τοῦ αὐγουσταλίου>, I waited until she had finished her prayer then, summoning one of her youths, I said: 'Call your mistress for me'. When she approached I told her what I supposed <to be her condition>. Again she dissolved into tears, saying: 'Oh, father, do you not know what my <trouble> is? God has abandoned me and not visited me. Today it is three years that I have not been ill, nor a child of mine nor a servant nor anybody else of my house, and I suppose that God has turned away from me because of my sin: that is why I am weeping, that God would visit me according to his mercy, and that right soon.' I was amazed at her intelligent <φιλόσοφος> soul and, having prayed for her, I went my way, glorifying God.

225. Nissen 6 *BHG* 1440s

A friend of Christ said:

We visited the community of a holy elder in the Thebaïd and as we arrived at the monastery, huge dogs used by goatherds were growling on top of the wall. I was afraid and I wanted to dismount from the horse, but those who were with me had previous experience of the dogs' barking and they said: 'Do not dismount, master; the dogs have the abba's command not to come down from the circuit <of the walls>.' We entered the monastery and received the prayers of the fathers. They brought us to the well at the time of psalm-singing. The camel which drew the water was at a standstill and did not move. When we asked why the camel was not going round, they replied: 'Our abba ordered it not to walk round at the time of psalm-singing, after the knocking <of the wooden signal> has sounded—until the congregation has been dismissed. Because once when it was <the time for> psalm-singing the well-keeper did not hear the signal on account of the noise of the machine, and he was not present in church. The abba came to the well and said to the well-keeper: "Why did you not come to the church when it was time?" He said: "Forgive me; the noise of the machine prevented me from hearing the signal". The abba stood there and ordered the camel that drew the water, saying: "Blessed be the Lord! When the knocking <of the signal> for church is given, do not budge until <the congregation> is dismissed", and the camel kept the commandment. And even if another camel, any <animal> whatsoever, is put to the machine, it keeps the same commandment. When we heard this, we glorified God.

226. NISSEN 7 *BHG* 1448i/1440kt

There was in the Thebaïd a man named Paul who frequented the holy catholic church of God day and night. When the diligent, hard-working <people> who were with him saw him, they said to him: 'Abba Paul, you have no parents and no wish to take a wife. Why do you not become a monk?' He said to them: 'You have spoken well; I will become a monk'. Off he went, and stayed alone in a cell, passing his time in ascetic exercises and other labours. He had a totally guileless disposition. When the evil demon saw what kind of a man he was, he disguised himself as an angel, foretelling certain illusions to him and leading him astray. When the demon knew that he had him under his thumb, he said to him: 'Christ is delighted with your way of life and he is going to come to you tomorrow to bestow gifts on you. You are to come out of your cell and worship him and you will receive the gift, then go back into your cell'. When he came out of his cell next day, he saw rank on rank of angels in splendid raiment, and a wheel of fire. In the midst of the wheel there was somebody represented whom he took to be Christ. As he bowed his neck to worship, suddenly a well-aimed hand gave him a blow and turned him around in the other direction so that he could not worship. He fell to the earth in prayer and he saw those splendidly attired beings by the wheel of fire no more. Perceiving the demon's deception, he remained weeping in the same place for two days and nights, saying before God: 'Woe is me, the sinner! I have sinned; I have ruined my whole life and I do not know what to do'. Now he had been hearing of an anchorite who had been in the Upper Thebaïd for some time, living alone in the field. He decided to go and lay before this man what had happened to him.

When he came near the place where that elder was, he cast himself face down on the ground, falling before him and saying: 'I have sinned; forgive me, and pray for me'. The elder shouted to him: 'Don't you come here, you laughing-stock of demons; don't come near', and he continued to rebuke him in similar terms. But <the man> remained, stretched out on the ground, weeping. So the elder felt sorry for him and said to him: 'If you go away to learn some skill or other, do you not expect to go to a craftsman and learn what pertains to his craft? But you went off to live all alone with your own self, without even explaining to anybody what you were up to. And if God had not helped you, and if the right hand of the holy angel.... for if you had worshipped <the wheel of fire> you would have destroyed your mind and you would have had to wander around in the cities like one of those who are possessed by demons. But, as things are, give thanks to God who helped you—and then come into the community'. The holy man then took him to one of the communities of the Thebaïd and handed him over to the abba, saying: 'Give him kitchen duties for seven years so he can serve Christ's command and be of service to the brothers'. Then he said to Abba Paul: 'In seven years' time I will come and speak to you'.

When <Paul> had served seven years, the elder came and said to the abba: 'Give him a cell outside the community', for the communities of the Thebaïd have little cells for anchorites so that when some men have grown old in the ascetic life, they can live in those cells five days a week, coming into the community with the brethren for Saturday and Sunday. And the elder said to him again: 'Spend another seven years in the anchorite's cell and I will come to speak to you again'. When he had fulfilled this command, the holy elder came and Abba Paul said to him: 'What do you command me to do now?' Then the elder said to him: 'You have no further need of me. The Holy Spirit dwelling within you will teach you all things'. Much honour having accrued to him on account of this saying, <Paul> departed and went away to Scêtê. The members of the community <there> came to him beseeching him <to join them> and they took him in with themselves. He came <to them>, and much honour accrued to him from the brotherhood, so he fled from there also. While he was living in the wilderness, it happened that I and three of the fathers (amongst whom was my abba, an elderly man), visited him. It is indeed the case that he had no bread, no <water->jar nor anything else pertinent to the needs of the body. He did no hand-work and he had no book. He tasted nothing during the five <week->days and he had a large body. He told us that he never had water in his cell. When some people visited him in the heat of the day who were very thirsty (and he had no water,) he stood and prayed. Contrary to what one might have expected, God made water to spring forth there, where he was praying. They drank and were refreshed; and they glorified God.

227. NISSEN 8 *BHG* 1322n

Abba Basil, the anchorite-priest who became a monk of the New Lavra, told us that he had heard some friends of Christ recounting a wonder like this:

In the land of the Palestinians there was a well-populated village in which there dwelt both Christians and Hebrews. They possessed large flocks and herds and this was their custom, handed down from <the time of> their forefathers: each day at dawn they used to gather the animals together at the gate of the village and each man would send either his son or his <slave-> boy with his own beasts. The young people would take the animals and also provisions for themselves. They would go out and stay in the field until evening. As the sun was setting, they would bring back <the flocks and herds>.

Now one day, as they went forth as usual to pasture, they gathered together at meal-time and the children of the Christians said to each other: 'Come, let us hold a eucharist like the clergy do in church'. One of them took the role of the bishop and he appointed one to be priest, one to be deacon, one subdeacon and others to be readers. They set up one of the stones that was flat to serve as an altar and they offered the sacrifice out of the provisions they had brought along. Now with them there as a Hebrew, the son of the chief rabbi, and he begged the children saying: 'Let me <play> with you so that I can give <communion> like you do'. They rejected him saying: 'You cannot come with us for you are a Jew'. He said: 'I too can become a Christian'. They said to him: 'If you become a Christian, then we will accept you'. When he agreed to this they accepted him and the pretending bishop baptised him after they had found some water there. So they did everything in an orderly manner and offered the bread and, as they were completing

<the service> and saying: 'One is holy',[1] fire came down from heaven and consumed everything lying <on the altar>. <The children> were so afraid that they fell down as though they were dead.

When evening came, the beasts went off, each to its own home. Early next day the neighbours went out and searched and they found the children lying half dead. Each one cared for his own child, and thus they brought them to their houses. They returned to their senses three days later; then their parents asked them what had happened to them. They confessed everything that had taken place, exactly as it is written above.

Bread was set before the chief rabbi's son and his father invited him to eat. But he would not agree to eat, saying: 'I am a Christian and I will not feed <on this>.' When that wretched fellow heard this he decided to hand his son over to bitter death. But God—who foresees <what will happen>, who *Tries the very hearts and reins* <Ps 7:10>—God, knowing the evil thoughts of that abominable <man>, contrived for the magistrate of the area whom they call the emir bitterly to complain against the district bath-house keeper for taking <his duties> too lightly and for failing to maintain the temperature of the bath <-house> according to instructions. He said to him: 'Just look how long you have been deceiving everybody! Whenever I come to bathe, I find it cold. I swear to you by the great God that if you do not obey instructions, and if <the bath> is found to be cold the next day <I come here>, I will cut off your

[1] The response in the orthodox liturgy to the invitation to communion, 'The holy things for the holy people *[ta hagia tois hagiois]:* 'one is holy one is Lord, Jesus Christ to the glory of God the father and to the fullness of the holy Spirit'; see 'The Byzantine Liturgy of the Ninth Century' in *Liturgies Eastern and Western,* ed. F.E. Brightman, vol. 1 (Oxford, 1896) p. 341. The point is that the children had celebrated the entire liturgy almost to the point of communion.

head'. The man undertook to do what would be of service to the emir.

The father of the Hebrew child knew all about this. Convinced that <the child> was in the grip of a diabolical subterfuge, he himself sent to the bathkeeper (a man who was in debt to him) and said: 'I am aware that you owe me ten pieces of gold'. 'Yes, that is correct', came the answer. 'If you will discharge the commission I am about to prescribe, I will excuse you all this debt'. 'In order to free myself of the weight of the debt, I will do whatever you require of me', he replied. The lawless false priest said to him: 'I hear you have received an order from the emir to fire up the bath. I want you to tell me when the furnace is burning and you are about to close it up, for I have a child who provokes me to anger. Then, no matter who it is I send to you asking "is the bath in order?" you are to seize him and hurl him into the furnace, shut it up and go away. This so that I might change his evil mentality'. When the bath-keeper heard this, he agreed to do what was prescribed in the hope of gaining relief from his debt.

He came <to work> and for fear of the emir's threats, he proceeded to make the furnace far hotter than usual. When he perceived that <it was time for> the furnace to be closed up....<he sent a message to the chief rabbi who then>....sent his son saying: 'Is the bath in order?' <The bath-keeper> said: 'Master, it is more than in order. If you don't believe me, look quickly—' and seizing the child, he hurled him into the fire, closed up the furnace and went away.

The emir came to bathe and found the bath even cooler than on the former days. He called the bath-master and said to him: 'Did I not instruct you to heat the bath well? Why have you not obeyed, but have rather made it cooler?' He swore on his oath: 'I stoked it with three times as much wood as usual in my desire to please you and I just do not know why things are like this. If you do not believe my testimony, come and see the furnace and you will know from the number of coals that I am not lying'. He went with him fuming with anger and when <the bath-keeper> uncovered <and removed> the slab of the furnace, he found the child sitting there as large as life. <The emir> said to the bath-keeper: 'How does this child come to be here? How do you explain him having been thrown in there?' The bath-keeper explained everything to the emir and <suggested that> perhaps it was because the child had been unjustly thrown in that so great a flame in the furnace had died away.

The emir came to the conclusion that there was not a word of truth in what he was saying. He said to him: 'Bring wood and heat up the furnace of the bath in my presence'. Whilst this was being done, the emir asked the child whose <son> he might be and for what reason he had been thrown into the furnace. When he learned that this was because the boy definitely wanted to be known altogether as a Christian and that he was unwilling to partake of Jewish food, the emir was beside himself with anger. Pouring derision on christianity (for the fear of the Lord is an abomination to the sinner) *he* took the child and thrust him into the furnace saying: 'Even if you put the fire to sleep by sorcery the first time, you will not escape from my hands now'.

But God *who is always doing great and wondrous things,* <Jb 5:9> *who is near to all who call upon him in truth* <Ps 144:18> —he quieted down the flames of the furnace as before and kept the child safe. When the emir came back to bathe, the bath was found to be even cooler than before, as though it had remained a whole week without being fired up. Flabbergasted at this the emir went and opened the furnace of the bath and found the child sitting quite comfortably within. And there was not even the slightest smell of burning in the furnace. Utterly confused by the strangeness of this wonder, the emir went off at a run to make these things known to what they call 'the counsellor'. When he heard he quickly came to the village, ordered the furnace to be fired up and the child to be thrown into it again, in his presence. He set a seal and guards at the door <of the furnace> and went in to bathe. When he entered the bath <-house>, instead of the heat of the bath there was considerable coolness so he came out immediately and, opening the mouth of the furnace, he found the child sitting there in good condition. And there was no smell of fire there. Then *he* questioned the child; whose son was he? When he learned that this was the child of the false priest of the lawless Jews and what had happened <to the child> in the field, as it is written above, and that it was because the child had committed himself to and remained <faithful to> the confession of christianity and would not allow himself to be polluted with the unclean food of his parents that he had been delivered into such a deadly punishment of fire by his own father; <when he learned, furthermore,> that having already been three times hurled into the furnace of fire he was not burned up but, on the contrary, it had comforted him just as the Babylonian furnace in ancient times <comforted> the three children;* <when he learnt all this,> he brought the father of the child and said to him: 'What excuse are you going to make to God for the devilish and filthy deed you have done? You thought you could escape the notice of God and of men. But God, who knows your evil deeds and purposes, did not grant his approval. On the contrary; he condemned the savagery of your soul. For if you were so heartless as to deliver the fruit of your loins to so bitter a death, what would you not have perpetrated if the right occasion had presented itself? Now, since you have committed this heinous deed and have contrived to make us accessories to your filthy undertaking, you shall suffer the death of evil-doers so that no other demon of like kind will work the same things in you <as this misdeed>.' And so saying he sent and ordered him to be beheaded outside the village in a desert place <and to be left there> as food for carnivorous beasts.

He summoned the children and learned exactly what play-acting had been done by them in the field. Then he put them in a monastery, granting an allowance for each one, according to the part he had played. To him who played bishop, a bishop's allowance; to those who played priests or deacons or subdeacons or readers, to each he ordered a support-allowance to be given appropriate to the rank of each of them.

The God and creator of all things was pleased to allow all this to happen for the help and support of us Christians and to make known to all the peoples who oppose us out of evil intent the utter hatred of the lawless Jews for our Lord and God and his only begotten Son and for us who truly believe in him. For the prophecy of the Lord had to be fulfilled, <the one> which he made to those who lacked understanding: *I came in my father's name and you received me not. Should another come in his own name, him you will receive and you will die in the sins of your evil deeds.* <Jn 5:43; Jn 8:24>

228. NISSEN 9 — *BHG* 1450ze

There was going to be holy communion in a community but when the deacons came in to put on their stoles, one of them could not be found by them. After much searching, they told the abba. He said to them: 'Search again'. When it was still not found, moved by the irregularity of the matter, the abba said: 'We are cohabiting with thieves. As the Lord lives, there will be no communion, nor will we take a morsel of food until the thief is found.' While the abba, together with the deacons, was searching the brothers' cells the brothers <all> sitting in church, the one who stole it said to his neighbour (who was a pious soul): 'I am in deep trouble! How I am going to suffer!' The other said: 'What for?' He said: 'I am the one who took the stole; it is in my cell, down in a wine-jar for exporting wine from Gaza>.' The other said: 'Do not upset yourself; go and put it in my cell'. So he went and put the wine-jar in the brother's cell. When the abba and the deacons came searching where the brother's wine-jar lay, one of the deacons put his hand down into it and brought up the stole. He began to cry: 'This pious man turns out to be a thief!' They came into church, laid their hands on him and gave him many wounds. They dragged him forth and threw him out of the community. He begged them, saying: 'Let me repent and I will never do it again', but they threw him out, saying: 'We cannot have a thief with us'. Then they went in to celebrate the holy communion. When the deacon came to draw the curtain, it would not move. They were at great pains to see if anything was obstructing it but they found nothing. Then the abba reasoned with himself: 'Perhaps it is because we threw out the brother that this happened to us. Go and bring him in, and we will find out'. When the brother came in, they drew the curtain and it followed <the cord> easily. Now behold: *that* is laying down one's life for one's neighbour. If we do not measure up to this standard, even though we neither speak ill of our neighbour nor condemn him <...?> so that we not be alienated from the joy in which the saints are going to delight.

229. NISSEN 10 *BHG* 1442cb

There was a stranger from among the fathers and he told a parable like this:

In my country they dig pits to trap lions. Now it so happened that a vixen fell into <one such> pit. Hard though it tried to do so, it was unable to get out. Then the master of the ditch came by to see if anything had fallen into it—and he found the vixen. The animal dissimulated; it lay there as though it were dead. The master of the ditch climbed down, grasped it by the tail and threw it up; <the vixen> made her escape on the double. Some days later the same animal saw another vixen which had fallen into the same ditch; and when she saw her, pacing to and fro but unable to get out, she said to her: 'I too did a good deal of pacing to and fro; and, if had not made myself dead, I would not have got out'. We too, brethren, if we want to....

[Nissen 11 (defective)/Mioni 6, below]

230. NISSEN 12 *BHG* 1450p

In Antioch the Great in Syria there are different kinds of social services. A man who was a friend of Christ was in charge of one of them. It was his custom to provide those in need with what each of them lacked on each occasion. He used to buy things with which to supply their needs. Amongst other things he used to get linen under-garments which came from Egypt and from this <supply> he would provide garments for those in need, in accordance with the pronouncement of the Lord which says: *I was naked and you clothed me* <Mt 25:36>. A brother came when the distribution of clothing (as I described it) was taking place, and he received a linen garment, not only once, but two and three times. That friend of Christ, realising that the man came a second and a third time, decided to speak to him about it. When he came a fourth time, moved on that occasion to single him out from the rest of the poor, he said to him: 'Look, you have received <a garment> a third and a fourth time and heard nothing from me. Do not do this again in the future, for there are others afflicted like you and in need of good works'. The poor man withdrew in shame. The next night, the supervisor of the <social->service saw himself standing in what is called the Place of the Cherubim. It is a very sacred place and those who know say that in that place there is a very awesome icon bearing the likeness of our Saviour, Jesus Christ. As he stood there in deep thought, he saw the Saviour coming down to him out of the icon and censuring him especially on account of the four garments which the poor man received. Then, falling silent again, <Christ> removed the tunic he was wearing and showed him the number of under-garments while saying: 'Behold, one; behold, two; behold, three; behold, four. Do not be dismayed; inasmuch <*cf* Mt 26:40> as you provided those things for the poor man, they became my raiment'. <The man>

recognised the clothes and fell down at his feet, saying: 'Forgive my faint-heartedness, Lord, for I reckoned this matter in human terms'. When he awoke, he gave thanks to God who had shown him this revelation; and from that time on, he gave to all who asked, with simplicity and joy. And all who heard <of it> glorified God.

231. NISSEN 13 *BHG* 1450u

The holy Abba Theodore of Adana told us that when he was staying in the area adjacent to the Holy City, a person from the regions of Asia came to the Community of Penthoucla near the holy Jordan, wanting to renounce the world. The higoumen took him in and, when he had been there some time and had been trained in the rule of the community, he brought the gold he possessed and gave it to the abba, saying: 'Since I have been trained in the rule of the place and (with God's permission) want you to tonsure me, and to grant me the sacred habit so that I can stay here with you, please receive this contribution'—he showed him the gold, 'and use it as you will'. The higoumen, a man of virtue, was in no great hurry to get his hands on the gold. He said to him: 'Child, we are in no need of these <pieces of gold> at the moment, for, as you know, we do not spend a great deal on our own needs but, as it happens, we manage on cheap fare and we live in a desert place. But follow the Lord's command: go and give them to our brothers, the poor, and, according to the true commandments, you shall have treasure in heaven'. <Mt 6:19-20> But the brother pressed him, urging him and saying: 'I have renounced the world, father, and where I renounce <it>, there I bestow these <pieces of gold>.' The elder said to him: 'Child, if I take them, I shall bestow them on the poor, for we have not been taught to lay up treasures on earth'. But he went on saying: 'Take them, father, and use them as you will, either for <the relief> of the poor or for some other use'. As the abba could not change his mind, he accepted the gold from him; and, a little while later, he tonsured him; and then, some time later still, he conferred on him the holy habit of monks.

By the providence of God, the abba did not dispose of the money, but waited, wanting to see the brother's progress. And, by the snares of the enemy, nobody, not even the brother himself, knew that <the abba> had retained the gold. At the beginning, in the zeal of his renunciation, <the brother> fulfilled every regulation, performing the duties he was required to undertake readily and without hesitation. When some time had gone by, he began to slacken (by the enemy's influence) and not to show the same diligence. Whispering and muttering to himself under his breath, he said: 'I gave gold enough to the community, and I do not eat bread that is freely given here'. Some of the brethren were offended when they heard this, especially those whose condition was the least favoured by riches. When the abba of the community learned of this, he called for the brother and said to him: 'Did you not forcefully entreat me to take your gold from you? Did you not hand it over for distribution to the poor? Maybe there is a misunderstanding between us, that you grumble and offend the brothers so? Let it not be so, brother, for it is written: *See that not one of these little ones be offended*' <Mk 9:42>. The abba administered these and many similar admonitions to the brother but he did not refrain from his diabolical rumination on account of the evil habits of thought implanted in him. Now when the abba perceived that he was not to be diverted from the road which leads in the wrong direction, one day he said to him: 'Come, brother; let us go down to the Jordan'. They went down, the two of them, alone, and as they were walking along the banks of the holy Jordan, the abba began to admonish the brother. He brought out the gold, sealed up, (the same which the brother had given him) and he said to him: 'Do you recognise this?' He said: 'Yes, master'. 'And the seal that is on it?' 'It is the same, father'. Then the abba said to him: 'Take the gold, child, and if you wish to give it to the poor as I recommended, give it. If you wish to keep it, keep it—to your own condemnation. I will not break the rule of the community or offend the brethren or enrage God for the sake of these pieces of gold. I took you in to be with us as one who serves just as the rest of the brothers serve and as I served in my youth—and still to this day labour to the extent of my ability'. When the brother saw the gold and heard the abba saying these things, he threw himself at his feet saying: 'Forgive me; I came to give them to God and I cannot take them back'. The elder said: 'Child, God does not need these. Everything that is made is his. He needs the salvation of our souls. It is inadmissible for me to keep them any longer'. <The brother> remained prone and said to him: 'I will not get up from your feet unless you give me your word that you will not be offended and that you will not oblige me to take the gold pieces'. When the elder perceived the persistence of the request, he said to him: 'Stand up, child, and believe me: I will not oblige you to take them, nor will I retain them'. When the brother got up, the abba loosened the knot and said to him: 'These are the pieces of gold, child'. He said: 'As you promised, father, do not say a word to me about them'. The elder smiled and said: 'No, child',—and, so saying, he hurled the pieces of gold into the river before his very eyes. And he said to the brother: 'We are taught by the Lord to hold all these things of little worth. Come back to the community and work with the brethren, performing shamelessly every task you are required to undertake, for Christ's sake, bearing in mind that he himself said: *'The Son of Man came not to be ministered unto but to minister'* <Mk 10:45>. When the brother realised the abba's godly intention, spurred on to greater fear of God, he returned to the community with him and acquired great humility and obedience toward everybody. And, by the grace of God, he died in the same monastery, having become a *choice vessel* <Acts 9:15>.

[Nissen 14 (incomplete)/Mioni 7]

232. Mioni 1

One of the fathers said:
There is a community near Nisbis and the superior there was a great elder. The people of the community sowed and reaped much barley and this they shared with the other monasteries. Now it so happened that a commander, coming on a diplomatic mission from Persia, met the holy elder and was greatly edified by him. He endowed the community with an income of thirty pounds of gold <2160 *nomismata,* x 4.55g = 9,828 grams of gold>. The brethren rejoiced, but they became totally unconcerned so far as the property was concerned. They sowed barley as usual, but the first year the land produced nothing; nor the second year, nor the third. The brethren said to the abba: 'What is going on? The earth does not produce barley like it used to'. The elder said to them: 'We took the thirty pounds <of gold> and that is why the earth does not yield its fruit. But go; sell all your property and give to the poor'. <Mt 13:44, Mt 19:21; Mk 10:21, etc.> The brothers did as the elder said, and the earth yielded up it fruit, and everybody glorified God.

233. Mioni 2 *BHG* 1322b

One of the fathers told us of a Christ-loving man named Martyrios, and he who told this story was a priest, a great ascetic:
We came to visit this Master Martyrios. We knocked at the door; his wife (who was within) heard us and, knowing who we were, went into the vineyard to call her husband. He came and embraced us and, putting water in the bowl, washed our feet. He led us into the upper chamber of his dwelling and set a table <before us>. He was full of the love of God. When we had partaken, his wife brought her son and placed him near the door of the upper chamber

where we were taking our ease near to its father, so it could be blessed by us. By the machination and enmity of the devil, the child fell out of the door of the upper chamber and died immediately. His father was reclining by the door of the upper chamber, receiving the things offered to us by his wife. He looked down and saw his son lying senseless; but he was not upset, not he nor his wife. He knocked for the child's mother <to come> and gave instructions to her; she came and found the child dead. She laid him on the bed. <The father> however merrily ate and drank with us and, when we had eaten and were ready to go our way, they joyfully bade us God's speed. When the <thanksgiving> prayer was said <the couple> seized the priest's hand and said to him: 'Come and say a prayer over the child because he is giving off a bad odour <ἀηδίζεται>.' The priest went in and made the sign of the cross over him and we went our way. A few days later, we visited them again and, when they saw us, they rejoiced greatly. We found the child sitting with its mother, and we glorified God who had endowed him with health. They took up the infant and told us, saying: 'This little child was dead and, through your prayers, God gave him back to us', and they told us the whole story, bit by bit: 'When you went out, we came into where the child lay, intending to carry him away, but we found him alive, thanks to your prayers'. They said of him that when he grew up, he was a man who lived a godly life.

234. MIONI 3 *BHG* 1448z

One of the fathers told us that when he was at Constantinople he saw a strange thing with his own eyes. There was a Christ-loving man whose name was Christopher, serving at the palace in what is known as the Regiment of the Protectors. All day long he was on regimental duty <ἐσχολάζε> at the palace, tasting nothing until sundown. In the evening he would go aside to eat some dry bread and some boiled vegetables with water <to drink>, and he was satisfied with these customary <victuals>, for he never partook of the highly-flavoured food which most people eat. For clothing, he wore a hair shirt within, but on the outside he wore splendid clothing in order to conceal it from people at large. Off duty, once he had dismissed his subordinates, he would come to a silver-smith-*cum*-money-dealer <ἀργυροπράτης> of his acquaintance and receive from him three purses: one of whole gold pieces, one of half gold pieces and one of one-third gold pieces; and going alone into the arcades and prisons, all night long he gave to those who asked. While he was thus engaged one night, he came to the cell of a brother. He took out something to give to him and urged the brother to rise and receive <it>, but he answered never a word. The man urged him again with a loud voice, but there was neither sound nor hearing. Then he touched him—and knew that he was dead. He went to a nearby shop, knocked and asked the shop-keeper to provide him with lights and a vessel of water so he could wash the brother; he gave the shopkeeper one third of a piece of gold. He went with the shop-keeper and washed <the brother>. Then he went to a shroud-maker's and got what was needed for a burial, paying the price. He likewise <obtained> footwear, candles, burial-clothes <? ἐνταφιάσας>, as is customary. He lit the candles and placed a piece of gold on his chest for those who buried him. Then he said to the dead man: 'Rise up and greet me with christian love'. <The corpse> sat up, embraced him, lay down again and slept. When the shopkeeper saw this, he began to tremble and ran away. He remained as though he were dead with fear. It was he who noised this extraordinary wonder abroad to people at large.

235. MIONI 4 *BHG* 1448z

And they told us something else about the same saintly Christopher. When he set out one night to pray in the houses of prayer, he would come to the Chalkê gate of the Palace, and from there into the so-called Phletrô of the Saviour. This is a very holy and venerated spot, with bronze doors. As he approached alone to worship, the doors would open to him of their own accord. He would enter and worship, offer incense and come out again without anybody knowing. When those who dwelt there got up on many occasions and found the doors open, they were both amazed and afraid—lest any loss had befallen the sacristy and they find their positions as guardians endangered. So they watched laboriously and were especially wakeful. They found that the only explanation lay in the presence of the aforementioned man. They went to the then-patriarch and told him about the man. In his amazement, <the bishop> would not believe until he had himself secretly kept watch in the gallery and, with his own eyes, seen him offering incense. Thus convinced, he glorified God. And let no man be disbelieving because what is said here is beyond reason. Let him rather remember the godly David who says: *He will fulfill the desire of those who fear him: he also will hear their cry and will save them* <Ps 144:19>.

236. MIONI 5 *BHG* 1442m

A person who loved Christ said that a good-looking young woman came into one of the churches of Constantinople and prayed in a loud voice with tears in her eyes: 'Lord, afflict me!' and she went on saying this many times. There was another person, one of the illustrious citizens, praying in the same building at the same time as she was saying this, and he yearned to know why she was praying like that. When she refrained from weeping, he came up to her and said: 'For the love of God, tell me why you say those things when you are praying. And, if you tell the truth, I hope in God that I will help you with all my strength'. He thought that she was in need, or being oppressed. When she realised that his enquiry was made with serious intent, she took him aside and said to him: 'My lord, I had a husband from the time I was a virgin, but he died some time ago, leaving me a widow. Now, my body rises up against me in its desire for intercourse with a man. That is why I call upon God: to humble me, so that I do not have the experience of a second husband.' After saying this, the woman went away to her house. He who had heard this was amazed and, wishing to know more, he sent his servant along after her to find out where she lived. The servant put a sign on her house. The master sent him again to see what had happened to her. He came and found her in the grip of a violent fever, lying groaning in bed. The servant came to his master and told him what had happened. When he heard, he was astounded at that chaste soul and he glorified God.

237. Mioni 6* *BHG* 1442mb

There was a virtuous anchorite who called upon God saying: 'Lord, make known to me what your judgements are'. He demonstrated frequent <acts of> asceticism in support of this prayer, but God made it known to him that, for men, this was not possible. He still continued beseeching God by an ascetic mode of life; and as God wished to inform the elder, he allowed the idea to come to him to go visit an anchorite who was settled not a few miles away. He got his sheepskin coat ready and set off. God sent an angel disguised as a monk who met the elder and said to him: 'Where are you going, good elder?' The elder said: 'To so-and-so the anchorite'. The angel who was pretending to be a monk said: 'I am going to <see> him too; we will travel together'. When they had travelled the first day, they came to a place in which there dwelt a man who loved Christ. He received them <as guests> and put them up. Whilst they were eating, the man produced a silver dish <πατελίκιν, *patella*> and when they had eaten, the angel took the dish and made it disappear into thin air. The elder was disturbed when he saw this. Then going out together, they travelled the next day and in due course encountered another man who loved Christ and monks, in the place where he dwelt. He received them as his guests, washed their feet and embraced them. Early next morning, he brought his son, the only child he had, to be blessed by them. The angel seized it by the throat and strangled it. The elder was flabbergasted, but he said not a word. The third day, although they travelled a great distance, they found nobody who would offer them hospitality. Then they found a long-deserted dwelling <αὐλή> where, sitting down in the shade of a wall, they partook of the dried-out crusts the elder had. And, as they were eating, the angel saw a wall about to collapse. Leaping up to safety, he began to take down the masonry <? πινσόν ~πλίνθον?> and to rebuild <it>. The elder could bear it no longer; he swore at him, saying: 'Are you an angel? Are you a demon? Tell me what you are; the things you do are not the sort of things a man does'. The angel said: 'What did I do?' The elder said: 'Yesterday and the day before, those friends of Christ put us up. You not only made the first one's dish disappear; you also strangled the son of the other. And yet here, where we have found no rest, you stand doing the work of a labourer'. Then the angel said to him: 'Listen, and I will tell you. The first man who received us is one who loves God and manages his possessions in a godly way. That dish was left to him as the inheritance of an unjust man. I made that dish disappear, you see, so that he would not lose the reward of his other good <deeds> on account of it, and <now> his record is clean. And the other man who made us his guests, he is virtuous. Had that small child lived, it would have <grown up> to be an instrument of Satan, so that the good works of his father would pass into oblivion. So I strangled him whilst he was tender to ensure the salvation of the father, and that his record remain unassailable before God'. The elder said: 'And what about here?' The angel said: 'The owner of this dwelling is a plague who seeks to harm many people; it grieves him that he cannot succeed in doing so. When his grandfather built this house, he put money into the masonry he was building. I restored the masonry, you see, so that he would not be able to harm those he intended to harm by means of the cash he would have found when the building collapsed; I deprived him of the means. Now go to <your> cell, for as the Holy Spirit says: *Your judgements are like the great deep* <Ps 35:6>.' Having said this to him, the angel of God disappeared. Then the elder returned to his senses; he went back to his cell, glorifying God.

238. MIONI 7 *BHG* 1442f

When we willingly forsook the commandments of God and boldly turned to sin, then, in proportion to our offenses against the walls of defence, God contrived for us (who were shown by <our> deeds themselves to be unworthy of the great gifts) to become subjects of the barbarians. We became foreigners at the Holy Places when (by the righteous judgement of God) the city of Jerusalem and all the surrounding area fell into the hands of the Persians <5 May 614>. Then a strange thing, worthy of being preserved in writing, happened at Jerusalem. Having heard this not from one <man> but from a variety of persons, we resolved to record it for the edification and imitation of those who love virginity and purity.

When the enemy had besieged the city, having slain thousands and tens of thousands, they finally entered the <Church of the> Resurrection of Christ our God and the other Holy Places. It was in these <places> that most of the people took refuge, but especially in the sacred temple of the Holy Resurrection. When <the Persians> found them, they massacred them without quarter, <except that> they chose out good-looking young children and pure virgins. Having laid their hand on many such <persons>, after the great slaughter was ended, the Persians were at liberty to drink together in the houses and, contriving to do the lawless deed to the worthy virgins, they drew them down to destruction. It was then that one lamb of Christ, a virgin who was truly espoused to Him, looking upon the destruction of the servants of God that was taking place, suffered as David suffered and said: '*I saw the transgressors and I pined away* <Ps 118:158>. She caused herself to pine away from want of food. For fifteen days she refused to take food or drink, even though she was strongly urged to do so. She did not give in, but instead exhausted what strength remained in her body by devoting herself to unceasing tears and sighs. She was more beautiful than all the woman who were with her. Now it so happened that he who held her was distinguished among the Persians. He urged her (by means of her fellow virgins) to destruction, but she hated the very mention of it. True indeed is that which is said by the Lord: *Many are called but few are chosen* <Mt 22:14>. For even if they were virgins, most of them did not hold fast to the promise. For they willingly took food and drink at regular hours and supported the shame of destruction <quite well>, urging her <to do likewise>, but she reproved them with sighs. When he who held her learned of this, he raged, but he spared her on account of the beauty of her body. But one evening he was drinking with some Persians and some falsely-named virgins. Moved by the devil to an insane passion for her, he bade her come and sit down to dinner with him. She was not willing <to do so>, so his servants dragged her forcibly <to table> and, although she sat down, she took nothing. When dinner was over, burning with abundance of wine and his licentious desire, he left everybody and bade her go to bed with him. When she declined, he was moved to anger and he dealt her such blows that she fainted. He tried to force her to cooperate with his wicked desire and when she utterly refused, he took her at that hour of evening and brought her up to one of the towers of the walls. He stood her there on the pointed roof of the tower and asked her whether she would cooperate with his desire. She rejected the idea with contempt, abominating even the sound of it. At that, he became utterly inhumane. He bared his sword and began to torment her very violently, urging her to perform the defilement of licentiousness. But the holy virgin remained piously faithful to her resolution. When he had given her many wounds with his sword and made her blood-stained all over, finally, putting the same question and receiving an answer in line with the first and with the pious profession of virginity, he commanded his servants to throw her down from the roof. And that is what happened at that very hour. Thus, fighting courageously, she surrendered her spirit to the Lord, receiving the confessor's crown from Christ who is God.

239. Mioni 8

There were some people living in the world who had a daughter and it came about that she was afflicted by a demon. Her parents asked various monks to pray for her but she was not healed. At last, a monk whom they loved said to them: 'If you want your daughter to be healed, go out into the wilderness. There are holy men there and I believe she will be healed by their prayers'. They heeded him and went off into the wilderness. Now it so happened that a young man was coming out <of the wilderness> and when they saw him from a distance, they rejoiced and said: 'Look, God has sent us one of them so that we will not have to go out into such a wilderness.' When they came near to him, they and their child threw themselves to the ground, beseeching him and saying: 'This, our little daughter is troubled by a demon, but for the Lord's sake, pray for her', but he said to them: 'I am not one of those <holy men>; I am a man who is a sinner'. They besought him, saying: 'For the Lord's sake, do not speak like that, but rather have pity on us and pray for her',—for they thought it was out of humility that he said these things. So they went on beseeching him, and he gave them the same answer again. When they persisted and put pressure on him, his heart was warmed. From his own arm-hole <μασχάλη> he produced a little book and said, with an oath: 'I stole that, and then I came out here'. When he had said these words, the demon made off, unable to tolerate the young man's humility. <The parents'> faith was in no way diminished by what the monk had said. They venerated him as a holy man and eagerly urged their intercessions <on him>.

240. Mioni 9

Abba Irenaeus said to the brothers:
Let us fight diligently and be patient in our warfare, for we are soldiers of the heavenly king. And as the soldiers of an earthly king <wear> helmets, so we have heavenly gifts <χαρίσματα>—the beautiful virtues. They have breast-plates of chain-mail and we have the spiritual breast-plate forged with the bronze of faith. They have a spear: we have the cross. They have a shield: we have our hope in God. They have the oblong shield: we have God. In war they shed blood whereas we surrender our <right to> choose. That is why the heavenly king conceded that the demons should do battle with us—that we not forget his benefits. Many men, in their slackness, do not pray at all; or, if they pray, do not pray continuously but <are> wandering in their thoughts. They will be found to be no better than those who do not pray at all. For how shall they be heard who speak to God with their lips while they are reckoned to be of the world in their hearts? When we are afflicted, *then* we soberly give ourselves to prayer (for <otherwise> we often sing with our lips but not with our attention), sending up the eye of our heart as we pray to God, speaking to him with sighs. So now, brothers, let us imitate the soldiers of the mortal king and fight with zeal, or rather <imitate> the Three Children <Dan 13> and tread down the furnace of passions by purity. Let us quench the coals of temptation by prayer. Let us put the imaginary Nebuchadnezzar (the devil) to shame, setting forth our bodies as a living sacrifice to God and offering a religious mind as a burnt sacrifice.

241. Mioni 10

A brother asked an elder saying: 'What shall I do, abba, if, when I see a person sinning, I hate him? Or, if I hear of a careless brother, I judge him—and lose my own soul?' The elder said: 'When you hear any such thing, quickly get yourself away from such thoughts and run towards the remembrance of that fearful day. See in your mind's eye the terrible judgement-seat, the impartial judge, the rivers of fire, those who are being judged before the tribunal and most vehemently scalded in the fire; those impaled on swords, the relentless punishments, the chastisement which knows no end, the moonless night, the outer darkness, the worm which shoots arrows, the unbreakable fetters, the gnashing of teeth, the wailing which cannot be comforted. Think, then, of these things, and of the inescapable condemnations. That judge will take no account either of accusers or of witnesses, of arguments or of affidavits, but only of what was actually done. Let him come into the midst of and before the eyes of all who have fallen into error; then no man who has done business and reduced the price somewhat <will find favour>, not a father or a son or a daughter, a mother or any other relative; not a neighbour or a friend or an acquaintance; not the giving of money or the abundance of wealth or authority, for all these are swept away as dust from the feet. Only he who is being judged will pay the price for what was done by him <and receive> the vote which sets him free or condemns him. Nobody will be judged for what another did wrong, but <only> on his own faults. Knowing this, child, condemn no man and you will be untroubled, in fear of no dread.'

242. Mioni 11 *BHG* 2102d

Abba Peter, the disciple of Abba Isaiah told us:

Once when I was at Abba Macarios' with my father, Abba Isaiah, some people came from the eighteenth mile-stone out of Alexandria. With them they had a consecrated virgin/widow <κανονική> fearfully possessed by a devil. They begged the elder to have pity and cure her, for the nun <μονάστρια> was violently devouring her own flesh. When the elder saw her so terribly afflicted and pulling her own flesh to pieces, he made the sign of the cross and reproached the demon. The demon replied to the elder: 'I will not come out of her; for it was unwillingly and against my own wishes that I went into her. It was your colleague and ally, Daniel, who interceded with God and sent me into her'. The elder said: 'By what means did you enter into her'? He said: 'She was my instrument. I taught her to go often to the baths, shamelessly and unblushingly adorned. I shot and wounded many with her <looks>—and her with theirs, ensnaring not only worldlings, but clerics too, and I titillated them, <inciting them> to shameful intercourse with her. By <their> assent to shameful thoughts and by what they saw with their eyes at night (for I made it all visible to them) I trapped them into ejaculation. Now it so happened that the hoary old glutton, Daniel, met her as she was washing at the bath and going back to her cell. He heaved a sigh to God and prayed for her to be sent a correction—for her own salvation, and for the other nuns who lived soberly, that they might be completely enclosed. It was on account of this that I dwelt in her. When the elder heard this, he said: 'He who handed over can redeem', and the elder sent them to Abba Daniel.

243. Mioni 12 *BHG* 1076k

There was a Jew at Constantinople, a glass-blower by trade, who had a wife and a son. He sent the son to school to learn letters, near to the Great Church. Now it often happened that the sacristan of Saint Sophia had a great deal left over from the holy table, and he despatched persons to the schoolmaster <asking> for children to be sent to consume what was superfluous from the holy eucharist. This they were accustomed to do. Now, when the children came, the Jewish boy followed too and, whilst they were there, the schoolmaster dismissed the other children. It was dinner time. The Jewish glass-worker also left his workshop and went to his house at the dismissal <-time, τῇ ὥρα τῶν μισσῶν>. When he failed to find his son there, he said to his wife: 'Where is the child?' When she realised that he had not yet appeared, she began to speak to the neighbours. Then, when the child came, she said: 'What has kept you, child?' He said: 'I went to the Great Church with the other children and we ate and drank very well there'. When his father heard this, he was very angry, but he kept his silence for the time being. Then, after dinner, he took the child to the workshop and learned from him more precisely <what had happened>, and that he said he had eaten the communion in the church. Then the father laid violent hands on the child and threw him into the furnace, shut it up and left the shop. He went away and found some shade, for it was midday. Now, moved by God and knowing how angry the child's father was with him, the mother came to the workshop. She looked in through the opening in the door and heard the child's voice inside the furnace. She broke open the door, went in and found her son in the fire. She opened <it> up and cast him out of the furnace. Then she said to him: 'Who put you in the furnace, child?' He said: 'My father'. Then she said to him: 'But how is it that you did not burn in the fire of the furnace, child?' He said: 'A woman dressed in purple came to me and gave me water and told me not to be afraid'. Greatly perturbed, <the mother> took him and went to the patriarch, the most holy Menas, and told him what had happened, asking that she and her child might become Christians. When the patriarch heard this, he was amazed. He took the woman and the child to the most dear<-to-God> and Christ-loving Emperor, Justinian, and told him this extraordinary wonder. The most dear-to-God emperor ordered the Jew, the father of the child, to give himself up and urged him to become a Christian. When he would not be persuaded, he commanded him to be put in the furnace, saying: '<This is> because he put his son in the furnace'. He commanded the woman to become a nun—<ἀσκήτρια> and the child to be a reader; the patriarch attended to this. And they all glorified God who performs great wonders for the salvation of the race of men; to whom be glory and power now and for ever and to the ages of ages. Amen.

NOTES

Currency:

The Later Empire, after the reforms of Diocletian (286-305) had a gold-based currency, the basic unit of which was the gold *nomisma* (also known as *solidus* and, later, as *bezant* in the west). In the translation the *nomisma* or its equivalent has been consistently rendered 'piece of gold'. The *nomisma* was 4.55 grams of pure gold.

For the calculation of large sums, the hypothetical *litra* (pound) of gold was used. This was seventy-two *nomismata* or pieces of gold, 327.6 grams.

The pound was divided into a thousand *miliarisia* (see c. 185).

The *nomisma* knew a number of sub-divisions: the half-piece *(sêmision)* and the one-third-piece *(trimêsion)* (see c. 234, Mioni 3).

One *nomisma* = twenty four *keratia* (thus 1728 *keratia* to the pound of gold).

One *keration* = twelve *pholleis, noummai, lepta, obols* or *pholera,* here translated 'coppers' or 'copper coins'.

Mention is also made a gold *denarius,* also called *kentênarion* (c. 195), obviously from the Latin *centenarium,* a hundred of something, but what? In the context a hundred *nomismata* would appear excessive, but a hundred *keratia* (just over four pieces of gold) would seem not unreasonable.

Some clues are given concerning the cost of things, but they may be misleading. For instance: in c. 134 three pieces of gold is the price for the entire New Testament written on fine skins *(i.e.* vellum or parchment as opposed to papyrus) whilst the daily wages of a labourer is five coppers. The proportions might be correct (the book representing well over half a year's labourer's earnings) but the sums seems very low. Note that in c. 192 a monk (at Rome) receives three pieces of gold to buy shirts while in the following story (c. 193) the Pope of Alexandria gives away fifty pounds of gold to one man, that is over 16kg! Probably nearer the mark are stories such as c. 107 where three gold pieces buys an ass, or c. 112 where twenty four gold pieces cannot be found to ransom three sick monks: only eight—yet in c. 34 the Patriarch of Antioch ransomes a *notarios* (an educated cleric) for eighty-five pieces of gold. It may of course be that John (and Sophronios) in their quest for the monastic virtue of *aktêmosunê,* indifference to worldly goods, simply did not take money very seriously and that John did no more than set down any sum which came to mind. At all events, there seems to be little consistency in the prices and costs mentioned. The reader may simply have to translate them into 'a large sum' or 'a trifling amount', as the case may be.

In the following notes, R signifies Rouët de Journel who translated the *Pratum* into French, and Chitty refers to Derwas J. Chitty, *The Desert a City,* as referenced in the Bibliography.

c. 1

The Monastery of Abba Eustorgius: founded by Eustorgios in the middle of the fifth century (prior to 466) near Jerusalem; the exact location is unknown, but it appears to have been on Mount Sion (Chitty pp. 93-94).

The Archbishop (apparently Elijah, 494-513) clearly assumed the responsibility of appointing the higoumen of this monastery.

'his own disciple': in the east one enters monasticism not by a novitiate as in the west, but by an apprenticeship to an experienced elder. The apprentice owes his master full obedience; hence, 'whither thou goest, I shall go'.

crossing the Jordan: *i.e.,* from west to east, into the desert.

Sapsas: a monastery was founded at this location when Elijah was patriarch of Jerusalem (494-516).

Wadi Chorath: the 'Brook Cherish' of 1/3 K 17:3. This is not the only location at which Elijah was thought to have been fed by ravens.

c. 3

Saint Sabas, (The Great Lavra of) was the most famous of the Palestinian monasteries. It is located in the Cedron valley and was founded in 478 by Sabas. At the height of its fame it contained over one hundred and fifty anchorites. It seems not to have been so much a community *(koinobion/coenobium)* as a lavra, that is, an assembly of independent ascetics living largely apart from each other but obviously with some central organisation to provide the weekend services for which the elders assembled. It still exists, and is known today as Mar-Saba.

Penthoucla was a monastery located a little to the west of the Jordan of which very little is known (see cc. 13 and 14 below). Its proximity to the Jordan is indicated by its popularity as a place of baptism.

Archbishop Peter(of Jerusalem) 524-55, would not break with tradition by allowing a 'deacon-woman' (lit) to perform the sacrament.

Sheepskin: *mêlôtê,* but here *mêlôtarion,* is the sheepskin or goatskin, hence a rough, hairy cloak worn by monks; see *Life of Anthony* c. 91 *(PG* 26:972B,) and Lampe, *s.v.* for further references. It is the cloak of the stranger-pilgrim (1 P 2:11).

c. 4
The *koinobion* founded by Saint Theodosius (d. 529) after 478 (Chitty pg. 100, n. 103) and bearing his name was between Bethlehem and Saint Sabas at a conspicuous hilltop now known as Deir-Dosi in the Wilderness of Judaea. In the time of its founder this community numbered around four hundred monks. It was famous for its hospitality and the care of those in need. It became the largest and the most highly organised of the Judaean communities (see Chitty, pp. 108-109). This was almost certainly John Moschos' own home monastery.

The New Lavra was originally founded (in the Valley of Tecoah) by Abba Romanos, but it was destroyed in 484 and then refounded by sixty monks expelled from Saint Sabas in 508. Its complex history is fully explained by Chitty.

Compare the ending of this story with the ending of c. 10.

c. 5
The Lavra of the Towers *(Pyrgia,* translated 'Turrets' by Chitty) was founded by James, a monk of Saint Sabas, at the beginning of the sixth century, west of Jordan and not far from Jericho. Cf. cc. 6-10, 100. It certainly seems to have consisted of towers (c. 10) perhaps indicating that the location was liable to attack at one time.

not keeping himself up to the mark: lit., 'failing to take care of himself <spiritually,>' ἀμελῶν ἑαυτοῦ.

Sunday duties: monks, whether resident in the lavra or in secluded hermitages were expected to assemble on the Lord's Day for common prayer, the holy eucharist and (usually) a meal.

c. 6

The Monastery of Saint Mary at Jerusalem was founded by Justinian the Great (527-565). It was named after the near-by church of the Mother of God (sometimes called Saint Mary the New) begun at the beginning of the sixth century but completed by Justinian and finally dedicated in 543.

The hospital at Jericho was run by men from Saint Sabas.

c. 7

Abba Anthony = Saint Anthony the Great *(ca* 251-356) whose *Life* [*PG* 26:837-976], now generally accepted to be the work of Athanasius of Alexandria (*ca* 296-373), is a basic handbook of eremitic monachism. By 'the others' is meant Pachomios and the immediate disciples of Anthony.

c. 8

Eutychios (or Eustochios), Patriarch of Jerusalem 552-563/4.

c. 9

poverty: lit., 'he was very without-possessions', *poly aktêmôn.* The ability to detach oneself from earthly possessions, indeed from all material concerns, was one of the great monastic virtues *(aktêmosynê;)* see chapter six of 'Pelagius and John' (the 'systematic' collection of apophthegmata).

c. 11

Saint Gerasimos was born in Lycia, went to Jerusalem in 451 and took up residence in the stony desert by the Dead Sea. He later founded the lavra which bears his name one mile from the Jordan (see c. 107). There were seventy cells. This monastery was destroyed in the twelfth century at which time the remaining monks went to the monastery of Calamôn ('the reed-bed') in the Jordan valley (see c. 26).

'Struck the wood'; to this day eastern monks are often summoned to prayer by the beating of a piece of wood *(sêmantron)* although at an increasing number of monasteries the western practice of ringing bells has been partly adopted.

'Take your rest'; the line recalls Mk. 14:41, 'Sleep on now and take your rest.' A very similar charge is given ('rest on now') in two stories in the *Alphabetikon,* Macarios 7 and Milesios 1 in which the dead are made to speak. Compare also the *Life of Saint Marcian the Oeconomos,* cc. 13 and 15 and c. 234 below (Mioni 3).

the stones: see Jos 4. 'Lapides illos quos levaverunt filii Israel de Jordane positi sunt non longe a civitate Hiericho in basilica post altarium magni valde', Antoninus (*anno* 578) in *Itinera Hierosolymitana,* ed. Geyer (*CSEL* 38) pg. 168, 16-18.

c. 12
'say something to him', (lit. 'give him a word, or saying', *i.e.* he was asking for an apophthegm) *eipon moi rhêma:* it is the frequently repeated invitation to an elder to utter a word of wisdom (often preceded by a long period of silence). *cf.* cc. 52, 69.

'a stranger': it is a constant teaching of eremitic monachism that 'we have here no abiding city' (Heb 13:14) but are 'strangers and pilgrims' (1 P 1:1; 2:11) in a foreign land.

c. 13
The frequent use of additional words to translate the reply of Abba Mark clearly illustrates the elders' extremely laconic way of speaking. Economy of words was counted a great virtue.

c. 15

'The holy place of the Bites' *(tôn Bitôn):* not yet identified. The text may be corrupt, for the Latin has *Betamarim,* also unidentified. Could it mean Bittir (formerly Bethar?) But then why 'holy'?

c. 16

The lavra of Abba Peter was founded in the fifth century.

Raïthoun on the Gulf of Suez, now Tor, not far from Sinaï.

perform a service, *diakonia:* not a religious service but rather as craftsmen or workers.

Thebaïd: a very long journey across the desert from the Gulf of Suez to the Nile and beyond.

easy going: *rhathumos* (Fra Ambrogio: *negligens est ac desidiosus;)* one who is careless of his own soul's health (cf. c. 5).

hospitable: I have followed the tradition of former translators in this rendering of *xeniteia* but (see Lampe, *s.v)* it probably should be interpreted to mean the virtue of *being* a stranger *(xenos)* rather than of entertaining one *(cf.* note on c. 12,) *i.e.,* in the sense of *peregrinatio.* Thus: 'Let us give to him for the extent to which he estranged himself from the world.'

we reached civilisation: a striking demonstration of the monastic antithesis of the wilderness *(erêmos)* and the inhabited land *(oikoumenê)* which underlies all monastic teaching.

c. 18

in his cloak: *palion, pallium:* originally any cloak, but increasingly an ecclesiastical habit, then a vestment *i.e.,* the eastern equivalent of the chasuble, *phelonion)* and finally the *omophorion pallium* of the modern bishop.

c. 19

the grass eater (or 'grazer') *ho boskos:* the word designates a well-recognised category of ascetics. Thus those of Mesopotamia: 'When they first entered upon the philosophic [*i.e.,* monastic] career they were denominated grazers *[boskoi]* because they had no houses, ate neither bread nor meat and drank no wine, but dwelt constantly on the mountains and passed their time in praising God by prayers and hymns according to the law of the church. At the usual hours of meals they each took a sickle and went to the mountain to cut some grass on the mountains as though they were flocks in pasture and this served for their repast. Such was their course of philosophy [*i.e.,* asceticism;'] Sozomen, *Historia Ecclesiastica* 6.33.2. Evagrios (*HE* 1:21) mentions *boskoi* in Palestine. Lampe gives other examples *s.v.* One would like to assume that the grass was cooked a little, but this is not said. *Boskoi* are frequently mentioned by John; see cc. 21, 84, 96, 92, 115, 129 part 2, 154, 159, 167, etc.

Macarios was patriarch of Jerusalem briefly in 552 and again 563/4—*ca* 575.

lewd thoughts: *logismoi,* literally 'thinkings', but the word is used often enough to leave the meaning unmistakable.

c. 20

standard bearer, *drakônari(o)s,* lat. *draconarius,* 'bearer of the dragon-standard.'

Thecla, the companion of Saint Paul, was martyred at Leucia in Isauria in the first century. To her are attributed many wondrous deliverences. See art. *s.v.* in *ODCC.*

lead a life of solitude: *hêsuchazô,* lit. 'lead a life of silence', but as the one is largely dependent on the other, the word tends to mean both solitude and silence—which makes it difficult to translate. Whenever possible the context has guided the translator in his choice of terms.

Kopratha: a lavra in the Jordan area but it is not known exactly where.

c. 21
The Monastery of Saint Euthymios was founded in the fifth century and lasted until the twelfth. Its ruins can still be seen at Khan el Amar, between Jerusalem and the Dead Sea.

c. 22
archimandrite: lit., 'the ruler of a [sheep-] fold.' The term was originally (fourth century) interchangeable with *higoumen,* but by the sixth century it meant 'one charged with several monasteries', and there were two in Palestine: one for communities *(koinobia)* and one for anchorites.

c. 23
a former soldier, *apo stratiôtôn:* 'a former officer' might be a better translation.

lying down: the Greek says 'on his side' *(epi pleuron)* but given the importance laid on not lying down to sleep, this would seem to be the meaning.

c. 24
The Lavra of Choziba is a fifth-century foundation, devastated in 614 by the Persians but rebuilt and still functioning to this day. It is in the Wadi-el-Qelt (the only stream in the area which never completely dries up,) north of the road from Jerusalem to Jericho.

See Chitty, pp. 150-152 for description. In c. 25 it is called the *koinobion* (community) of Choziba. A member of that community is called *Chozibite.*

c. 25

'the words used ...', *hê proskimidê tês hagias anaphoras:* the phrase is difficult to translate. It obviously *means* 'the words of the eucharistic liturgy which brought about the transformation of the bread and wine', but which words are intended? The western answer to this might well be the 'words of institution'; contemporary orthodox would say the *epiklêsis,* the prayer to the Holy Ghost to consecrate. In the seventh century it more likely meant the entire prayer which would have been called 'the canon of the mass' in the west, *i.e.,* the holy *anaphora.* The story implies that it was not only priests who could consecrate the eucharist. There is a tale (W931, Garitte 13) of a deacon who did.

'in the holy sanctuary' could equally mean 'on the holy altar.'

'the coming of the Holy Spirit', *epiphoitêsis;* see cc. 27a and 150. There is a story of how at Scêtê the clergy (only) customarily saw the descent of the Sprit like an eagle, but once the sign was not seen. The priest asked a certain deacon to withdraw and the sign reappeared (Nau 68). The story is a little different in the Pseudo-Amphilochian *Vita Basilii;* there a golden dove suspended over the altar (and containing the reserved sacrament) would usually move at the *epiphoitêsis,* but once failed to do so because one of the deacons was looking at a woman (*BHG* 251). In the same collection there is the story of a chaste priest at whose eucharist fire was said to descend at the elevation *(BHG* 254).

'The elder laid down a rule ....' rarely is the argument from silence of any value, yet here the fact that there is no reference to a *silent* recitation of the prayer is almost certain indication that it was not yet said silently (as it later came to be).

c. 26
Dara: probably Dara in Mesopotamia (a heavily fortified roman border-post in the wars with Persia,) but possibly the remote town of the same name on the Euxine coast of Pontus. Two other towns of this name are known to have existed, one in Greece and one in Phoenicia.

lewd thoughts: see most recently on *porneia* and the desert fathers chs. 11 and 12 in Peter Brown, *The Body and Society: Men, Women and Sexual Renunciation in Early Christianity* (Princeton, 1988).

Nestorians: followers of Nestorios who taught that in Christ there were two persons, one human, one divine. Hence he objected to calling Mary 'Mother of God' *(theotokos).* Nestorianism was centered at Ctesiphon on the Tigris and flourished outside, rather than within the Empire.

Theodore [of Mopsuestia,] Eutyches etc.: a list of the better-known persons suspected of heresy.

c. 29
Severus was the monophysite patriarch of Antioch who had persuaded the Emperor Anastasios to desist from persecuting those who had not accepted the definition of the Council of Chalcedon in 451, *i.e.,* the monophysites. His deposition by Justin I in 518 led to a schism which carried his name. C. 48 suggests that he also bore the name *Akephalos,* 'the headless'.

c. 33
The text is confusing for *Theoupolis* is used sometimes to mean Jerusalem (as in Ps 45:5 etc.,) sometimes to mean Antioch. The

second is not incorrect as Justinian the Great conferred the title upon Antioch early in his reign (Theophanes p. 178, 5-7) possibly in response to a recently discovered prophecy (Malalas p. 443, 16—p. 444, 4). In cc. 33 and 34 Antioch is clearly intended for the patriarchal lists of that city include a Theodotos (d. *ca.* 428) and an Alexander (d. 424).

c. 36
Ephraim was patriarch 527-545 (see note to c. 37).

Akephalites: ('having no head or leader';) a strict monophysite *(i.e.,* Severan, see note to c. 29) sect originating in Alexandria in the mid fifth century. See Gibbon, *Decline and Fall;* ed. Bury, vol. 5, note on p. 141.

apostolic throne: meaning Antioch, *cf* Theophanes p. 416, 7: 'the throne of Theoupolis.'

omophorion: a long scarf, formerly of wool, embroidered with crosses, which an eastern bishop wears about his shoulders *(cf* the western *pallium,* not to be confused with the eastern *pallion).*

c. 37
The Holy City (in the title) would normally mean Jerusalem, but it is clear from what follows that the story is located in Antioch-Theoupolis. Ephraim, Count of the East, did indeed become Patriarch of Antioch and a strong defender of the Chalcedonian orthodoxy against the monophysite (Severan) heresy (Theophanes p. 173, 21 *et passim).*

'but you add what you can by way of almsgiving'; the meaning is less than clear here and the sequence of thought somewhat deranged. A lacuna is suspected.

c. 39

There is a 'doublet' of this story at c. 205, probably an earlier (simpler) version of this one.

c. 40

The Monastery of the Byzantines was at Jerusalem, on the Mount of Olives; it was an early-sixth century foundation.

Theoupolis=Antioch, of which Gregory was patriarch 569-584.

two swords: Lk 22:38. The Lord replies: *hikanon estin,* 'it is enough/adequate' or 'it suffices.' *cf* Abba Theophilos' explanation.

c. 41

Anazarbos (Navarza today) is in Cilicia.

solitary life: *hêsychazôn:* this word and its cognates signify the truly solitary or anchoritic life as opposed to the communal life of brotherhoods. Strictly speaking the root indicates only silence (as it would for *hesychastic* movement but it was used in a more general sense of solitude in the early christian centuries.

c. 42

Readers are reminded that there is a general comment on money and currency at the beginning of these notes, page 231.

the fellow-monk, *sygkellos, i.e.,* one who occupied a neighbouring cell. The next phrase makes little sense when we have just read that he died in the patriarchal hospital. Perhaps the reading should be 'leaving them both he *struggled to be made perfect* in the desert.'

c. 44

Antinoë (Antinoöpolis), a city founded by the Emperor Hadrian to mark the spot on the Nile where his beloved Antinoüs died in 130 AD.

c. 45

'wicked old man' *(kakogêre)* lit. 'bad elder', but definitely pejorative, which the word 'elder' is not.

c. 48

Severus Akephalos: see notes on cc. 29, 36.

c. 52

three virtues: *aktêmosunê, praotês, egkrateia.*

c. 53

—echoes Cyril of Scythopolis' *Life of Saba* c. 26.

c. 54

discernment: *diakrisis,* the ability to perceive what is in the hearts of men, discernment. But it can also mean doubt or hesitation; *cf* c. 55.

c. 55

a book of sayings *(biblion gerontikon,)* possibly a collection of apophthegmata or a collection similar to Moschos, *The Lausiac History* perhaps or *The History of the Monks in Egypt.*

The Cells *(Kellia)* was a well-known collection of cells in the Nitrian Desert, not far from Scêtê. See Chitty, pp. 29-33.

c. 56

God performed many signs, *sêmeia,* the word used for the great Dominical miracles in the Fourth Gospel.

'but also after his death:' *i.e.,* his relics also had healing power.

c. 57
This is not the famous Symeon Stylites (d. 459) whose pillar was in Syria, but one of the many who mounted a pillar *(stylos)* in imitation of his example.

This story is something of a *topos; e.g.,* in *The Life of Saint Paul the Less of Latros,* ed. Hippolyte Delehaye, *Analecta Bollandiana* 11 (1892) 19-74 & 136-181, at the moment at which the saint died, far away in Constantinople (says the hagiographer, c. 44,) a monk named Photeinos—who was living there—heard angels in the air, singing in a most unusual way. He immediately took himself off to Paul, the Bishop of Monembasia, who happened to be there at the capital. 'Quick' Photeinos cried to him, 'get your thurible and start offering incense.' ('Yes' the writer adds, a little scandalised it would seem; 'he spoke to the bishop like *that!')* The bishop naturally wanted to know what this was all about. 'I have just seen Paul of Latros being carried to heaven by angels' was Photeinos' reply.

c. 61
New Church: see note to c. 6.

c. 66
'In black-face' is a literal translation of the Greek *aithopes* (whence Ethiopians), the most common way of describing demons and devils in early monastic and hagiographical literature.

c. 70
This recluse is called Addas in the Latin title (which does indeed sound Mesopotamian) but Adolas in the Greek text. As the second is very close to a Greek expression meaning 'without guile', we can suspect a play on words. Fra Ambrogio's reading is probably to be preferred here.

c. 77

Pope Eulogios: Patriarch of Alexandria 581-608. In John Moschos' time (and for many year afterwards) the words 'pope' and 'patriarch' were frequently used interchangeably.

prodigal: *asôtos,* 'not to be saved', the same word used in the Parable of the Prodigal Son (Lk 15). An allusion is obviously intended.

c. 78

Since this is the only known reference to the Monastery of the Giants, it is impossible to say whether Theoupolis is here meant to designate Antioch or Jerusalem.

[...] Readers are reminded that square brackets indicate passages found in the Latin text of Fra Ambroggio, but not in the Greek of Migne. <...> indicate words supplied by the translator.

penances *(epitimia:)* this word does not have exactly the same significance as the western *penance,* as the context shows.

c. 79

The word translated 'species' means, literally, 'communions' and a number of words are used to distinguish them. From the context it is clear that this was not reservation in *both* kinds, but rather of portions of the one kind (which might however have been intincted and then toasted after the modern Greek method).

c. 92

Even today monastic ovens in the east are huge round constructions, sometimes large enough for two or more men to climb into.

c. 96

This is a difficult passage, important for linguistic purposes as it uses the two terms *proskomidê* and *anaphora* interchangeably for the eucharist. It would appear that Abba Julian is contemplating withdrawal from his monastery as a protest, thinking perhaps that all clergy are schismatics and all monks tainted with *porneia.* Symeon (the Stylite, d. 459), holds up the example of Patrick not only to show Julian that all is not bad, but also to give an example of how the prayer of one just person can prevail for many. In this passage Antioch, as often, is referred to as *Theoupolis,* the City of God.

c. 98

'my spiritual duties', *ton kanona mou. kanôn* in a notoriously difficult word to translate. The Latin translator put: 'whilst I am performing the work of God *(opus Dei)* or singing psalms at the appointed hours', thus assuming it to mean a *monastic* rule, but *kanôn* can just as well mean a *personal* rule of life.

c. 99

(cf Cyril of Scytholpolis, *The Life of Sabas,* c. 14)

Coutila: the 'utter desert', towards the Dead Sea, the region of Qumrân.

c. 100

Saint Menas: the town and sanctuary of this name lay half way between Alexandria and Wadi Natroun, in the Desert of Mareotis (Chitty p. 147). This was a popular place for pilgrims to visit; an overnight journey with donkeys or mules would bring one there from Alexandria.

c. 101

The Abba is named Pardos in the Latin translation, but Paul in the Greek text. Presumably the former is his pre-monastic name; *cf* Paul of Monembasia's Tale 2 *(BHG* 1449c) where a Pardos becomes Peter on being made a monk.

c. 102

The commencement of this passage is somewhat controversial, and of considerable importance for dating the lives of John and Sophronios. The Greek *could* mean: 'When Sophronios was about to die', (literally: 'was about to be perfected',) but it is more likely to mean *perfected* in the sense of completing his commitment to the monastic profession. This is convincingly argued by Henry Chadwick in 'John Moschus and his friend Sophronius the Sophist', *Journal of Theological Studies* N.S. 24/1 (1974) 41-74; see especially p. 57 and note 1.

c. 105

Holy Sepulchre: in Greek, always 'Holy Resurrection' *(anastasis).*

c. 107

penultimate paragraph: the Greek text reads: 'The abba's disciple *and* Abba Sabbatios (omit "the Cilician") saw it.' There appears to have been a confusion between *kai* and *kilix* and the Latin to have preserved the better reading.

Chitty (p. 143) claims that this is the earliest version of the story of Gerasimos' lion, surely another 'monastic novel', and one which could have been much improved by reference to Cyril of Scythopolis' stories about lions.

c. 108

'the same city on Samos': reading *Samiôn* for *Sabiôn.*

c. 112
Tiberius: 578-582.

Nobody from Cappadocia ever reigned: is this a simple statement of fact, or a proverb?

Maziques: the invasions of these barbarians from Mauretania show that the stability of the Empire was already cracking at the beginning of Maurice's reign, since they were now able to terrorise the country around the Great Oasis, even if they hesitated to attack the town. C. 155 shows similar evidence in another area.

the recollection, the poverty...*hêsychia* is, strictly speaking, the keeping silent, *aktêmosunê* 'indifference to material possessions.'

c. 113
continence, *egkrateia,* yet another of the great monastic virtues. It means all forms of self-control; the domination of one's passions, whether for food (abstinence) or for the other pleasures of the flesh (continence). *(Cf* c. 130 and note.) It will readily be appreciated that there are no English words which precisely reproduce the meanings of these monastic virtues.

An interesting medical detail is recorded here: that a disorder of the spleen (?) might be treated with vinegar. Note also the brother who bled from all parts after being struck by a snake (c. 124) and the case of ophthalmia in c. 164.

c. 116
Messenia is in the south-west Peloponnese.

c. 118
It is hard today to understand how an eye falling out could signify forgiveness, but a sign was promised and expected; this was assumed to be it.

c. 120
Paran (or Pharan) is in the Sinaï Peninsular.

They wore habits... As the square brackets indicate, from here to the end of c. 122, the published Greek text has a lacuna. We follow the Latin text of Fra Ambroggio (see Translator's Note).

c. 125
Eulogia is a word of many meanings, ranging from the eucharistic species to any gift of alms. It seems to indicate a regular monastic dole of bread for John Moschos.

c. 127
syncellos: literally, one who occupied an adjacent cell; hence, the lieutenant of adjutant of a senior cleric.

This is one of the few passages in which *abbas* (with an 's') is used in the western sense of 'abbot', *i.e.,*=higoumen. See also c. 143.

Maurice, 590-602.

c. 130
self discipline and indifference to worldly goods: *egkrateia... aktêmosunê.*

c. 131
lawyer: *scholastikos,* according to Lampe: a graduate lawyer. But Rouët thought the older meaning of *un littré* was better here.

c. 133
a pagan Saracen: the Greek says: 'A Saracen who was a Hellene'. By the end of the sixth century, Hellene meant one who practiced a non-Judaeo-christian religion. *Cf.* c. 136: 'Are you a Christian or

an Hellene?' and c. 138, the man from the west whose parents were Hellenes and did not know whether he had been baptised or not.

c. 134
The opening passage [...] I have supplied to fill a suspected *lacuna.*

c. 135
The Monastery of the Eunuchs was originally founded (near Jericho) in 473, but in 528 it passed to the eunuchs of Julienne, the mother of Valentinian. It was at that time that it took the name of its new inhabitants (R).

c. 138
attendant *(diakonêtês):* it was by no means unusual for monks to have attendants (who might or might not themselves be monks) to take care of their physical needs and, in the case of solitaries, to communicate with others on their behalf.

c. 139
Gregory was patriarch of Antioch 569-584.

cc. 146, 147
both use the unusual term *koinobiarchês* (ceonobium-ruler) to denote the superior of the community.

c. 147
Flavian was the Patriarch of Constantinople (446-449) who excommunicated Eutyches and was virtually martyred for it. See H. Chadwick, "The Exile and Death of Flavian of Coonstantinople: a Prologue to the Council ofChalcedon," *JTS* NS 6 (1955), 17-34.

c. 149
This fear of ordinations is a frequent trait of monastic literature; *cf* Theodore of Phermê 25 (*PG* 65:193AB).

c. 150

This story is remarkably similar to an incident in the Pseudo-Amphilochian *Vita Basilii, BHG* 251, *de diacono ventilante.*

rhipidion: In the eastern liturgies, the deacons used to agitate ceremonial fans, originally (?) to keep insects away from the holy gifts. The fans can still be seen, often in the form of six-winged seraphim and cherubim, behind most orthodox altars and are still sometimes processed. A very similar story is to be found in the pseudo-Amphilochian *Vita Basilii.*

c. 156

Note that there are no names mentioned in this story (unless one assume John and Sophronios are the two philosophers, which seems somewhat unlikely). It is a story which ends with a memorable saying too; hence, it has the marks of a characteristic 'spiritually beneficial tale'.

c. 157

Soubiba: this appears to have been a region on the lower Jordan, and those who lived there to have been known as Soubibites (but there is doubt). Three monasteries are mentioned here; Besoi may well be another name for Thracians.

c. 158

Mardes: a lavra founded in 425 on a mountain in the Desert of Judah. On the summit of the same mountain was the Monastery of Castellium (see c. 167). The anchorites lived in caves but had coenobitic communities nearby (R).

c. 164

Eleousa (El-Khalasa today) was in the Desert of Beersheba. There was both a lavra and a bishop there, a suffragen of Petra (R).

c. 165

Who might this 'friend of Christ' be who tells the story? Note the end: 'I <John Moschos presumably> and John, priest of the Lavra of the Eunuchs, met this man', presumably the robber. In which case it is the converted robber himself who tells the tale.

c. 166

The Lavra of Abba Firminos was founded at the beginning of the sixth century in the gorge of the Wadi-es-Souenit which separates Djeba from Machmas. The monks there fell into 'Origenist' errors in the middle of the sixth century (R).

Dorotheos did not found this monastery; but he did retire to it and live there many years (R).

Maïouma is the port of Gaza. Jerome says that this area was the cradle of Palestinian monachism; Hilarion of Thavatha began solitary life there when he was fifteen years old, possibly *ca* 330. There was a monastery there by 444. See Chitty, pp. 13, 88.

c. 167

Castellium was built 492-493, on the ruins of the Herodian prison of Hyrcania. See Chitty, pp. 108-111 for a description.

c. 170

Sampson could be the Sapsas mentioned in cc. 1 and 2 above (R).

c. 176

The Greek and Latin texts have quite different beginnings.

Gregory the Theologian: see Gregory of Nazianzen, *Oratio* 39.

fellow with initiative: *philoponos,* strictly, one who likes hard work, an industrious fellow. An energetic, enthusiastic worker. It is stretching a point to translate 'with initiative', but as the story shows, that is what is meant.

Hypotyposes (literally, images or figures of speech). No work of this name by Clement of Alexandria *(ca* 150-215) is ever mentioned elsewhere, but Clement does speak of *hypotyposes* in Book Four of his most famous work, *Stromateis* ("Miscellaneous studies").

c. 177
Evagrios of Pontus, 349-399 is not universally reckoned to be a heretic. He was made deacon by Gregory of Nazianzus and became a respected preacher at Constantinople. But in 382 he withdrew to Nitria where he became a friend of Macarios the Egyptian. He was one of the first monks to undertake serious scholarship. His extensive writings (by which the ideas of Origen were diffused) greatly influenced a number of later writers. Evagrios was several times condemned for his Origenist 'errors', hence the epithet *heretic* here.

c. 180
This story is told in the acts of the Seventh Oecumenical Council (Nicaea II), act. 5, but reading *Saraphas* for *Araphas.*

c. 188
The Old Lavra of Saint Chariton, or Souka, is to be distinguished from the New Lavra (c. 4) and the Great Lavra which was the Lavra of Saint Sabas (c. 3). The Old Lavra was founded by Saint Chariton in the mid-fourth century. It was fourteen stades from Tekoa and the ruins of it may still be seen (R); see Chitty pp. 14-15 *et passim.*

tavern-keeper, *kapêlos;* the word more commonly means 'tavern-keeper', but also 'swindler', which makes more sense in this context; an interesting comment on the reputation of tavern-keepers.

Great Church: at Constantinople, always Hagia Sophia.

c. 189

their honour, *eleutheria:* the prime meaning of the word is 'freedom', but the context suggests 'honour'; *cf* c. 188 where the elder says the brother 'has destroyed an honest woman, *eleutheria.*' *cf* note on c. 203.

c. 190

was connected with the civil authority, *ho kata ton dêmarchon,* as Lamp corrects *zêmarchon:* this phrase does not appear in the Latin text and its meaning is less than clear.

c. 192

Anastasios of Sinaï's tale, No. 57.

c. 197

This story is found in the Book 14 of the *Ecclesiastical History* of Rufinus (d. 410), *PL* 21:486B-488A.

he summoned the parents: two different versions of the same story (which exists in many forms) seem to have been conflated here.

Ps 2:2 the kings of the earth etc: an oblique reference.

c. 203

the good man, *ton eleutheron:* the honest, generous, man of integrity etc., more usual of a woman *cf* cc. 188, 189.

c. 211

the vessels: τὰ σκεύη, *ta skeuê* (see also c. 212). This word in fact covers all the things used by a cleric in worship and administering the sacraments, vessels, vestments, books, and all, usually called 'sacred equipment' *(ta hiera skeuê),* an expression found in Thucidides 2.13 to mean sacred vessels and implements.

c. 212
The apophthegm in question is in the *Systematikon,* 'Pelagius and John' 16,13, Nau 337, where the purse is not *hanging* but *hidden* in the cell, which makes a little more sense of this story.

c. 220
Readers are reminded that the following tales are not found in any of the published texts of John Moschos' work, but that many of them may very well be included in the definitive edition when it appears.

c. 227
The story of the Three Children, Shadrach, Meshach and Abednego (in Greek: Ananias, Azarias and Misael) in the burning fiery furnace (celebrated on 12 December in the Orthodox calendar) is in Dan 13.

c. 237
This story bears a remarkable likeness to the well-known episode of The Hermit (L'Hermite) almost at the end of Voltaire's *conte philosophique, Zadig ou la destinée.* As the commentators on Voltaire point out, the origins of this episode are to be sought in the Talmud and so, presumably, are those of the present tale. This makes it of particular interest for, whilst Talmudic origins might well be suspected for several of the tales, in only two cases have these been definitely established. The other one is *BHG* 1322zk /1438p, W600, Nau 450: *de Hebraeo divite/de lapide pretiosa in veste Aaron, Systematikon* 5.48. A man at Jerusalem who had acquired great riches by unjust means, prompted by Prov 19:17, sold all and gave to the poor, thereby lending to God. But nobody helped him in *his* poverty. Until one day he had the good fortune to buy, very cheaply, a stone which a jeweller recognised as the

much sought-after gem which had fallen from Aaron's ephod. In return for it, the high priest generously awarded the man—and made him rich again. (George the Monk, *Chronicon,* ed. DeBoor, p. 216, 24-218, 8; *PG* 110:268-269).

LIST OF ABBREVIATIONS

A/B	*Alphabeticon* (see *Apophthegmata)*
AASS	*Acta Sanctorum*
Anal.Boll.	*Analecta Bollandiana*
BHG	*Bibliotheca Hagiographica Graeca*
CSCO	*Corpus Scriptorum Christianorum Orientalium*
HE	*Historia ecclesiastica*
HL	*Historia Lausiaca* (see *Palladios)*
HME	*Historia monachorum in Ægypto*
HR	*Historia religiosa [Φιλόθεος 'Ιστορία]* (see *Theodoret)*
N	Nau, F, "Histoires des solitaires"
PA VB	*The pseudo-Amphilochian Vita Basilii* (ed. Combefis, *q.v.)*
PMB	*Paul of Monembasia* (ed. Wortley, *q.v.)*
PE	*Paul Euergetinos*
Pl	*Plerophoriai of John of Maïouma, q.v.*
PS	*Pratum Spirituale, see Moschos, John*
R	*M.-J. Rouët de Journel*
SLNPNF	*A Select Library of Nicene and Post-Nicene Fathers,* ed. Henry Wace and Philip Schaff, 14 vols, 1890-1900 (also known as 'Wace and Schaff').
SCH	*Sources Chrétiennes*
Sys	*Systematicon* (see *Apophthegmata)*
Synax.CP	*Synaxarium Ecclesiae Constantinopolitanae*
W	Wortley, J., *A Répertoire of Byzantine "Beneficial Tales"*

BIBLIOGRAPHY

Anastasios the Sinaïte,'Le texte grec du moine Anastase sur les saints pères du Sinaï' [1-40 + appendix,], ed. F. Nau, *Oriens Christianus,* (1902) 58-89, and 'Le texte des récites utiles à l'âme d'Anastase (le Sinaïte)' [42-59] Paris, 1903.

_________. *Homily on Psalm vi. PG* 89:1105A-1109B (W863 and W955).

_________. *Homily on the Synaxis. PG* 89:849 (W868).

Apophthegmata Patrum, *collectio alphabetica* [*A/B]* J.-B. Cottelier's edition of the Greek text with Latin translation is in *PG* 65:71-440, supplemented by J.-C. Guy, *Recherches sur la Tradition grecque des apophthegmata patrum.* Brussels, 1962.

_________. French translation by Lucien Regnault, *Les Sentences des Pères du Désert, collection alphabétique.* Solesmes, 1981.

_________. English translation by Benedicta Ward, *The Sayings of the Desert Fathers,* Oxford and Kalamazoo, 1975.

Apophthegmata patrum, *collectio systematica [Sys]* the Greek text (as yet unpublished) is about to appear, ed. J.-C. Guy and Bernard Flusin, in *Sources Chrétiennes. interim,* see Nau.

_________. Latin translation of 'Pelagius and John' (6th-7th century) in *PL* 73:851-1052.

_________. French translation, Lucien Regnault, *Les Sentences des Pères du désert, série des anonymes.* Solesmes-Bellefontaine, 1985, and *Les sentences des pères du désert: nouveau receuil,* Solesmes, 1970.

Barlaam and Joasaph, trans. G.R. Woodward and H. Mattingly. London, 1914.

Basilii, the pseudo-Amphilochian *Vita;* ed. François Combefis, with Latin translation: *Sanctorum patrum Amphilochii Iconiensis, Methodii Patarensis et Andreae Cretensis opera omnia quaesupersunt.* Paris, 1644. Pp. 155-225.

Baynes, Horman H., 'The «Pratum Spirituale»', *Orientalia Christiana Periodica* 13 (1947) 404-414.

Bibliotheca Hagiographica Graeca; ed. François Halkin, third edition, Brussels 1957 *(Subsidia Hagiographica* No. 8a); and *Novum auctarium Bibliothecae Hagiographicae Graecae,* Brussels 1984 *(Subsidia Hagiographica* N° 65).

Chadwick, Henry, 'John Moschos and his friend Sophronios the Sophist', *JTS,* NS 25 (1974) 41-74.

Chitty, Derwas J., *The Desert a City.* Oxford 1966, rpt. Crestwood, New York 1977.

Daniel of Scêtê, 'Vie et récits de l'Abbé Daniel de Scété'; ed. Léon Clugnet, *Revue de l'Orient Chrétien,* 5 (1900) 49-73 and 370-391.

Dorotheos of Gaza, *Instructions* [Διδασκάλιαι διάφοραι]; ed. and trans. L. Regnault and J. de Preville. Paris, 1963.

Euergetinos, Paul, *A Collection of the Words and Sayings of the Fathers* (in Greek with modern Greek translation,) 4 vols., Athens, 1557-1966.

Evagrius, *Historia ecclesiastica;* ed. J. Bidez and L. Parmentier. London 1898, repr. Amsterdam, 1964.

_________. French translation by André-Jean Festugière OP, 'Evagre, *Histoire Ecclésiastique', Byzantion* 45 (1975) 187-488.

Follieri, Enrica, 'Dove e quando morì Giovanni Mosco?', *Rivista di Studi Bizantini e Neoellenici* NS 25 (1988) 3-39 (claims that John Moschos died at Rome after 11.xi 620 but before spring-summer 634).

Garitte, Gérard, '«Histoires édifiantes» Géorgiennes,' *Byzantion* 36 (1966) 396-423, and also *CSCO* 202/203 (Iberian 11/12), *Captivitas Heriosolymae,* cc. 20, 21.

Geerard, M., *Clavis Patrum Graecorum III.* Turnhout, 1979. Pp. 379-381.

George the Monk: Chronicon; ed. Charles de Boor, 2 vols. Stuttgart 1904.

Gregory the Great, *Dialogues;* ed. A. de Vogüé, with French translation by Paul Antin. Paris. *Sources Chrétiennes* 260, 265, 1979, 1980.

Guy, J.-C., *Recherches sur la tradition grecque des Apophtegmata Patrum,* Subsidia Hagiographica No. 36. Brussels, 1962.

Historia Monachorum in Ægypto, [HME]. Subsidia Hagiographica No. 53. ed. André-Jean Festugière OP Brussels, 1971.

_________. French translation by the same, *Les Moines d'Orient* IV/1: *Enquête sur les Moines d'Egypte.* Paris, 1964.

_________. English translation by Norman Russel, *The Lives of the Desert Fathers.* London, Kalamazoo, 1981.

John Climacus, Κλίμαξ τοῦ παραδείσου *[Scala Paradisi, The Ladder of Paradise]; PG* 88: 585-1248. English trans. by L. Moore. London 1959.

John Rufus, Bishop of Maïouma, *Plerophoriai, [Pl.];* ed. F. Nau, with French translation, *Patrologia Orientalis* 8:1-161.

Macarios the Egyptian, [pseudo-] Homilies; *PG* 34: 221-229.

Moschos, John *Pratum Spirituale;* ed. J.P. Migne (after Fronto Ducaeus and J.-B. Cotelier,) with the Latin translation of Ambrose Traversari ('Fra Ambroggio' 1346-1439, Florentine humanist); *PG* 87:2851-3112.

_________. French translation by M.-J. Rouët de Journel, *Le Pré Spirituel. (Sources Chrétiennes* 12). Paris 1946.

_________. Italian trans. by Riccardo Maisano, *Giovanni Mosco, Il Prato.* Naples, 1982.

Mioni, Elpidio: 'Il Pratum Spirituale di Giovanni Mosco: gli episodi inediti del Cod. Marciano greco II.21', *Orientalia Christiana Periodica* (1951) 61-94.

_________.'Jean Moschus, Moine', *Dictionnaire de Spiritualité* 7 (1973) colls. 632-640.

Nau, F. 'Histoires des solitaires égyptiens', *Revue de l'Orient chrétien* 12 (1907) through 18 (1913) *passim.* Greek text of the first four hundred tales found in Cod. Paris. Coislin 126. Also French trans. of tales 1-215.

Nissen, Th. 'Unbekannte Erzählungen aus dem Pratum Spirituale', *Byzantinische Zeitschrift* 38 (1938) 351-376.

Palladios, Bishop of Hellenopolis, *Historia Lausiaca, [HL];* ed. E.C. Butler, *The Lausiac History of Palladius II, Texts and Studies* VI.2 (Cambridge 1904) 3-169.

__________. English translation by W.K. Lowther Clarke, *The Lausiac History,* London 1918; *The Lausiac History,* and by R.T. Meyer, *Ancient Christian Writers* 36, Westminster, Maryland 1965.

Paramelle, Joseph and Bernard Flusin: 'De syncletica in deserto Iordanis, *BHG* 1318w', *Anal. Boll.* 100 (1982) 305-317.

Patlagean, Evelyn: 'L'histoire de la femme déguisée en moine et l'évolution de la sainteté feminine à Byzance', *Studi Medievalis.* III 17 (1976) 597-623.

Pattenden, Philip, 'The Text of the Pratum Spirituale', *JTS NS* 26 (1975) 38-54.

Poussines, Pierre. *Thesaurus asceticus sive syntagma opusculorum octodecim a graecis olim patribus de se ascetica scriptorum.* Paris 1684.

Radermacher, L. *Griechische Quellen zur Faustsage.* Vienna and Leipzig 1927.

Synaxarium Ecclesiae Constantinopolitanae; ed. Hippolyte Delehaye, Brussels 1902. *(Propylaeum ad Acta Sanctorum novembris).*

Theodoret, Bishop of Cyrrhus, Φιλόθεος Ἱστορία—*Historia religiosa Sources Chrétiennes* 234, 257.ed. and trans. Paul Canivet, Alice Leroy-Molinghen, *Histoire des moines de Syrie.* Paris, 1977, 1979.

Theophanes, *Chronographia;* ed. Charles de Boor, 2 vols. Leipzig, 1883, 1885.

Tobler, Titus and Augustus Moliner. *Itinera Hierosolymitana et descriptiones terrae sanctae bellis sacris anteriora.* Geneva 1879.

Wortley, John. *Les récits édifiants de Paul, évêque de Monembasie et d'autres auteurs,* Paris 1987.

__________. English translation (with notes and more tales). Forthcoming from Cistercian Publications.

INDEX OF NAMES, PLACES AND IMPORTANT EVENTS

SUBJECT INDEX

SCRIPTURAL INDEX

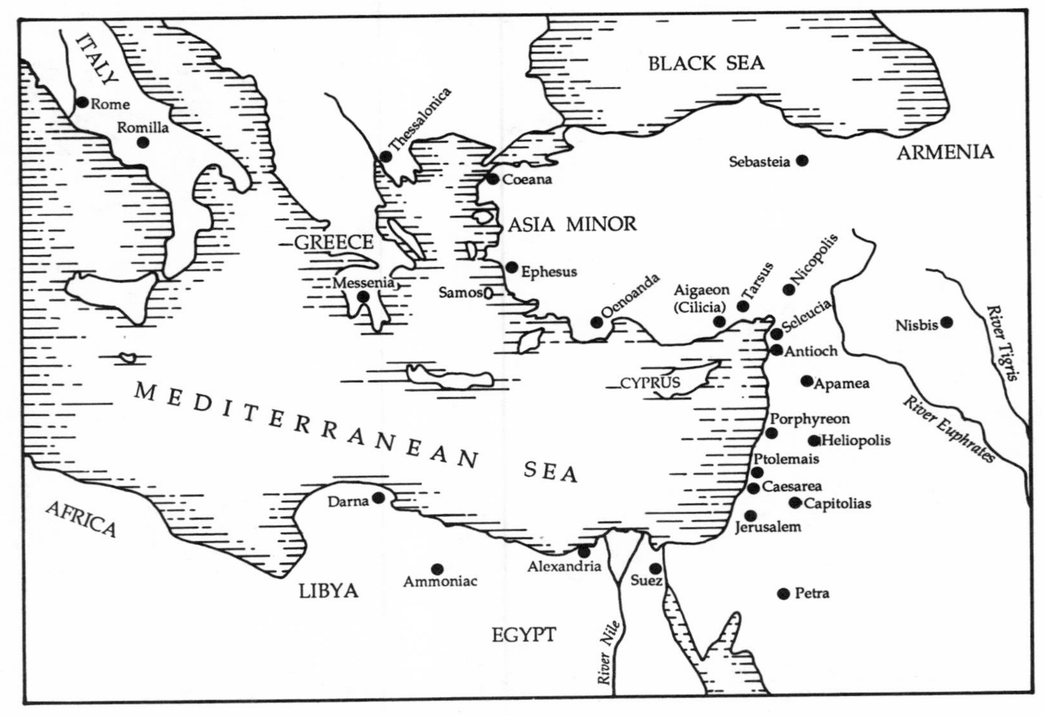
ITALY
Rome
Romilla
Thessalonica
BLACK SEA
Sebasteia
ARMENIA
Coeana
ASIA MINOR
GREECE
Ephesus
Messenia
Samos
Oenoanda
Aigaeon
(Cilicia)
Tarsus
Nicopolis
Seleucia
Antioch
Nisbis
River Tigris
Apamea
CYPRUS
MEDITERRANEAN SEA
Porphyreon
Heliopolis
River Euphrates
Ptolemais
Caesarea
Capitolias
Jerusalem
Darna
AFRICA
Alexandria
Suez
Ammoniac
LIBYA
Petra
EGYPT
River Nile

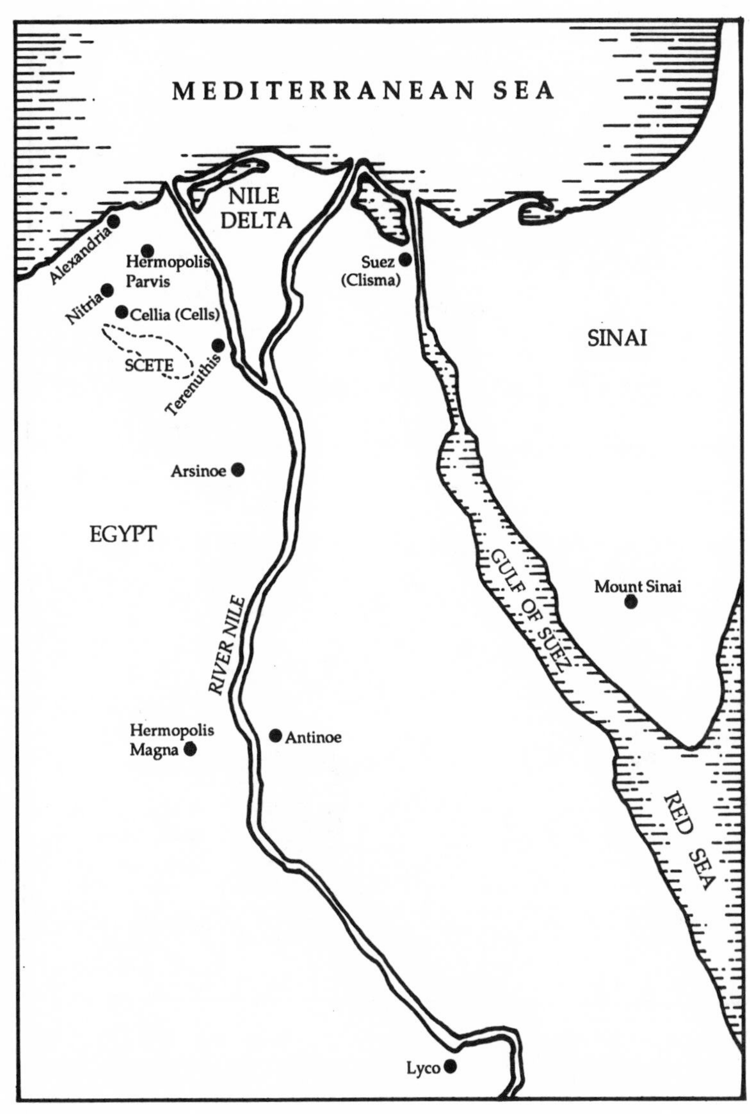
MEDITERRANEAN SEA
NILE DELTA
Alexandria
Hermopolis Parvis
Nitria
Cellia (Cells)
SCETE
Terenuthis
Suez (Clisma)
SINAI
Arsinoe
EGYPT
GULF OF SUEZ
Mount Sinai
RIVER NILE
Hermopolis Magna
Antinoe
RED SEA
Lyco

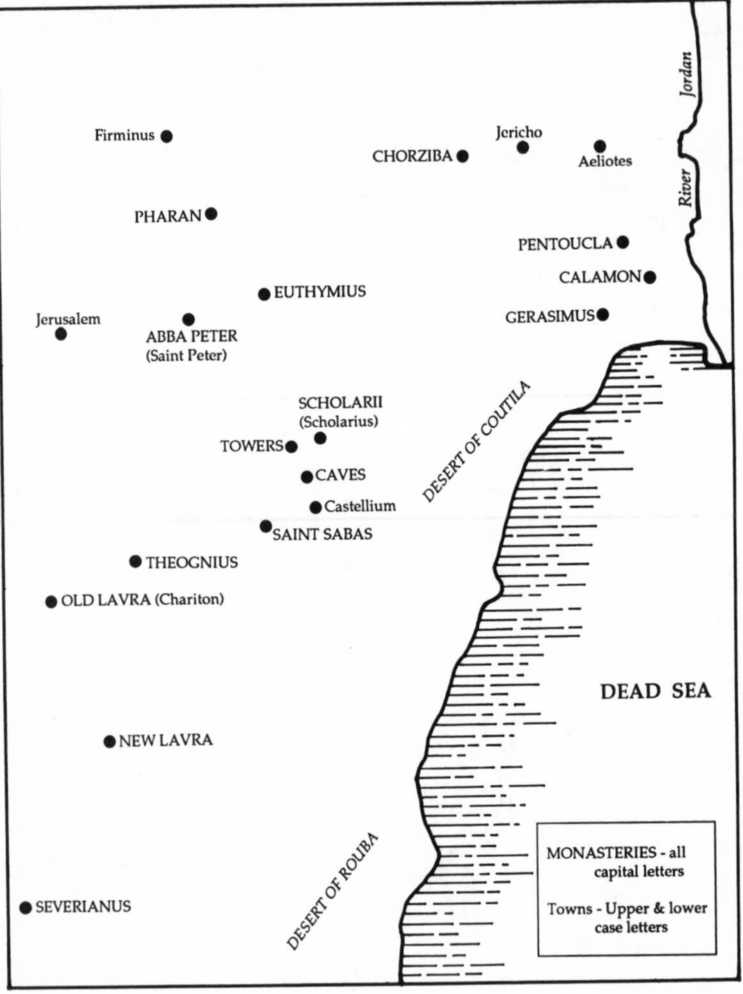

Jordan
River
Firminus
Jericho
CHORZIBA
Aeliotes
PHARAN
PENTOUCLA
CALAMON
EUTHYMIUS
GERASIMUS
Jerusalem
ABBA PETER
(Saint Peter)
SCHOLARII
(Scholarius)
DESERT OF COUTILA
TOWERS
CAVES
Castellium
SAINT SABAS
THEOGNIUS
OLD LAVRA (Chariton)
DEAD SEA
NEW LAVRA
MONASTERIES - all capital letters
Towns - Upper & lower case letters
DESERT OF ROUBA
SEVERIANUS

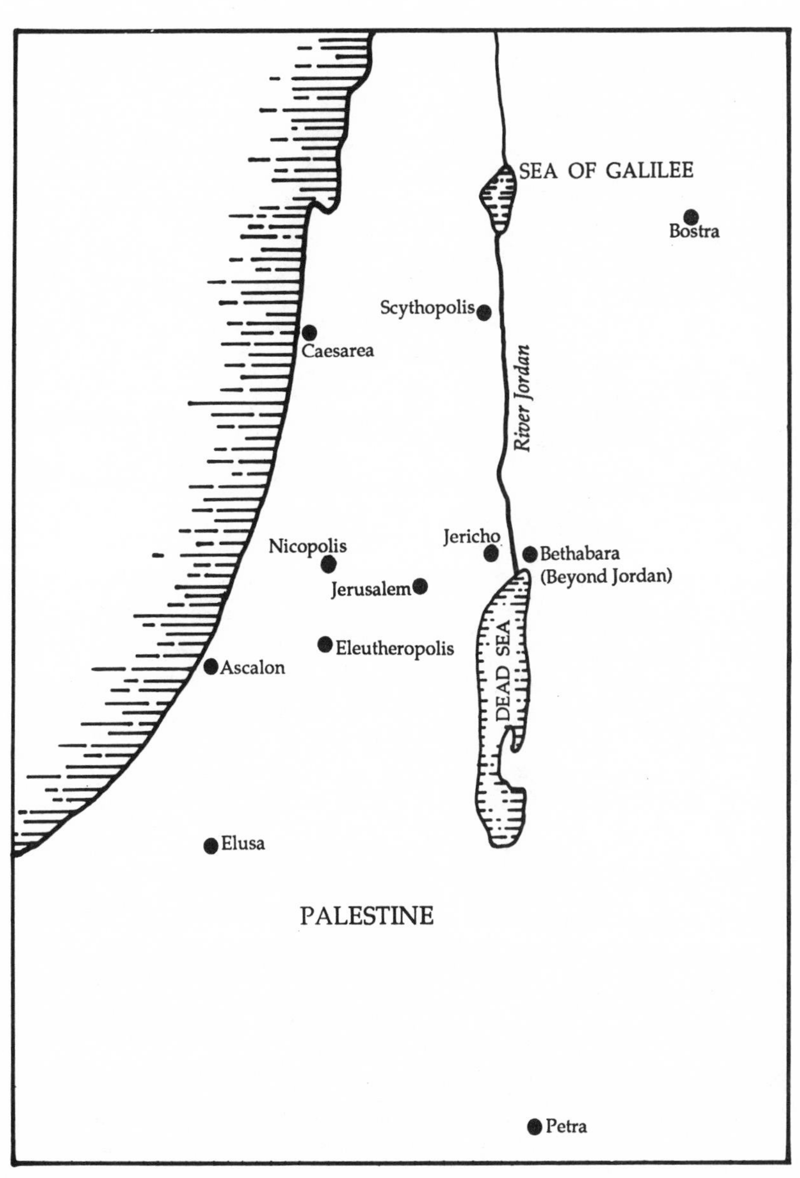
SEA OF GALILEE
Bostra
Scythopolis
Caesarea
River Jordan
Nicopolis
Jericho
Bethabara
(Beyond Jordan)
Jerusalem
Eleutheropolis
Ascalon
DEAD SEA
Elusa
PALESTINE
Petra

CISTERCIAN PUBLICATIONS, INC.
TITLES LISTINGS

CISTERCIAN TEXTS

THE WORKS OF BERNARD OF CLAIRVAUX

Apologia to Abbot William
Five Books on Consideration: Advice to a Pope
Grace and Free Choice
Homilies in Praise of the Blessed Virgin Mary
The Life and Death of Saint Malachy the Irishman
Love without Measure. Extracts from the Writings of St Bernard (Paul Dimier)
The Parables of Saint Bernard (Michael Casey)
Sermons for the Summer Season
Sermons on the Song of Songs I - IV
Steps of Humility and Pride

THE WORKS OF WILLIAM OF SAINT THIERRY

The Enigma of Faith
Exposition on the Epistle to the Romans
The Golden Epistle
The Mirror of Faith
The Nature and Dignity of Love

THE WORKS OF AELRED OF RIEVAULX

Dialogue on the Soul
The Mirror of Charity
Spiritual Friendship
Treatises I: On Jesus at the Age of Twelve, Rule for a Recluse, The Pastoral Prayer

THE WORKS OF JOHN OF FORD

Sermons on the Final Verses of the Song of Songs I - VII

THE WORKS OF GILBERT OF HOYLAND

Sermons on the Songs of Songs I-III
Treatises, Sermons and Epistles

OTHER EARLY CISTERCIAN WRITERS

The Letters of Adam of Perseigne I
Baldwin of Ford: Spiritual Tractates I - II
Gertrud the Great of Helfta: Spiritual Exercises
Gertrud the Great of Helfta: The Herald of God's Loving-Kindness
Guerric of Igny: Liturgical Sermons I - II
Idung of Prüfening: Cistercians and Cluniacs: The Case of Cîteaux
Isaac of Stella: Sermons on the Christian Year
Serlo of Wilton & Serlo of Savigny
Stephen of Lexington: Letters from Ireland
Stephen of Sawley: Treatises

MONASTIC TEXTS

EASTERN CHRISTIAN TRADITION

Besa: The Life of Shenoute
Cyril of Scythopolis: Lives of the Monks of Palestine
Dorotheos of Gaza: Discourses
Evagrius Ponticus:Praktikos and Chapters on Prayer
The Harlots of the Desert (Benedicta Ward)
Iosif Volotsky: Monastic Rule
The Lives of the Desert Fathers
Mena of Nikiou: Isaac of Alexandra & St Macrobius
Pachomian Koinonia I - III
The Sayings of the Desert Fathers
Spiritual Direction in the Early Christian East (Irénée Hausherr)
The Syriac Fathers on Prayer and the Spiritual Life (Sebastian Brock)

WESTERN CHRISTIAN TRADITION

Anselm of Canterbury: Letters I - [III]
Bede: Commentary on the Seven Catholic Epistles
Bede: Commentary on the Acts of the Apostles
Bede: Gospel Homilies I - II
Bede: Homilies on the Gospels I - II
Cassian: Conferences I - III
Gregory the Great: Forty Gospel Homilies
Guigo II the Carthusian: Ladder of Monks and Twelve Mediations
Peter of Celle: Selected Works
The Letters of Armand-Jean de Rance I - II
The Life of Beatrice of Nazareth
The Rule of the Master

CHRISTIAN SPIRITUALITY

Abba: Guides to Wholeness & Holiness East & West
A Cloud of Witnesses: The Development of Christian Doctrine (D.N. Bell)
Athirst for God: Spiritual Desire in Bernard of Clairvaux's Sermons on the Song of Songs (M. Casey)
Cistercian Way (André Louf)
Fathers Talking (Aelred Squire)
Friendship and Community (B. McGuire)
From Cloister to Classroom
Herald of Unity: The Life of Maria Gabrielle Sagheddu (M. Driscoll)
Life of St Mary Magdalene and of Her Sister St Martha (D. Mycoff)
The Name of Jesus (Irénée Hausherr)
Penthos: The Doctrine of Compunction in the Christian East (Irénée Hausherr)
Rancé and the Trappist Legacy (A.J. Krailsheimer)
The Roots of the Modern Christian Tradition
Russian Mystics (S. Bolshakoff)
The Spirituality of the Christian East (Tomas Spidlék)

MONASTIC STUDIES

Community & Abbot in the Rule of St Benedict I - II (Adalbert De Vogüé)
Beatrice of Nazareth in Her Context (Roger De Ganck)
Consider Your Call: A Theology of the Monastic Life (Daniel Rees et al.)
The Finances of the Cistercian Order in the Four teenth Century (Peter King)
Fountains Abbey & Its Benefactors (Joan Wardrop)
The Hermit Monks of Grandmont (Carole A. Hutchison)

TITLES LISTINGS

In the Unity of the Holy Spirit (Sighard Kleiner)
Monastic Practices (Charles Cummings)
The Occupation of Celtic Sites in Ireland by the Canons Regular of St Augustine and the Cistercians (Geraldine Carville)
The Rule of St Benedict: A Doctrinal and Spiritual Commentary (Adalbert de Vogüé)
The Rule of St Benedict (Br. Pinocchio)
Towards Unification with God (Beatrice of Nazareth in Her Context, II)
St Hugh of Lincoln (D.H. Farmer)
Serving God First (Sighard Kleiner)

CISTERCIAN STUDIES

A Difficult Saint (B. McGuire)
A Second Look at Saint Bernard (J. Leclercq)
Bernard of Clairvaux and the Cistercian Spirit (J. Leclercq)
Bernard of Clairvaux: Man, Monk, Mystic (M. Casey) Tapes and readings
Bernard of Clairvaux: Studies Presented to Dom Jean Leclercq
Christ the Way: The Christology of Guerric of Igny (John Morson)
Cistercian Sign Language
The Cistercian Spirit
The Cistercians in Denmark (Brian McGuire)
The Cistercians in Scandinavia (James France)
The Eleventh-century Background of Cîteaux (Bede K. Lackner)
The Golden Chain: Theological Anthropology of Isaac of Stella (Bernard McGinn)
Image and Likeness: The Augustinian Spirituality of William of St Thierry (D. N. Bell)
An Index of Cistercian Works and Authors in the Libraries of Great Britian I (D.N. Bell)
The Mystical Theology of St Bernard (Etiénne Gilson)
Nicholas Cotheret's Annals of Citeaux (Louis J. Lekai)
The Spiritual Teachings of St Bernard of Clairvaux (J.R. Sommerfeldt)
Wholly Animals: A Book of Beastly Tales (D.N.Bell)
William, Abbot of St Thierry
Women and St Bernard of Clairvaux (Jean Leclercq)

MEDIEVAL RELIGIOUS WOMEN
Lillian Thomas Shank and John A. Nichols, editors

Distant Echoes
Peace Weavers

STUDIES IN CISTERCIAN ART AND ARCHITECTURE
Meredith Parsons Lillich, editor

Studies I, II, III now available
Studies IV scheduled for 1992

THOMAS MERTON

The Climate of Monastic Prayer (T. Merton)
The Legacy of Thomas Merton (P. Hart)
The Message of Thomas Merton (P. Hart)
Thomas Merton: The Monastic Journey
Thomas Merton Monk (P. Hart)
Thomas Merton Monk & Artist (Victor Kramer)
Thomas Merton on St Bernard
Thomas Merton the Monastic Journey
Toward an Integrated Humanity (M. Basil Pennington et al.)

CISTERCIAN LITURGICAL DOCUMENTS SERIES
Chrysogonus Waddell, ocso, editor

The Cadouin Breviary (two volumes)
Hymn Collection of the Abbey of the Paraclete
Molesme Summer-Season Breviary (4 volumes)
Institutiones nostrae: The Paraclete Statutes
Old French Ordinary and Breviary of the Abbey of the Paraclete: Text & Commentary (2 vol.)
The Twelfth-century Cistercian Psalter
The Twelfth-century Usages of the Cistercian Laybrothers

STUDIA PATRISITICA
Papers of the 1983 Oxford patristics conference
edited by Elizabeth A. Livingstone

XVIII/I Historica-Gnostica-Biblica
XVIII/2 Critica-Classica-Ascetica-Liturgica
XVIII/3 Second Century-Clement & Origen-Cappodician Fathers
XVIII/4 *available from Peeters, Leuven*

Cistercian Publications is a non-profit corporation. Its publishing program is restricted to monastic texts in translation and books on the monastic tradtion.

North American customers may order these books through booksellers or directly from the warehouse:
Cistercian Publications
St Joseph's Abbey
Spencer, Massachusetts 01562
(508) 885-7011
fax 508-885-4687

British and European customers may order these books through booksellers or from:
Brian Griffin
Storey House, White Cross
South Road, Lancaster LA1 4QX
England

Editorial queries and advance book information should be directed to the Editorial Offices:
Cistercian Publications
Institute of Cistercian Studies
Western Michigan University
Kalamazoo, Michigan 49008
(616) 387-8920

A complete catalogue of texts in translation and studies on early, medieval, and modern monasticism is available at no cost from Cistercian Publications.